The Many and the Few

HILDA SABATO

The Many and the Few

POLITICAL PARTICIPATION

IN REPUBLICAN BUENOS AIRES

Stanford University Press, Stanford, California   2001

The Many and the Few: Political Participation in Republican Buenos Aires was originally published in Spanish in 1998 under the title *La política en las calles: entre el voto y la movilización, Buenos Aires, 1862–1880,* by Editorial Sudamericana S.A., Buenos Aires, ©1998 by Editorial Sudamericana S.A.

Stanford University Press
Stanford, California
© 2001 by the Board of Trustees of the
Leland Stanford Junior University
Printed in the United States of America

Library of Congress Cataloging-in-Publication Data

Sabato, Hilda
  [Política en las calles. English]
  The many and the few : political participation in republican Buenos Aires /
Hilda Sabato.
      p.   cm.
  Includes bibliographical references and index.
  ISBN 0-8047-3943-9 (alk. paper) — ISBN 0-8047-3944-7 (pbk. : alk. paper).
    1. Political participation—Argentina—Buenos Aires—History—
19th century.   2. Buenos Aires (Argentina)—Politics and government.
3. Buenos Aires (Argentina)—History—19th century.   I. Title.

JS2328.B82   2001
323'.042'098211—dc21   2001020193
                                                                   CIP

This book is printed on acid-free, archival quality paper.

Original printing 2001
Last figure below indicates year of this printing:
10   09   08   07   06   05   04   03   02   01

Typeset in 10/12 Palatino

To Charly

Contents

The Many and the Few

Introduction

Nothing is more surprising to those who consider human affairs with a philosophical eye, than to see the easiness with which the many are governed by the few.
—David Hume, 1758[1]

The Many and the Few in Buenos Aires

This book poses the question of the relationship between the few and the many, and of the conflicts and political bonds generated between them, in a specific time and place: the city of Buenos Aires, Argentina, in the 1860s and 1870s. The issues it raises, however, refer to the almost universal human problem of the construction and exercise of political power. In our case, as in many others, this process involved not only the few at the top but also the rest of the Buenos Aires population, "the many," who played a particular role in the political experiment inaugurated in Argentina in the early 1860s. We shall explore the difficulties and complexities of their mutual relations. In our story, the "easiness" that puzzled Hume remains the backdrop for the many different dramas played in the foreground of the political arena.

In the history of Argentina, the fall from power of Juan Manuel de Rosas and his regime in 1852 marks the beginning of a decade of decisive political transformations. Two main events contributed to this change: on the normative side, the drafting of the Constitution of 1853, reformed in 1860, which established Argentina as a nation and as a modern, federal republic; on the institutional side, the ascent to power of a new political elite in the powerful province of Buenos Aires that would initiate the long process of state-building and the consolidation of a national polity. After the final unification of the country in 1862, this elite devised and strove to impose a new regime that would create a national order with themselves at the top. In this last objective they failed. The success of the nation-state came together with the political decline of the Buenos Aires elite and of the regime they had tried to shape. But for almost twenty years they had been relatively successful in their attempts at building and keeping political power.

What was the place of the rest of the people of Buenos Aires, the *porteños*, in this story? The constitution allotted them a space in the construction of political power. Argentina was a republic; popular sovereignty and modern representation were the founding normative principles of government. These principles were also embedded in political practices and traditions that went back to the early nineteenth century, when the imperial dominance of Spain over the Viceroyalty of the River Plate collapsed, and the institutions of the *Ancien Régime* were replaced by new forms of governance.

This normative framework provided the basic rules for the establishment of a representative system in the period under study. Suffrage became a key piece of that system. Elections were the main legal road to government posts, while voting was indicated as the ideal form of exercising political freedom. Not all the population had the right of suffrage, and many of those who did chose not to exercise it. Nonetheless, elections were a decisive moment in the relationship between the few and the many.

It was not the only one, however. This relationship was also maintained through other channels. Some of them were traditional forms, resting in family or kinship ties or in the different kinds of personal, deferential, or paternalistic bonds between those in power and other sectors of society. Typical of this period of profound social change in Buenos Aires, however, was the formation of a public sphere, which became a space of mediation between civil society and the state, and for the participation of vast sectors of the population in the public life of the city. Within that new and expanding space, different groups and sectors of society voiced their opinions and represented their claims directly, avoiding the specifically political path but translating their demands into the language of local political disputes. At the same time, those in power were attentive to the signals stemming from this public sphere as it became a source of legitimization for political action.

In their attempt to build a national polity, devise a stable political order, and keep power, the *porteño* political elite rested heavily on the people of Buenos Aires. The city and the rest of the province were important sites of electoral confrontation, where the different leaders operated to create their networks of caudillos and clienteles. Also, they made use of the electoral power accumulated at the provincial level when playing the national game and negotiating with the political groups of the other states.

The city itself acquired a unique quality for this elite as the site par excellence of public opinion, whose verdicts were increasingly relevant for the legitimacy of any government or regime. Contemporaries understood the institutions of the public sphere—the different types of associations, the press—as the breeding ground and the material incarnation of public opinion. Therefore, the leadership paid special attention to the word and deeds of these institutions. The latter, in turn, also participated in the public and political life of the city. Created to represent, protect, voice, and look after the interests of their members, they also established an ongoing dialogue with the state and its authorities.

The people of Buenos Aires, therefore, occupied a special place, different from that of the other Argentines, in the political experiment of the 1860s and 1870s. Electoral practices and participation in the public sphere were key dimensions in their relationship with the government and the political realm. They were not the only ones, but this book will privilege those two dimensions and explore their main features and mutual relations.

Citizenship and Representation

The people or the nation cannot speak, cannot act but through their representatives. This widely repeated statement formulated in revolutionary France by the Abbé Sieyès summarizes the basic principle of modern representative government.[2] The election of the representatives was prescribed as the main and the ideal form of political action on the part of the people. Modern representatives differed from those of *Ancien Régime* societies. They were not supposed to act as delegates of any group or sector in particular, nor were they to be limited by the traditional imperative mandate. They represented, and at the same time produced, the will of the nation, that abstract community formed by individual citizens. Hence elections became a key aspect of the new system of government and a crucial moment in the relationship with the governed. The right to choose and to be chosen constituted the core of the political rights enjoyed by the citizens.[3]

Modern representation constituted a founding principle for most nations of Spanish America, among them the Argentine Republic, and the configuration of a citizenry was a central aspect in the construction of the new polities. Most of the constitutions drafted after independence defined, and at the same time presumed, the ideal citizen, the free and abstract individual who was granted political rights and made a member of the national polity. The legal limits to citizenship varied with time, albeit not in a linear fashion. The actual shaping of a citizenry, however, had only partly to do with those normative boundaries, and has been the subject of various studies and interpretations.

A classical perspective, formalized almost fifty years ago by T. H. Marshall, assimilates the shaping and enlargement of the citizenry to the gradual expansion of the suffrage. The extension of the franchise to include all adult men is considered a turning point in the formation of democratic societies. In terms of historical development, this turning point is placed in the first half of the twentieth century, when the process of enfranchisement that led from the restrictions typical of nineteenth-century political citizenship to universal male suffrage was completed in several Western countries.[4] This perspective has frequently been adopted in the study of citizenship in Spanish America—not least in Argentina. Until recently, the scholarly and non-scholarly literature alike considered that in the nineteenth century, citizenship was restricted, and voting a prerogative of the privileged few.[5]

The problem with the former interpretation is that it overlooks the fact that the history of the franchise in most Spanish American nations did not follow the path of gradual expansion described in, and prescribed by, Marshall's model. To the contrary, immediately after independence, in most places of the region, the right to vote was widely extended among the male population. The normative notion of citizen that prevailed came closer to the postrevolutionary French *citoyen* than to Locke's property owner. In most countries, however, the initial boundaries were modified in the 1820s and 1830s, when attempts were made in different places to restrict the franchise by introducing qualifications to the suffrage. These proposals did not always find their way into legislation, and, from this point onward, the electoral history of each country, and even each locality, followed a different and zigzagging path not easily included in a general pattern.[6]

The former Viceroyalty of the River Plate had a complex record in this respect. That territory gave birth to several nations, among them the Argentine republic. The latter became a unified nation only in the 1860s, and therefore, until then, each state of the confederation had its own electoral laws. In this context, the State (later Province) of Buenos Aires passed a long-lasting electoral law as early as 1821 (five years after independence from Spain) establishing universal male suffrage in its territory. There were no qualifications in terms of income, property, or literacy. In 1853, the National Constitution adopted the same principle for the country as a whole. From then on, all adult men, born or naturalized Argentine, enjoyed the right of suffrage.[7] There was, therefore, no place for a gradual extension of the franchise.

Nevertheless, it has been frequently argued that in spite of the law, electoral participation was actually very limited. Until 1912, a very low percentage of the enfranchised population exercised their voting rights. The principle of universal suffrage was violated by electoral practices, and, for all practical purposes, it was as if there had been explicit restrictions to those rights. Different interpretations share this basic argument.

Some scholars underscore the distance between the liberal orientation of the constitution and the corrupt electoral practices devised to keep "the people" from voting. In the words of Luis Sommi:

This electoral system excluded the people from the polls. . . . There existed a great civic apathy. . . . The oligarchy did all that was possible to keep the creole and immigrant people away from the political life. . . . To that effect, they adopted the theory that the people were not capable enough to vote and that the vote had to be a privilege of the cultivated ones; that is to say, of those who had money.[8]

According to this view, the political regimes of the second half of the nineteenth century had ignored the principle of popular sovereignty, and were, therefore, illegitimate.

A second interpretation was advanced by Gino Germani, in a compelling book that has become a classic of Argentine political sociology. He emphasized the exclusion of the new, modern, social sectors:

The elites did not seem willing to share, nor to give away, power to the new groups that were being incorporated into the national life. Their aspiration was to keep a liberal democracy, with participation restricted to the upper strata of society.[9]

The deep social changes that had occurred since the mid-nineteenth century were not accompanied by an equivalent transformation of the political system. This contradiction was at the heart of a system established by an elite that was conservative in political terms, albeit very progressive when dealing with the economic, social, and cultural aspects of modernization. This elite kept the majority of the population out of public life, establishing a restrictive republic with limited citizenship. The massive presence of immigrants only made matters worse, as they were given the right of suffrage only after naturalizing, a step they very seldom chose to take. Thus, they were cut off from formal participation in the political arena.[10]

These interpretations equate citizens with voters, and assume that voting was the only legitimate form of political participation on the part of the people. They presume, moreover, that elections were the single way to power, and the key moment in the relations between the few and the many. These assumptions are anything but arbitrary; they are explicitly contained in the constitution, whose aim was to shape a polity according to those principles. Yet in 1853 this process lay ahead, and in Argentina—like in many other areas of the world—"the invention of the sovereign people" and the collective acceptance of modern representation were the result of a long and often contradictory historical development.[11] The continuous reference to representation and citizenship in the political discourse of the nineteenth century does not imply, in itself, that voters were the citizens prescribed by liberal theory and the constitutional norms, nor that elections were understood as the only means of political representation. At the time, moreover, the legitimacy of a political regime did not depend necessarily on the transparency of elections, nor were the latter the only efficient and accepted means to reach power or participate in politics. By presuming the contrary, the standard interpretations on the formation of the Argentine political system equate low electoral participation with indifference to politics or an explicit marginalization imposed from above. Also, they conclude that any regime based on electoral manipulation was illegitimate.

These assumptions have precluded the interrogation on actual elections, voters, and voting practices in different periods of Argentine political life. They have inspired readings of our electoral history that discount the importance of the institution of universal male suffrage in the Argentine case, and dissolve the latter's specificity by subsuming it into the more general model of restricted citizenship. This model is applied to characterize the political regimes between 1862 and 1916, thus including very different situations into a single pattern.

In recent years, the interpretations based upon these premises have come under revision. Citizenship and representation have become crucial topics of contemporary academic and political debate, and the electoral history of many countries of the world is being revisited. In Argentina, as well as in most of Latin America, new approaches and original research have seriously undermined interpretations based on the model of gradual democratization. The nineteenth century, from the Revolution of 1810 to 1916—the date of the first general election held after the passing of the Sáenz Peña Law of 1912—has acquired new density for historians of the political realm. Scholars are studying periods and regions that formerly were either ignored or subsumed into the national and secular picture. These ongoing efforts have resulted in a diversity of works that pose new questions and interpretations concerning the political history of Argentina.[12] The second part of this book may be read in this context, as an attempt to explore the electoral practices of Buenos Aires in the formative years of the republic.

Elections

Buenos Aires had a turbulent electoral history. In the violent decade of 1810, arms were more effective than votes in the struggle for power. In the 1820s there were attempts to modernize the political system, however, and elections became increasingly important. The political elites of the city sought to solve their internal fragmentation and rivalries by negotiating candidatures in advance and presenting unified lists to the electorate. According to the electoral law of 1821, all free, adult men were enabled to vote, but actual participation depended almost entirely on the capacity of the leadership to attract potential voters. This they did by mounting electoral networks strongly tied to government employment and state institutions. For some time, they were quite successful in mobilizing and, at the same time, controlling the electoral process. Soon, however, the conflict between factions of the elite proved too intense for negotiations. The elections became a terrain for factional, often violent, confrontation, and, in the end, the final showdown took place in the battlefield.[13]

During the following two decades, Buenos Aires witnessed the rise to, consolidation in, and fall from power of Juan Manuel de Rosas (see Chapter 1). Under the new political regime, elections were held regularly, but the rules of the game had changed. Competition was eliminated. The electoral results were always unanimous. But the systematic mobilization of voters persisted. The government mounted a careful organization to promote and secure electoral participation, and the turnouts remained similar to those of the 1820s. In this system, elections were staged to obtain the confirmation of the official candidates rather than to select representatives.[14]

The fall of Rosas in 1852 inaugurated a new political era in Buenos Aires. The renown historian José Luis Romero labeled the city of the following three decades "patrician." A renewed political elite, "who felt the protagonist of a saga illuminated by the torches of liberalism and progress," set out to organize the state and build a nation.[15] After unification, presidents Bartolomé Mitre (1862–68), Domingo Faustino Sarmiento (1868–74), and Nicolás Avellaneda (1874–80) led a program of social change and political foundation.[16] "They belonged to the elite . . . a republican and austere elite . . . ," which mounted an institutional organization that "guaranteed the political operation of a society where the mass of the people accepted as legitimate the monopoly of power exerted by a minority." The people "saw [in the elite] certain authentic republican virtues," although they also "felt the oppression of the new ways of life."[17] In this way, Romero distinguished this period from the one inaugurated in 1880, when "the old ideals of

liberalism fell, defeated by class interests," and the social transformations triggered by the liberal program generated a "divorce between
the masses and the elites," which turned into an oligarchy.[18]

Thus Romero argues that in these decades, a peculiar political and
institutional system, initially headed by the local elites of the city, consolidated in Buenos Aires. Historian Tulio Halperin Donghi has studied the way that system operated. His perceptive interpretation of the
political life of the period constitutes an indispensable reference for
this work. Under the leadership of Bartolomé Mitre, the political life of
the city experienced important changes, and so did the relationship
between the few and the many. A new institution played a key role in
this system, the political party. Mitre organized the Partido de la Libertad, which differed from previous political structures but also from
present-day parties. The party, contends Halperin Donghi, was established as a collective that was something more than the aggregation of
political figures, inasmuch as it aimed at incorporating large sectors of
the people into the political life of the city. It was supported by the
propertied and educated classes but also succeeded in mobilizing the
urban population. These "liberals," furthermore, identified their own
invented past with the history of the province, and presented themselves as the expression of "all legitimate political aspirations" and
the representatives of all of the good society. They were at the same
time the heirs of a heroic past and the heralds of the only legitimate future. When competing forces appeared in the electoral arena, the liberals accused them of factious behavior incompatible with the values
cherished by the people of Buenos Aires and incarnated in their only
"party of principles."[19]

Elections are not a central topic in the work of Tulio Halperin
Donghi, although he refers to them when analyzing the division of the
Partido de la Libertad that took place after unification and the ascent
of Bartolomé Mitre to the presidency of the country. From then on, two
main groups competed for power in Buenos Aires. The urban mobilization that had gained momentum in the late 1850s and early 1860s
gradually disappeared, Halperin Donghi argues, and "the political life
of Buenos Aires was more and more in the hands of two electoral machines, which sometimes resembled war machines, whose rivalries
only concerned themselves."[20]

According to this forceful view, by the mid-1860s the political life
of the city was reduced to a struggle between two organizations that
monopolized the electoral game. Rather than settling the issue of the
relationship between the few and the many, this assertion opens a vast
field for investigation. Who participated in this electoral game and
why? Which were the formal and informal rules of that game? What

was the electoral stage like? Which were the actual results of such a system? How did public opinion view it? These are some of the questions inspired by Halperin's work that will be addressed in the second part of this book.

The law and the constitution established that elections were the ideal mechanism to institute political representation. The people, on their part, did not always consider voting a relevant or desirable means of participation. In fact, during these decades of universal male suffrage, only a small minority of the population of the city actually showed up on election days. The image of a people ready to exercise their voting rights is, therefore, anachronistic. A widespread reluctance to exercise the prescribed form of political freedom was a common feature in many nineteenth-century societies. Quite often, electoral machines were employed not only to control elections but also to make them possible, to devise active mechanisms for recruiting voters. Argentina was no exception to this pattern, whose causes are variable and complex. In any case, it is evident that in Buenos Aires many people found other forms of participation in the public life of the city more appealing and seemingly more effective.

One of these forms was armed intervention. In Argentina, like in other Latin American countries, political citizenship was closely associated with participation in the militia. The notion of an active citizen implied the right and the obligation to bear arms in defense of the country. Inscription in the national guard was required of voters. Throughout most of the century, armed rebellions were deemed legitimate when those in power abused their functions, violated the constitution, and became "tyrants." The armed road to power was frequently followed in Argentina. As the national state consolidated, however, it gradually lost legitimacy. All the revolutionary attempts launched after 1862, including those originating in Buenos Aires in 1874 and 1880, were defeated. These revolts were supported by large sectors of the city's population and probably attracted more people than the polls. They constitute, therefore, an important, albeit transient, aspect of the relationship between the few and the many. In this book, however, I have privileged the more permanent forms of participation in the political life of Buenos Aires.

A Public Sphere

While armed rebellions gradually tended to subside, the opposite was true of another form of participation that flourished with increasing vigor. I refer to a set of practices that originated in civil society and may be encompassed in the Habermasian notion of public sphere. The use of these concepts is problematic. In the recent Latin American literature, scholars have favored different definitions of "civil society." Increasingly the term has been employed to refer to the realm of the social that is not within the sphere of the state, nor under the domain of the market. But other, more traditional variants have also been used that are closer to the dichotomous conception of Hegelian undertones, a conception that includes the market within the orbit of civil society, and therefore, confronts the latter with the state.[21] As for the concept of the public sphere, Habermas's formulation, originally drafted in the early 1960s, gained wide circulation in the last decade and gave rise to heated theoretical debates.[22] In spite of the controversial nature of the two concepts, historians have frequently made a rather eclectic use of both. They have rendered visible a new set of questions and problems hitherto seldom addressed when studying our past.

In the decades under study, the city of Buenos Aires experienced deep and swift social transformations, in the context of a rapid process of capitalist development and state consolidation (see Chapter 1). The shaping of an autonomous civil society was a visible development. The creation and expansion of an increasing number of associations was the most clear symptom of that trend. Mutual aid societies; social, cultural, and sports clubs; Masonic lodges; immigrant associations; literary circles and learned societies; festive and carnival groups; committees of all sorts to promote the building of a hospital, the celebration of a public event, the collection of funds for the victims of an earthquake, a fire, a war—all of these and many other forms of joint action operated in Buenos Aires in the late 1850s and 1860s, and more vigorously still, in the 1870s.

This type of institution was not new in the River Plate area. The first half of the nineteenth century had witnessed the emergence of modern forms of sociability in Buenos Aires. The new associations were not based upon custom or the law, as in the colonial past, but on the free will of their individual members, who gathered to pursue an explicit end. In the second half of the century these institutions experienced a sustained and rapid development. At the same time, a vigorous press flourished in the city as newspapers, journals, and other periodicals multiplied and broadened their readership. The first papers were closely related to the government and the political groups of the day, but by the 1870s an increasing number of autonomous periodicals were being published in the city and circulated among its growing population.[23]

The expansion of associations and the press has been frequently connected to the political life of modern societies. They occupied a central place in Alexis de Tocqueville's sharp analysis of the American democracy. He observed that

In aristocratic societies men do not need to combine in order to act, because they are strongly held together. Every wealthy and powerful citizen constitutes the head of a permanent and compulsory association, composed of all those who are dependent upon him or whom he makes subservient to the execution of his designs. Among democratic nations, on the contrary, all the citizens are independent and feeble. . . . They all, therefore, become powerless if they do not learn voluntarily to help one another.[24]

In the United States, the vigorous presence of associations resulted from widespread civil liberties and political freedom, and became a powerful antidote to despotism.

Contemporaries of Tocqueville, such as Saint-Simon, Fourier, and Mazzini, emphasized the fraternal and solidarity sides of the associative movement, which occupied a central place in their utopian projects. For all these men, associations played a political and social role that transcended the specific purposes of their creation.

In recent theoretical and historical works, the topic of civil society has gained increasing relevance. The role of associations and the press in the transition from *Ancien Régime* to modern societies is strongly emphasized in the literature. They are considered a breeding ground of democratic values and practices, a space of communicative exchange presumably governed by the laws of reason.[25] They also play a decisive role in Habermas's conceptualization of the public sphere as a space of mediation between civil society and the state.[26]

The proliferation of associative practices and the expansion of a periodical press in Buenos Aires may be read in that light as symptoms of the formation of such a sphere.[27] These institutions created a "space of mediation" and were, at the same time, its leading actors, providing the organizational network that structured the population of the city as a public. They also played an active part in the mobilization of that public.

The people of Buenos Aires were increasingly prone to collective action. The theaters, streets, and plazas were the favorite spots to meet for celebrations, protests, commemorations, and demonstrations of various sorts. These different events gradually developed a pattern of common practices that will be explored in the third part of this book. Thousands of men and women took part in these frequently colorful and peaceful acts. And for large sectors of the population, these forms of collective mobilization became a significant means of participating in the public life of the city, and of addressing those in power.

The political elite of Buenos Aires was aware of the increasing visibility of the institutions of civil society, and its members were particularly sympathetic to the urban public. This awareness did not result only from the massive presence of the people in the public arena. It was also motivated by the role that public opinion increasingly came to play in the legitimization of political rule. For the republican elite, the *tribunal de la opinión* represented the most genuine expression of the common will of the nation. Different concepts of public opinion circulated at the time among those in power and beyond, but all versions considered it a centerpiece of political legitimacy. This shared understanding enhanced the political importance of the public sphere and increased the efficacy of collective action.

Associations, newspapers, and mobilizations can thus be interpreted in terms of the construction of a public sphere, of a space of mediation between civil society and the political realm. The people of Buenos Aires were actively involved in the formation and development of that space and participated actively in its institutions and practices. This topic constitutes, therefore, the second large theme of this book. Chapter 2 describes the development of the associative movement and the press in Buenos Aires, while all chapters of Part III explore the practices and patterns of public mobilization.

Finally, in the Epilogue, I venture an interpretation of the connections between the two main forms of public and political involvement on the part of the people of Buenos Aires discussed in the book. Natalio Botana has perceptively distinguished the political participation through electoral means from the one that results from taking part in the public sphere. He associates the latter with civil liberties (he calls them "public liberties") and the former with political freedom, with the right of the people to participate in government and freely choose their representatives. This last form, he argues, is essential to modern republics, and its absence or distortion affects the legitimacy of any such regime.[28]

Yet in the actual Spanish American republics of the nineteenth century, the exercise of political and civil rights did not follow a uniform pattern. The fate of the liberties established by the constitutions and the laws differed in each time and place. In all of them, however, the access to, and exercise of, political power was not a question that pertained only to the elites and would-be elites, who kept these matters to themselves. The relationship between them and larger sectors of the population was a crucial aspect of the political life of these republics. By exploring the ways in which the people of Buenos Aires practiced their political and civil liberties, and participated in the electoral and public arenas, this book seeks to bring to the foreground a dimension that is frequently neglected: the relations established between the few and the many in the construction of political power in modern republican polities.

This work bears the signs of a very particular period of Argentina's recent past, marked by the transition to democracy. In the agitated atmosphere of the final stages of the military dictatorship, a question haunted many of us: did our society harbor any democratic reserves, after so many years of pervasive authoritarian practices? At the time, we searched for an answer in civil society, and advanced a rather optimistic hypothesis. The Argentine popular sectors, we argued, had shown in the past a great capacity to organize themselves and establish "nests of democracy."[29]

In 1984, we entered the institutional road to democracy. As in many other Latin American countries, in Argentina the new situation created great expectations of a renewed expansion of citizenship. It was widely believed that with the recuperation of a democratic order, civil, political, and social rights would be extended to benefit increasing sectors of the population. That picture, drawn in the 1980s, now seems too optimistic. The arbitrary ways of the dark years have been left behind, but authoritarian attitudes and practices have not altogether disappeared. Furthermore, the economic crisis and the policies adopted in order to face it are excluding increasing numbers of people from the labor market, from education and welfare, and from access to the public sphere. Electoral participation, in turn, attracts fewer and fewer people. Citizenship seems to be shrinking, rather than expanding. This situation is not limited to Argentina or Latin America; many societies seem to be arriving at a similar predicament.

In this context, representation, citizenship, and political participation have become crucial terms in the political and intellectual debates of the last decade, both in Argentina and elsewhere. Scholars—historians among them—are using this new lens to revisit some very old questions regarding the production and reproduction of political power. In Latin America, an increasing number of works address these topics with a historical perspective. This book is one of them. I first became interested in these problems in the 1980s, but I developed my ideas in their present form in the 1990s, when the main part of my research was carried out. In this English version, I have introduced some changes to the Spanish original, both to make it more accessible to readers not familiar with Argentine history and to sharpen some of my arguments and prose.[30]

In the long road that led to this book, published in Spanish in 1998, I became indebted to people and institutions whose help has been invaluable. When my research started, I was a member of the Program

on Economic and Social History (PEHESA) at the Centro de Investigaciones Sociales sobre el Estado y la Administración. With the "return
to democracy," the program became part of the University of Buenos
Aires, and I was incorporated both to the Facultad de Filosofía y Letras
of that university and to the Consejo Nacional de Investigaciones
Científicas y Técnicas (CONICET). The main part of my work, therefore, was carried out with the academic and financial support of those
institutions. I also received financial aid from Fundación Antorchas
and the Social Science Research Council. Ema Cibotti and Elías Palti
were my research assistants during the initial stages of my work. Later
on, Graciela Bonet colaborated with me in the arduous task of revising
and collecting materials from the periodical press.[31]

Throughout these years, I have received the help, encouragement,
and intellectual influence of friends and colleagues. I would particularly like to thank Leandro Gutiérrez, who was, before his deeply lamented death, a permanent source of ideas and inspiration to those
who had the privilege of enjoying his company; Juan Carlos Korol,
who followed closely the ups and downs of my research, discussed my
hypotheses, revised my writings, and granted me the benefit of his
critical comments and suggestions; Luis Alberto Romero, friend, col-
league, and editor, with whom I kept up a permanent dialogue about
many of the issues addressed in the book; Tulio Halperin Donghi, who
encouraged me throughout the years and to whose powerful ideas my
work is deeply indebted, and my partners of the editorial board of
Punto de Vista—Carlos Altamirano, María Teresa Gramuglio, Adrián
Gorelik, Beatriz Sarlo, and Hugo Vezzetti—for providing me with a
challenging intellectual milieu for the discussion of ideas and perspectives.

In 1990/91, I was a member of the School of Social Sciences of the
Institute for Advanced Study in Princeton. There I had the privilege of
presenting some of my work to my colleagues. My special thanks to
Gary Gerstle, Albert Hirschman, Jacek Kochanowicz, Peter Wagner,
and Michael Walzer; also to Arcadio Díaz Quiñones, of Princeton
University. In the following years, I participated in a joint project on
the electoral history of Latin America in the nineteenth century,
directed by Antonio Annino and José Carlos Chiaramonte; co-
ordinated a collaborative initiative on political citizenship in Latin
America supported by the Joint Committee on Latin American Studies
of the Social Science Research Council; and took part in a comparative
project on these topics in Argentina. In these groups, as well as in my
classes and graduate seminars, I benefited from the intellectual
exchanges with, and critical comments of, the participants. In
particular, I wish to thank Antonio Annino, Marta Bonaudo, Gerardo

Caetano, Marcello Carmagnani, José Carlos Chiaramonte, Carlos Forment, Pilar González, Richard Graham, Francois-Xavier Guerra, Eric Hershberg, Alicia Hernández Chávez, Alberto Lettieri, Mirta Lobato, Elías Palti, Gonzalo Sánchez, and Marcela Ternavasio. I would also like to emphasize my intellectual debt to Natalio Botana and José Murilo de Carvalho, whose works were a permanent source of inspiration. Finally, my gratitude to Jeremy Adelman, who insisted that this book be translated into English, for his comments and his help in this endeavor.

The research work was made possible by the collaboration I received from the librarians and other personnel of the Archivo General de la Nación, the library of the Instituto de Historia Argentina y Americana, Dr. Emilio Ravignani of the Facultad de Filosofía y Letras (University of Buenos Aires), and the staff of the Biblioteca Nacional (Argentine National Library). I thank them for their efficiency, patience, and goodwill.

My last, and warmest, acknowledgments go to my family, and particularly to my sister Celia who, with her excellent English, came to my rescue when the translation was too demanding; to my husband, Carlos Reboratti, to whom I dedicate this book; and to our sons, Julián and Andrés.

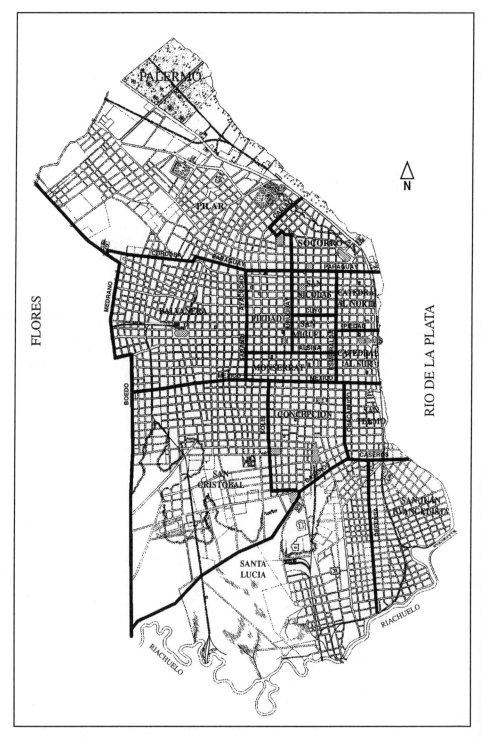

Map 1. Buenos Aires—parish boundaries (c. 1880). Source: Censo Municipal de Buenos Aires, 1887.

1 Buenos Aires, A World in Transition

The City

"Karlsruhe, Darmstadt, Berlin, Saint Petersburg, and many cities in the USA are extraordinary uniform, but I don't know of any city quite like Buenos Aires, cut across by straight lines and divided in identical square blocks. . . . The same uniformity that has regulated the width of the streets rules the construction of the houses."[1]

Flat, low, and irregular—that is how Xavier Marmier saw Buenos Aires in 1850. The domes of a few churches and the tower of the old Cabildo were the only constructions that protruded above the low contour lines of the city. Built on the edge of the Argentine prairie, the pampas, its smooth undulations barely altered the flatness of the horizon, prolonged to the east by the estuary of the River Plate, wide as a sea. In colonial times, the town was designed to follow the regular pattern of the Hispanic grid, but as the years passed its strict forms were often left behind and a more irregular plan took shape. With the Revolution of 1810, the new enlightened elite who aspired to turn Buenos Aires into the leading city of the new republic found their main representative in Bernardino Rivadavia. His urban reforms of the 1820s focused on the regularization of the grid and the organization of the public space. Although the project was resisted by many, it was carried through with success, and the results were soon evident: straightening of the streets, normalization of the fronts and facades, zoning by type of activity, consolidation of the city center as the place par excellence for public buildings and spaces, and enhancement of the role of the square (la plaza).[2] But neither these changes nor those that took place during the Rosas regime in the thirties and forties succeeded in altering the aspect of uniformity that so impressed Marmier when he first arrived in the city.

Some of the basic features that confirmed such a perception persisted even after the vast transformations of the following decades.

The extension of the grid, the regularity of streets and blocks, and the relatively low height of the buildings gave the city a touch of homogeneity that caught the eye of visitors. This regularity, however, was home to a diversity of styles, forms, and urban designs that multiplied to the rhythm of the city's rapid changes.

The reformist mood of the 1820s operated as a model for the elites who came to power after 1852. The city was at the center of their modernizing republican project, and they sought to control and regulate the swift process of urban expansion that was taking place, triggered by economic development and population growth. Successive governments devised and implemented public policies in different urban matters, with uneven success.

In the 1860s and 1870s, new public buildings contributed to alter the profile of the city: the customshouse, by the river, with its five floors and its pier crowned by an *Arc de Triomphe* and a lighthouse tower; the post office on the side of the Plaza de Mayo; the National Congress on the other side, with a seating capacity for eight hundred people; and the mint, a bit farther to the south. The riverside was remodeled to accommodate a tree-lined promenade. Idle common lands (the old *huecos*) became new plazas, while some of the traditional plazas were modernized. President Sarmiento went ahead with his ambitious project to create a large park in Palermo, to the north of the city center.[3]

At the same time, private construction thrived. It produced the huge train stations, with their imposing ironworks; large market and storage buildings; factories and workshops; theaters and churches; and all sorts of housing, to cater to the different sectors of the growing population.

Renowned architects, such as Carlos Pellegrini and Eduardo Taylor, designed some of the most prominent buildings. Yet their styles and techniques coexisted with the more traditional ones, and with the many assorted forms that resulted from the chaotic expansion of the city. Together with more solid buildings, a large number of precarious constructions sprung up all over town. Tin and wooden cabins, improvised yards, and poorly assembled sheds were erected even in the downtown area, and they bore witness to the hectic pace of urban expansion.[4]

New railway and tramway lines formed a network of public transportation. The installation of gas lighting, running water, and sewerage, plus the paving of many streets, were the visible signs of a modernization that seemed to have no limits. The periodic economic crises experienced by the country, however, put a temporary halt both to optimism and investments. And in difficult years, like 1867 or 1875/76, the construction sector was one of the most severely hit by the recession.

Throughout the period, the complex where today stands the Plaza de Mayo kept its symbolic role as the civic center of the city and the country. It was then formed by two squares, separated by an arcade where small shops and street vendors traded in retail goods. The square on the west side, known as the *Plaza de la Victoria,* was home to the small pyramid that commemorated the Revolution of 1810. It was also the favorite place for civic celebrations and public demonstrations. The construction of new buildings and the remodeling of several old ones facing both squares gave a modernizing air to the site. To the north there stood the new Colon Theater, and the restored Cathedral and Palace of the Archbishop. To the east, the old fort was renovated to house the national executive. In 1873, the post office building was erected on the same side, and behind it, the large customshouse. To the south, the new Congress Building was built, and to the west, the Cabildo was remodeled to accommodate the supreme court, the municipal council, and the police headquarters.[5]

The rest of the public buildings, the main stores, several of the oldest churches, the banks, the theaters, the principal newspaper presses, and the residential homes of the families of the old and new elites were all located in neighboring blocks, to the north and south of the plazas, in the districts known as La Merced or Catedral al Norte, and San Ignacio or Catedral al Sur.[6] Yet this area also housed small shops and artisan workshops, popular tenements, brothels, and taverns next to the riverside.

To the south of these neighborhoods, San Telmo was a more popular district, and one of intense traffic of carts and wagons, and San Juan Evangelista, also known as *La Boca,* was a site of recent settlement connected to the river trades. To the north of the elegant stores and residences of La Merced, the district of El Socorro was sparsely settled, the site for marketplaces, slaughterhouses, factories, and the spacious Plaza de Marte (named San Martin after 1878). The rest of the neighborhoods to the west of this strip (that ran by the river from La Boca to El Socorro) combined old working-class quarters such as Monserrat; districts of recent settlement such as Balvanera; and areas of orchards and vacant lands, on the outskirts of Santa Lucia and El Pilar (see Map 1).

The occupied area expanded rapidly, and between 1867 and 1880 it tripled in size from ten thousand to almost thirty thousand acres. Buenos Aires became more and more heterogeneous, variegated, and subject to constant and multiple changes, yet it always kept that imprint of regularity observed by Marmier in 1850. Urban blueprints, public policies, and public and private actions, although originating in different projects, had impressed their indelible mark upon the city.

The People

In the early 1860s, Buenos Aires was home to 120,000 people. Already the largest town and the main business center in Argentina, by 1862 it had become the seat of the national government; in 1880 it was designated the country's federal capital. Those decades witnessed an extraordinary economic growth, as the country found a leading place in the world market as an exporter of wool and other agricultural products to several European countries. The city harbored the main port, and it became a hub for the transportation, commercial, and financial networks that catered to the export trade. Its population grew steadily, generating a thriving internal market for goods and services that were increasingly supplied by local purveyors. Retail stores, workshops, banks, schools, theaters, and churches multiplied in number and spread all over town.

More than 300,000 people lived in the city by 1880. Massive European immigration was the main cause of the increase. Tens of thousands of men and women arrived every year in Argentina through the port of Buenos Aires. Many of them stayed there for good, and some of those who left for the countryside came back once and again to live temporarily in the city. In 1869 the resident immigrants numbered 90,000, a figure that was similar to that of the natives. Among the adult men, almost four out of five were foreign born (55,000 against 15,000), while the number of native women slightly surpassed that of immigrants. Two decades later, in 1887, the figures had more than doubled; the proportion remained the same for the adult men, but foreign-born women now outnumbered natives.[7]

"Foreigner" and "native" are census categories that say very little about the social and cultural attributes of the city's population. The immigrants came from very different places: half of them from the Italian peninsula, 20 percent from Spain, and the rest from France, Germany, Great Britain, and the rest of the Americas. The diversity of origin was actually even greater, however, as Italy and Germany were only then becoming unified nations, Great Britain comprised an assortment of kingdoms, and Spain harbored strong regional differences. As for the natives, they also had different origins: some had a long line of *porteño* ancestors; others were migrants from the rest of the provinces; yet others were the children and grandchildren of foreign immigrants.

This motley population was composed mostly of young adults, more men than women. The men were employed mainly in commerce, transportation, and the service sector, and to a lesser degree in manufacture and the building trades; women worked in the domestic service and in the garment industry.[8] A high proportion of the workers were hired as wage laborers in a market that chiefly required an unskilled and highly mobile work force to supply the expanding but sharply fluctuating labor demand. Wages varied greatly, following the oscillations of the market, and although sustained economic growth tended to keep the labor demand on the rise in the long run, seasonal and cyclical drops were recurrent, spelling uncertainty for workers.

While wage labor expanded, self-employment was also on the rise. Small proprietors of different sorts, chiefly connected with petty commerce and manufacture as well as the service sector, were significant in number and bore witness to the upward occupational mobility characteristic of the period. They were a very visible presence in the city, many of them being active promoters of, and participants in, the associative life that flourished during those decades (see Chapter 2).

Economic growth and modernization affected everyone, but their benefits were reaped largely by those at the top. Merchants, *estancieros*, financiers, bankers, and urban speculators increased their fortunes and refined their taste. Political leaders and enlightened intellectuals were also part of the Buenos Aires elite, and though most of them could not match the wealth of the rich, they shared many of their social habits and spaces. This elite was in the making, and the rapid and fluctuating pace of economic development favored social ascent—but could also bring about displacements and decline.

This was a dynamic and unstable society. New and old social relations and inequalities overlapped. The polarization between *gente decente* and *plebe* typical of the colonial and postcolonial order was gradually replaced by an increasingly complex stratification. New forms of economic exploitation, social control, and political dominion were taking shape. The traditional bonds that had articulated the social fabric, as well as the tensions that had run through it, were being replaced by those that emerged from the capitalist order in the making. This was not, however, a fully bourgeois order, but rather a world in transition.

Social actors perceived these changes in different ways. On the one hand, change was celebrated by many, as faith in progress and civilization was common to several of the ideological perspectives that circulated in Argentina, from liberal republicanism to utopian socialism. This mood coexisted with more traditional worldviews, which were sometimes used to resist modernity. On the other hand, the perception of change did not seem to affect the representation that the different social actors had of their society and of their own roles in it. The economic and social cleavages originating in the diffusion of capitalism did not result in explicit class conflict. The renewed elite did not feel that its role was at risk, and no group beyond it seemed willing to challenge its place. The *porteños* were divided by other issues. Tension ran high on several accounts: political and religious rivalries; the coercive action of the state, particularly upon the popular sectors; and the strained encounters among peoples of different cultures and traditions. Violence was pervasive, and it came in various forms: the individual manifestations that were increasingly labeled "criminal"; the collective and ritualized violence of elections and other political acts; the bloody one of the armed rebellions; and, last but not least, the various forms of violence exerted by the state itself upon the people.

At the same time, Buenos Aires witnessed the development of an institutional network that established connections and fostered communication among men and women of different social and cultural backgrounds. Rather than displaying or reproducing the existing lines of tension, a large number of associations of various sorts and a vigorous press—described in Chapter 2—aspired to bridge the gaps that cut across the social fabric.

Buenos Aires was, in the words of José Luis Romero, a "patrician city" that harbored a society in transition, no longer traditional but not yet "bourgeois." Like other Latin American capitals, Buenos Aires was the breeding ground of "the fundamental process of the country's constitution" and of "a new ruling class."[9] In this way, Romero stressed the social dimension of a political experience, that of the urban "patricians." These men belonged to the established propertied classes, but they formed a new political elite that sought to lead the consolidation of the republic.

The Politics

Beginning in the early days of the nineteenth century, Buenos Aires became a key political center in the southern cone of Spanish America.[10] Designated as the capital of the new Viceroyalty of the River Plate in 1776, it was the seat of the colonial authorities in that area for the following twenty-five years. It was also the birthplace of the Revolution of 1810, which started the long process that led to the severance of the links with the metropolis and the declaration of independence for the "United Provinces of the River Plate" in 1816. The first experiments to form a republic originated in Buenos Aires, but by the 1820s the territory of the former viceroyalty was no longer under one rule. Some areas, such as Upper Peru (later Bolivia), Paraguay, and, a bit later, Uruguay, split to form new states. The rest of the region was divided into provinces and organized into a confederation. The attempts to unify the nation under the hegemony of the province of Buenos Aires had failed. In the following decades, however, the province would exert increasing political influence over the rest of the confederated states. Under the strong and despotic rule of governor Juan Manuel de Rosas, Buenos Aires developed a prosperous economy and a strong army and soon became the most powerful of the provinces. Rosas tightened his political control over all.

After almost twenty years in command, in 1852 the governor of Buenos Aires and head of the confederation was defeated by an army led by Justo José de Urquiza, the governor of the province of Entre Ríos and a former ally of Rosas. For his enterprise, Urquiza had obtained the support of the Brazilian and the Uruguayan governments, who contributed men and arms to the cause. In command of his triumphant forces, he entered Buenos Aires, established his headquarters in the vicinity of the city, where Rosas had formerly had his own, required the support of the rest of the governors, and convened a general congress to decide on the institutional future of the country. Most of the provinces expressed their approval of the new measures, accepted Urquiza's leadership, and sent their representatives to the Congress that finally drafted the constitution in 1853. The only exception was Buenos Aires. Its legislature rebelled against Urquiza, rejected the new institutional arrangements, and seceded from the confederation. The *porteño* revolution of 1852 was, in the words of Halperin Donghi, "one of the not too many Argentine revolutions that constitute a landmark in the political development of the country."[11] For almost ten years, the rebellious province remained as an autonomous state, separate from the rest.

Rapid political rearrangements followed the fall of Rosas in Buenos Aires. No one wished to be associated with the old order, and the members of the elite who had endorsed it now posed as relieved victims of his despotic rule. They soon converged with returned exiles, men who had been compelled to leave the country because of their opposition to the regime. Many of them had belonged to the enlightened circles of young intellectuals that developed in Buenos Aires in the 1830s. Forced to leave sometime during the late thirties and early forties, they had settled in Uruguay, Chile, or Bolivia, where they embarked on a systematic publicity campaign against Rosas. They also endorsed all military initiatives to topple his government and, in 1852, enthusiastically supported Urquiza's crusade. But once Rosas was ousted and they returned to Buenos Aires, they were not willing to submit to the new leader or relinquish the hegemonic place that the province had gained during the fallen regime. Thus they joined forces with the established elite, and together they led the secession and started a new political experiment.

The initial struggles against Urquiza were the breeding ground of the Partido de la Libertad. The party was organized by a young former exile, Bartolomé Mitre, and attracted many of his peers as well as some older politicians. It soon became the chief political force in the province, that both developed strong (though by no means subordinate) ties with the social and economic elites and appealed to large sectors of the population, particularly the urban public. This party claimed to represent and defend "the cause of Buenos Aires."

During the 1850s, the autonomous state and the confederation maintained a strenuous relationship, based alternatively on peaceful negotiations and military clashes. The last armed episode took place in 1861, when the confederated forces left the battlefield to the triumphant army of Buenos Aires. Unification followed, now under the leadership of the rebellious state. Bartolomé Mitre was elected president of the republic in 1862, and the constitution of 1853 (slightly modified in 1860) became the law of the land.

The new government had to meet the challenge of consolidating the nation, while at the same time building a legitimate political order. Mitre used the institutions of the newborn national state as well as his own party to try to achieve control and gain power. Most provinces had long been in the hands of the federalists, a heterogeneous but very consolidated political force that had reigned supreme during both Rosas's and Urquiza's regimes. In some of the provinces, such as La Rioja, for example, the federalists resisted and were crushed by the "national" army. In others, such as Santiago del Estero, they were displaced by the influence of a local leadership turned liberal. And in Urquiza's own province, Entre Ríos, the federalists kept their leading place, in an unstable but negotiated relationship with the central government.

By 1865, this political process was interrupted by a war. Argentina, Brazil, and Uruguay entered an alliance against Paraguay. Notwithstanding its international character, this conflict was initially sparked by the rivalry between two enemy factions that operated both in Argentina and Uruguay and knew little of "national" loyalties. As on previous occasions, a fight between the *colorados* and *blancos* in Uruguay immediately triggered the respective support of the liberals and the federalists in Argentina. The intervention of Brazil to aid the *colo-*

rado/liberal tandem, and of Paraguay, which sided with the *blancos*, turned the political conflict into a war between nations. It was a long and costly war, particularly for Paraguay, which lost a large proportion of its male population in combat.

In Argentina, President Mitre obtained Urquiza's support for the war and succeeded in making the conflict a national enterprise. He crushed the military revolts launched by federalist caudillos in the interior provinces who supported the *blancos* and refused to go to war against Paraguay. In spite of these successes, he could not consolidate his own political power. In Buenos Aires, his Liberal Party split. In 1864, Adolfo Alsina, the young son of a prestigious anti-Rosas émigré who had been governor of Buenos Aires in the 1850s, created an electoral club—Club Libertad—opposed to Mitre's leadership. The president's followers, on their part, formed the Club del Pueblo. Both clubs were meant to be ephemeral electoral organizations that were to dissolve after the electoral period was over. Each of them claimed, therefore, to represent the "true" Liberal Party, and accused its rival of factious behavior. This division soon became permanent, and it gave way to the consolidation of two stable political forces: the Partido Nacionalista, which aspired to subordinate the province to the nation, and the Partido Autonomista, which adopted the opposite view. The former was led by Mitre, the latter by A. Alsina.

This development initially proved controversial, as it contradicted some of the prevailing ideas on political representation. The nation was then widely understood as an indivisible whole. Elections, for their part, were considered a means to select the best men to represent the whole, rather than to guarantee the representation of the various interests and sectors of society. Therefore, in Buenos Aires, as in other areas of Latin America, for a good part of the nineteenth century, the concept of "party" was controversial, and parties were critically labeled "factions," a word that had negative connotations of divisiveness and partisanship.

In spite of these misgivings these parties existed, and during the 1860s and 1870s the political life of Buenos Aires revolved mainly around the antagonism and competition between the two parties. This opposition did not preclude internal divisions within each party, or crosscut arrangements and alliances between groups in both. Scholars have stressed the inorganic, personalistic, factional nature of these parties. Yet they also became important centers for the convergence of different political interests and for the development of material networks and symbolic webs that defined political traditions.

Competition between the *nacionalistas* and *autonomistas* covered different grounds, from the most obvious one of electoral confrontation to other, more permanent battles to gain the favor of the urban public or the support of the socially powerful. They also struggled to gain positions in the national and provincial administrations. Beyond Buenos Aires, Mitre and the *nacionalistas* achieved some influence in the rest of the provinces, while the *autonomistas*, though unable to set foot elsewhere, entered into political and electoral alliances with former federalists and other provincial groups. Both parties, however, were based in Buenos Aires, and from there they tried to build their authority over the whole nation.

In the end, they failed. In the second half of the 1860s, Mitre's party gradually lost ground in its own province. In 1866, the *autonomistas* won the governorship and the majority in the legislature, and in the general elections 1868 the *nacionalistas* were again defeated. The War of the Triple Alliance against Paraguay had lasted too long. Mitre had spent many years away from Buenos Aires, as commander in chief, leaving Marcos Paz, the vice president, in charge. The *autonomistas*, however, could not go too far. The presidential race of 1868 was won by Domingo Faustino Sarmiento, a man with no party affiliation who was traveling in the United States at the time of his nomination. His name had been proposed by members of the officer corps that had participated in the war. Although he was not a military man, his victory reflects the political influence of the army after the campaigns against the federalist caudillos and the war. The *autonomistas* had barely managed to include Alsina as the candidate for the vice presidency.

The *nacionalistas*, now in the opposition, tried to recover some of their local and national political potential. Mitre was able to recuperate his prestige, but his power was limited to Buenos Aires. They continued to struggle with the *autonomistas* for the control of the city and the province. Both parties created new electoral clubs, entered various alliances, competed for seats in the provincial legislature, the National Congress, and the governorship, and debated through the press as partners in an animated political game. Meanwhile, beyond Buenos Aires, powerful political groups from the rest of the provinces were building a new coalition of forces. In 1874, Nicolás Avellaneda, their candidate, won the presidential elections. The *autonomistas* entered the coalition at the last minute, to include—once more—one of their men as candidate for the vice presidency.

In that same year, Mitre's followers launched a revolution against "the oppressors that keep treading upon the rights of the people."[12] They accused their rivals of committing fraud in the parliamentary elections and claimed their right to bear arms against "despotism." Those in power, on their part, considered this episode to be a regression to a deplorable past, when political differences were "solved" mainly by armed struggle. The government acted swiftly. The revolution was crushed, and the rebels were deported.

In spite of the rapid success of the government forces, the episode alarmed the authorities. It challenged the aspirations on the part of the state to a monopoly of violence and put the recent and precarious institutional order at risk. In the following years, the president devoted an important part of his energy to the reconstruction of that order. On the one hand, he consolidated the coalition that had initially driven him to power in 1874. On the other, he tried to change the political habits of the *porteños*, particularly their turbulent republicanism and their competitive electoral practices, all of which did little to favor the desired order. To that effect, he first granted an amnesty to the deported, then initiated a round of negotiations both with the *mitristas* and the *alsinistas*. Men from these two groups were incorporated as ministers to the government; and, at the time of elections for Congress, shared electoral lists with candidates from the three different parties were drafted. It was a way of avoiding the violent clashes that were typical of Buenos Aires elections. This move was not favored by all, however, and both within the *nacionalistas* and the *autonomistas* there was resistance to the pact. Among the latter, the dissidents formed a new party, the Partido Republicano, that had a short but boisterous existence. Thus the efforts to control and pacify the political life of the city had little success, as the discontents from all sides reenacted the tumultuous practices that had been typical of the city before 1874.

The main sources of political power were, however, increasingly found elsewhere. The central administration, with the support of a large number of the provincial governments, was preparing the presidential succession of 1880. The creation of the Partido Autonomista Nacional (PAN), and the nomination of General Julio Roca as presidential candidate, resulted from a coalition of forces that had no place for the Buenos Aires political elite. Some of its traditional figures migrated to the new party, but a great number of *mitristas* and *alsinistas* kept their old allegiances and stayed in their respective parties. The antagonism between them and the PAN escalated until violence erupted. The *porteños* opposed Roca's official candidacy, as well as the change of status of the city, designed to become a federal district and the national capital. By June 1880 they had turned the streets into an armed bastion of resistance. The president summoned the army, which under the command of General Roca soon defeated the urban militias. Thus the province of Buenos Aires was finally "conquered" by the national forces, its main city became the federal capital, and its chief leaders were displaced from the ranks of the most powerful. After subduing the last province to resist the centrality of the national state, the newly elected President Roca succeeded in establishing law and order throughout the territory.

In the midst of the political struggles and conflicts of the 1860s and 1870s, the state had, nevertheless, consolidated. In the words of Halperin Donghi: "Roca's victory was that of the central state, which had proved hardly controllable by either the political factions . . . or the dominant groups of civil society."[13] The role of the city of Buenos Aires in this process had been rather ambiguous. On the one hand, it had been the seat of the national government and the administration since the 1860s. Also, it had always occupied a key symbolic place in the history of the nation. On the other, the province had once and again insisted on the autonomous right of its authorities to resist the federalization of the city. And all attempts at designing Buenos Aires as a national capital had failed. By 1880, this ambiguity ended when the central power imposed its rule through the use of force.

Factious confrontations gave way to national unity, while the central state became the main site of political power. At the same time, there were clear symptoms of the increasing strength and autonomy of a civil society, as we shall see in the next chapter.

2 The Institutions and Networks of Civil Society

The drawing entitled "Today's Celebration—the Inauguration of Mazzini's Statue" portrays the meeting that took place on the occasion of the inauguration in Buenos Aires of a statue of one of the main figures of Italian republicanism, Giuseppe Mazzini. In the foreground are the main opponents to the event: in the center, the official newspaper, *La América del Sud* (represented by the pig); to the right, Archbishop Antonio Aneiros; to the left, a member of the municipal board. The text reads:

[Archbishop Aneiros]—You have finally succeeded in erecting a statue to that damned freethinker, and I, I cannot obtain a simple [cardinal's] hat!

[Municipal board member, Mr. Perisena]—And I thought that by allowing the carnival's final celebration to take place today, this inauguration would be a fiasco!

Rivadavia's Centennial

Few, very few people did not attend the day before yesterday the celebrations in honor of the illustrious citizen Bernardino Rivadavia. . . .

It is hard, almost impossible, to give the idea of those immense masses of men who, from the early hours of the day, filled up the streets and avenues where the procession was going to pass. . . .

The parade was carried out in the following manner:

The first column . . . is formed by members of the National Government. There, you can see the President of the Republic and his ministers . . . the generals Mitre and Sarmiento [former presidents], the Senators and Representatives of Congress, the members of the Supreme Court of Justice, and a group of head officers of the Army, all dressed up for parade. Behind them, the representation of the Province of Buenos Aires. . . . Also, the Centennial Commission. . . . It stops at the corner to look at the great parade. The stage is then occupied by the "Club Español," which advances into the Plaza [de la Victoria]. . . . Behind the Spanish Club with its banners and flags, and its happy music, there follows the "Club Catalán," and other innumerable and diverse Spanish associations.

When they finish passing, the French societies come by. . . . The first is the mutual aid society "Minerva," followed by other associations of the same nationality. There come the tailors, with their truly regal banner. It is made of red velvet, embroidered in gold, with cords and tassels also in gold. The banner is shaped as a cone, and on the top, it carries the cap of liberty.

"The column of the liberals" shout one thousand voices. And there it is, the large column presided by the chief editor of El Nacional, and by Dr. Eduardo Wilde. . . . Heading the column, a group called the "Negros Orientales" [Uruguayan blacks]. They carry three flags: the Oriental, that of their own nation [neighboring Uruguay]; the English, as a sign of deference toward England for having abolished the slave trade; and the American for the abolition of slavery. . . . Go ahead!

The large column moves forward. . . . The Masonic societies, compact and numerous, follow. Their banners with squares, compasses, and other Masonic symbols drawn or painted on a white, violet, or red field, line up in the central row and offer a beautiful and picturesque view. Their march is closed by the largest of the Masonic societies, one that exhibits a white flag with the [Italian] words "Patria é laboro."

Here comes the great Italian colony. First comes the society "Republicanos italianos," with their beautiful and rich banner. In the center, it has a large, circular emblem, with a red field encircled by two laurel boughs. In its center, the following words shine: "To Rivadavia, the Italian Republicans!" Here we have the "Stella di Roma" with its large music band. . . . Open the way to the "Lago di Como," headed by its glorious flag, with the green field, the golden embroideries, and the shiny letters in its center! The next is "Unione e Benevolenza," the oldest, the most beneficent, and the richest of the Italian societies in Buenos Aires. The Italian colony keeps passing for over half and hour, until the Swiss arrive, admirably organized.

In a moment, the eyes of the twenty or thirty thousand spectators who occupy the Plazas are raised toward the sky. They follow the march of a large balloon that has the inscription: "Education is peace." It rises to great height and then releases a large number of small Argentine flags that flap in space. . . .

The gigantic parade continues.

The Typographical Society, one of the oldest in the country, which has over two hundred and fifty members, carries a banner and two flags. . . . The Board of Trade follows, then the "Sociedad Rural" and the German residents. Heading the latter, the students of the German school, dressed with their nice uniforms. The German Club follows, made up of one or two hundred gentlemen dressed up in their most formal suits.

After them, there follow the "Sociedad Lusitana" and innumerable carnival groups. The march ends with a large column of Army regiments. . . . Finally, a huge wave of people closes the splendid civic procession.

—La Tribuna, May 22, 1880

A "Splendid Civic Procession"

The long quotation that opens this chapter refers to the celebration of the centennial of Bernardino Rivadavia, born on May 20, 1780, which culminated in a grand parade that ended in the Plaza de la Victoria.[1] The narration offers a snapshot of Buenos Aires and its residents that presents the space and the people in a very peculiar way. The place is the city center; first the streets, then the Plaza—a civic site par excellence. Thousands of people march to render tribute to an illustrious "citizen." This is not, however, the image of a spontaneous or undifferentiated crowd. To the contrary, a strict order rules the scene. The public appears behind its organizations. Immigrant associations and clubs, Masonic lodges, mutual aid societies, political parties, and even carnival groups occupy the center of the stage and of the newspaper account. There is, however, a reference to "a wave of people" that closes the march, and— in another paragraph—to "the masses . . . who occupy the roofs and balconies." Flags and banners give color and glow to the symbols of the different groups, and bands provide the music. Republican, liberal, and patriotic patterns are displayed everywhere.

Here, *La Tribuna* has put together a picture of Buenos Aires as a site for the exercise and glorification of civic virtues, public life, and associative practices. It portrays one among many other possible images of the city; one that introduces the people via their associations, which occupy the center of the scene. This is not a unique picture, as many similar ones may be found in the newspapers of the period. Yet it is not a well-known one. The history books have generally paid attention to other faces of the city. They have described its political life, analyzed its demographic and social features, studied its spatial configuration and changes. But little has been said about the dimension put forward by *La Tribuna*, which refers to the networks of civil society, to a public sphere in the making. It is only recently that those aspects have become visible to scholars, both in Argentina and elsewhere, as a result of a more general concern for the problems of political citizenship, representation, and participation in modern democracies (see the Introduction).

The formation and differentiation of the state and civil society have been generally considered to be typical of the transition from traditional to modern, bourgeois societies. Argentina was not an exception to this rule, and during the second half of the nineteenth century, the development of a vigorous civil society was soon as evident as the consolidation of the state, in the context of a capitalist economy in the making. That process was particularly noticeable in Buenos Aires, where a thick web of associative and communicational institutions became visible from the 1850s onward. The creation of a dense network of voluntary associations and periodicals was a symptom both of the development of a civil society and of the formation of a public sphere.[2] That is the subject of the present chapter, which will describe the main characteristics of the associative movement and the press in Buenos Aires, their mutual relationships, and their role in the genesis of a "culture of mobilization."

Associative Life

After the fall of Rosas, Buenos Aires experienced an unprecedented expansion of associative practices. Mutual aid societies, social and cultural clubs, literary circles, Masonic lodges, learned societies, festive groups, committees for the collection of funds for different purposes: these and other institutions sprung up throughout the city at an increasing pace.

These activities were not new in Buenos Aires. At the beginning of the nineteenth century, all main cities in the Spanish territories showed signs of the development of certain modern forms of sociability that differed from those that had prevailed during most of the colonial era. In those days, the organization and membership of brotherhoods, confraternities, artisan guilds, and the like had rested mainly on tradition, ascription, and custom. In contrast, the new associations were organized on a voluntary basis by free and equal individuals brought together by a common purpose. Deliberation and action within them were presumably governed by the laws of modern rationality. These novel forms played an important role in the transition from the *Ancien Régime* to the republic, as institutions where values and practices based on the principles of equality and freedom prevailed. They not only served the specific purposes that led to their creation; they also functioned as sites for the development and diffusion of modern social and political practices.[3]

The difference between traditional and modern patterns of social action was not as clear-cut as our classification suggests, and the institutions and practices of the first half of the nineteenth century probably show many combinations of both types, as well as forms that may not quite fit any of them. But the emphasis on that difference is not just a product of our own definitions. It was a matter of concern at the time, particularly when the revolutionary and postrevolutionary enlightened elites gained power and influence. They considered the modern forms of sociability an ideal site for the breeding of new citizens, and thus they promoted the creation of civil voluntary associations of all sorts. These efforts from above were only partially successful in the 1820s and 1830s, as there was little action from below in that direction. Rosas's years put a temporary halt to the move, but after his fall there was a sudden burst of associative life. The provincial and national authorities encouraged this expansion and re-established freedom of speech and association. This time, however, the main impetus for the expansion did not come from the government but, rather, from civil society.

Until recently, scholars had considered this drive toward associating as typical of the immigrant groups that were then settling in Argentina in increasing numbers, and of an incipient labor movement.[4] We now know that their reach was not restricted to those groups, and that voluntary associations could vary greatly in purpose, organizational means, and recruitment patterns.[5] "The association is the idea that marches at the avant-garde of universal civilization"[6]—those words, pronounced by the president of the Sociedad Tipográfica Bonaerense in 1862, express a conviction that was widely held at the time in Buenos Aires. In spite of the ideological and cultural differences that existed among the inhabitants of the city, the so-called associative movement was praised by all as a breeding ground for the values of equality and fraternity, a field for the practice of solidarity, and a solid foundation for a free and republican society.

This positive valuation of associative practices contributed to their expansion, which was both supported by the political elite and cherished by the rest of the people. The former found not only that associations were an indication of civilization but also that they could become legitimate voices in the political dialogue. As for the latter, several factors may account for their enthusiasm for associative practices. The massive presence of immigrants in Buenos Aires has been generally considered to be the key factor in this respect. The absence of primary links in their new place of residence led them to seek other forms of fraternal relationships. Many of them had previous associative experience, particularly among the republican political exiles from Italy, France, and Spain, who championed both the values and the practices of the associative movement. Rather than contributing to segregate the foreign population from the locals, that movement actually encouraged their integration, insofar as it "presumed the existence of a community of values" shared both by immigrants and natives.[7]

Immigrants constituted a potential public for associations, and their presence may have helped to create the conditions for the expansion of the movement. To account for its rapid and wide success in Buenos Aires, however, would require a broader look at the social and cultural life of the city. Rather than attempting to cast such a look in order to explain the success of associations, in the following pages I will explore their main characteristics and interrelations.

The city census of 1887 registered sixty-one associations in Buenos Aires, with a total of 60,258 members. These figures refer only to the leading institutions and they underestimate the scope of associative life in the city, as reflected by other sources.[8] Mutual aid societies ranked first in terms of numbers (they were more and had a larger membership) as well as public standing. According to Pilar González Bernaldo, their number increased from forty-one in the 1860s to over two hundred, twenty years later.[9] They constituted one of the main pillars upon which the whole movement relied.

Mutual Aid Societies

Mutual aid was the main purpose of many of the city's leading associations. They were created in order to gather funds and develop the means to assist and support the members and their families in matters of health care, unemployment, disabilities, and sometimes, education. Only one association of this sort was established during the first half of the nineteenth century, in 1832, by a group of French artisans, but it had a short life. After the fall of Rosas it was again the French who created the Sociedad Filantrópica de Beneficencia de los Peluqueros de Buenos Aires in 1853, and from then on many others followed.

According to their membership, these associations fell into three different types. Some institutions brought together people of the same national background; others, of the same occupation or profession; and yet others—a few—defined their membership on ethnic lines, as belonging to the "black community."

IMMIGRANTS ASSOCIATE

The associations founded by immigrant groups, and particularly by the Italians, were the largest. They were created in order to assist the immigrants of the same country or region and nucleated members of different social background. In 1854, the French established the *Société Philanthropique de l'Union et Sécours Mutuels*. Two years later, Spanish immigrants created *La Viguesa* and in 1857 the *Asociación Española de Socorros Mutuos*, which had a long and successful life and coexisted with other institutions of the same community established in the following years. Soon, however, they were superseded in number and membership by the associations originating among the Italian immigrants.

Unione e Benevolenza, founded in 1858, was the first Italian mutual aid society, and it has survived until today.[10] It was created with the declared purpose of assisting its members in case of sickness, covering their burial expenses, and helping the women and children in case of need. It later incorporated other services related to health care and education as well as social and cultural activities. Although its initial membership was predominantly from the regions of Liguria and Lombardia, the society always included members from other areas of Italy (even before Italian unification).[11] By the mid-1860s it had around three thousand associates. That figure dropped to fewer than one thousand at the beginning of the following decade, but growth soon resumed. By 1881 membership had again risen to three and a half thousand. It was the largest mutual aid society in the country.

The society's social composition was heterogeneous. Skilled and white collar workers, shopkeepers, and merchants were predominant. The directive posts were held mostly by those who came from the highest social ranks among the membership, particularly by professionals and merchants. Compared to other similar institutions, Unione e Benevolenza shows a relatively intensive participation of the rank and file in the meetings, elections, and assemblies convened during the first years after its creation. Later, this participation tended to decline, a pattern that was common to most institutions of this sort, both in Argentina and in other countries.

The rivalry between monarchists and republicans during the process of Italian unification was replicated within the association. A republican group, under the ideological influence of Mazzini, headed Unione's first steps. In 1861, after the ascent of the House of Savoy in Italy, some of the members, who had monarchical inclinations and acted under the protection of the Italian consul in Buenos Aires, were expelled and founded a new society, the *Nazionale Italiana*. Three years later, the republicans themselves suffered a split, a moderate group took over the association, and the Mazzinian radicals were separated from the leading posts. The latter finally created a new institution, the Società degli Operai Italiani. This replacement produced a reorientation in the internal organization of the Unione, as well as in its relationship with the Italian consul, the rest of the Italian associations, and the local political elite. The new leadership left political definitions behind, declared their aim to be to achieve efficient institutional performance, and sought to reach out to all Italian immigrants, regardless of their political inclinations. During this period, Unione e Benevolenza succeeded in becoming the main representative of the Italian community in Argentina, although by 1880 there were thirteen other Italian mutual aid societies in Buenos Aires.

The leadership of those associations aspired to exert a guiding role among the Italians in Argentina and worked to transform the "multifarious conglomerate" of immigrants into a "homogeneous and singular subject," a subject that it would later define as the "Italian colony."[12] The leaders also sought the recognition of the Buenos Aires political and intellectual elite. In order to meet both these aspirations, they led their associations to act well beyond the strict limits of mutual aid. To advance in community building, they organized social, political, and cultural events. The cause of Italian unification was the favorite motive for celebration, although the internal split between monarchists and republicans led the former to prefer the commemoration of regal heroes and dates, while the latter celebrated the actions of Garibaldi and his men. This duality would later be replaced by an appeal to a single *italianità* made by the moderate leadership that managed to control the Unione after 1864 and exerted its influence over the rest of the associations. In the 1870s, September 20 became the accepted date for the major celebration of Italian unity.

Besides all these activities based around community building, the leaders of the Italian associations developed strong links with those of other immigrant institutions, as well as with Argentine politicians and intellectuals. These ties were initially cemented by ideological affinities, particularly between Italian republicans and some conspicuous members of the local elite known by their republican inclinations. Bartolomé Mitre, for example, developed a lasting relationship with the community. He participated in most celebrations, was an honorary member of several associations, and was invited to talk at meetings and other collective events. On their part, members of the Italian community supported Mitre in his political struggles, and even in his military endeavors. Italian brigades took his side in the battle of Pavón in 1861 and in the Revolution of 1874.[13]

The case of the Italian associations shows how these mutual aid societies founded by immigrant groups did not limit their action to the specific purposes for which they were created but displayed intense activity in other fields. Although not all the immigrant groups were as numerous, culturally heterogeneous, or politically diverse as the Italians, most associative life shows similar patterns of concern regarding both the process of community building and the relationship with local political and intellectual elites.

THE TRADES

A second group of mutual aid societies brought together men, and occasionally women, of the same occupation or profession. Their main purpose was not only to provide for their members in matters of health care, unemployment, and education but also to defend the trade. Therefore they have frequently been considered the predecessors of the workers' unions and resistance societies, and sometimes also as the successors of the colonial artisan guilds. Yet they differed greatly from both: from the latter, because, in principle, membership in a mutual aid society was based on voluntary association among free and equal individuals who practiced a particular trade; from the former, because mutual aid societies were not defined in terms of social class. They recruited their members not only among dependent workers but also among the self-employed and even among owners and bosses.

The first institutions of this sort that we know of were established in the 1850s. In 1853, a group of French hair dressers created the *Société Philanthropique et de Bienfaissance des Coiffeurs de Buenos Aires*. The shoemakers organized their own in 1856, and in 1857 it was the turn of the seamstresses, the cooks, and the typographical workers. They were followed in the 1860s and 1870s by the carpenters, masons, bakers, construction workers, tailors, and harness-makers. The historical narratives of the labor movement underline the importance of these institutions, considered to be the first autonomous attempts on the part of the working classes to organize. There are, however, few traces of them, as they were probably small and short-lived. In the context of the associative movement, they occupied a minor place, both in terms of their number and the size of their membership.[14]

The Sociedad Tipográfica Bonaerense was the exception to the rule.[15] It had a long life and it became a visible public presence in the city. It brought together the workers of the different trades that were connected to the production and sale of printed material, both of which experienced a sustained growth during these decades. These trades, albeit requiring different levels of ability and training, demanded mostly skilled labor. Native workers made up 66 percent of the men employed in the printing jobs, a figure that was higher than in most other industries, where immigrants prevailed. The workers engaged in these trades had privileged access to information of different sorts, national and international, and they were in contact with different sectors of the population. They regarded "their mission on Earth [to be] that of propagating civilization, and cooperating efficiently . . . to the diffusion of the enlightened and healthy ideas of the peoples. . . ."[16]

To the initial aims of "promoting the advancement of the typographic trade . . . assisting its members who fall ill or become unable to work . . . protecting those who need help . . . and securing that its workers are paid according to their skills and knowledge . . . ,"[17] the society soon added new purposes of a social and cultural nature. It organized a library, established its own printing press, and edited the periodical *Anales de la Sociedad Tipográfica Bonaerense*. The city's newspapers regularly published information on the society's program and activities. Its reports show, however, that the authorities found it hard to bank the fees, pay the bills, and even "maintain order and discipline."

The membership was relatively small when compared with that of other mutual aid societies. In 1880, when the industry employed around 500 workers in printing jobs, the *Tipográfica* had 187 associates. Since its creation, however, it had included some important figures of the Buenos Aires political and cultural world. The first president was Mariano Varela, a typographer and journalist by trade but also a well-known member of the local elite, founder and director of one of the main newspapers, *La Tribuna*, who later served as national minister and senator. Other such personalities acted in the *Tipográfica* and frequently sat in its board. Moreover, it appointed as honorary members some very distinguished national figures, such as Bartolomé

Mitre and Domingo Faustino Sarmiento, and international ones, such as Prussian prince Friedrich.

Besides establishing these links with people in power, the society championed the cause of mutual aid. In the *Anales*, Bartolomé Victory y Suárez claimed that the associative form was the ideal institutional basis of society, as it was governed by the principle of reciprocal cooperation and "the doctrine of all for one and one for all." Another regular commentator, José María Méndez, lectured on social revolution, peaceful and egalitarian, that would put an end to "the exploitation of man by his fellow men." According to Ricardo Falcón, the *Tipográfica*, through some of its members, established some contacts with the International Workers' Association in Europe.

Today, it might seem rather contradictory that an institution that basically nucleated workers and proudly announced that it was "the most fraternal association founded among the workers in our soil" at the same time sought to ensure a fluid relationship with sectors of the elite. At that time, however, this combination was feasible and welcome, inasmuch as the institutional leadership considered themselves to be part of both worlds. Among them, we could find typographers who were also journalists and held important posts in one or more of the city's newspapers. Many of them could, simultaneously, act as ideological advocates of the mutual aid cause and even some sort of socialism; participate in the political and cultural life of the city, sharing places and interests with the local elite; and develop strong links with the rest of the workers in the trades where they held the highest positions. The above-mentioned Victory y Suárez is a good example of this combination. He was born in the Baleares, arrived in Argentina in 1860, worked as a typographer, founded the periodical *El Artesano* in 1863, and participated in the activities of the Tipográfica, where he collaborated in *Anales* and apparently acted as a link between the Argentine institution and the Barcelona section of the International Workers' Association. He also joined the Spanish mutual aid society and the Masons. Yet Victory y Suárez also cultivated other relationships in Buenos Aires. He was, for twenty years, manager of the Sociedad Rural Argentina, which nucleated some of the richest landowners of the country. He also developed close ties with President Sarmiento, who named him the director of the bulletin published on account of the national exposition held in Córdoba.[18] Victory y Suárez was no exception among the Tipográfica's leadership, as many of its members had a similarly multilayered public life.

For almost twenty years, this style of action and rule did not generate any visible controversy within the institution. In 1877, however, a group of associates split off and founded the Sociedad Unión Tipográfica, whose main purpose was to intervene in labor relations in order to impose wage standards upon employers for all the labor force. Chapter 9 describes how this new association promoted the first strike declared in the country, in 1878, which ended with favorable results for the workers. Nonetheless, in the following year both societies merged, and the yearly report of 1879/80 stressed "the transcendental importance of the fusion . . . and the high moral implied in the extinction of the nefarious antagonism that gave way to the division."[19]

THE BLACK COMMUNITY

The mutual aid movement also had representatives within the black community, formed mainly by the descendants of African slaves.[20] This community had developed strong associative traditions in Buenos Aires. The first organizations were devoted to the celebration of ritual dances related to their original ethnic groups or "nations." During the last decades of colonial rule and the first after the revolution of 1810, these activities were banned by the authorities, and only in 1822 did the provincial government authorize the creation of the Sociedades africanas. Many were founded in the following years by the different "nations," who congregated for purposes of festive and ritual dancing.[21]

In the 1850s, the new associations that had formed—*Abaya, Protectora Brasileña, del Carmen y Socorros Mutuos*, and *de Morenos Criollos Nuestra Señora de Luján*—included mutual aid and cultural activities as their main purposes. Nevertheless, they kept the religious, ritual, and festive roles that had been typical of the *Naciones*. Two opposed views soon developed within the community: while some leaders defended the old ways, others championed the cause of mutual aid. Finally, by the 1860s the *Naciones* had disappeared, but new forms of festive sociability developed. In the 1870s, for example, groups organized to prepare for, and participate in, the carnival celebrations that proliferated in the city. Meanwhile associations especially devoted to mutual aid had a moderate expansion. The main institution of this sort, *La Protectora*, was created in 1877, and a short time later, it reached three hundred members.

The Associative Fervor

Mutual aid societies shared the stage with other types of associations. Some of them, such as the above-mentioned cultural clubs, literary circles, professional societies, and Masonic lodges, were institutions that aspired to some degree of continuity in their action. The Masons, for example, experienced a sustained expansion during these decades. Many lodges were founded, which brought together people of different social and national backgrounds. They published several journals and had a very visible public presence. Professional societies were slower to prosper, however. The physicians, for example, had several failures before they organized the *Asociación Médica Bonaerense* in 1860 and, a decade later, the more successful and long-lasting *Círculo Médico*. The pharmacists, on their part, organized their own society in 1856, which represented and defended the interests of the trade and was considered a "truly scientific corporation." In the 1870s, the university students displayed an intense associative life whose main purpose was the reform of the university and particularly the medical school.[22]

The associative fervor was so intense that even a festive, subversive, event like the carnival came under its organizational spell. This traditional festivity had been highly controlled by the authorities during the Rosas regime, but after 1852 it became a great, joyous occasion in the city. The Spanish residents created the *orfeones*, organizations that prepared hundreds of men and women to parade with their regional costumes and musical bands.[23] The young *porteños* of the propertied classes imitated the Spanish and formed the *comparsas*, to prepare their dances and satirical songs for the carnival, a practice that soon expanded to other social sectors. In the 1860s and 1870s, men and women of different ages as well as social and national origins organized their own *comparsas* whose imaginative names bear witness to the various cultural traditions involved: *Salamanca, Lago di Como, Stella, Los Habitantes del Carapachay, Orión, Los Negros*. The latter did not include, as the name suggests, men of color, but its members posed as such in the carnival's parades, a practice that was soon adopted by other groups. They painted their faces black, played the drums, and performed traditional African dances, imitating the old *Naciones*, long absent from the streets of Buenos Aires. The black community, in turn, copied this copy and organized its own *comparsas*, to parade and dance in imitation of its ancestors. In 1869 they founded *Símbolo Republicano*, and ten years later there were twenty-nine of them that included only men and fifteen that were for women.[24]

Although the main purpose of all these organizations was to prepare for the parades that took place every February, during carnival season, they soon extended their field of action to include social, cultural, and recreational activities all year round. Thus they became one of the many permanent expressions of the associative life of Buenos Aires, and they were praised for contributing to the incorporation of the young to public sociability. *La Broma*, one of the main papers of the black community, considered the *comparsas* to be the first step that would later "produce newspapers . . . , establish libraries, offer literary conferences, [and] establish mutual aid societies. . . ."[25] In this way, the disruptive nature of the carnival was subsumed into the progressive march of civilization.

More ephemeral forms of collaboration also proliferated in these decades. *Porteños* were inclined to create committees and commissions for specific purposes, such as collecting funds for a particular cause, erecting a statue, paying homage to a public figure, or organizing a celebration. The study of all these different forms, both permanent and ephemeral, is well beyond the scope of this chapter. It is possible, however, to point to some of the more visible traits of these associative practices and institutions.

First, the associative movement attracted people from all walks of life. Native and immigrant, black and white, men and women, old and young, worker and employer, rich and poor—all could be found among its members.

Secondly, most of the associations cut across the social spectrum and included men, and sometimes women, of different social backgrounds. Recruitment very seldom followed class lines, and even institutions that prima facie presumed a socially limited composition—such as the Sociedad Rural or the workers' societies—always had a larger membership. Predisposition to participate was higher among those that belonged to the middle ranks, but neither the upper nor the lower classes were excluded. In the immigrant mutual aid societies, for example, the bulk of the members were skilled workers, both wage laborers and self-employed; small proprietors of different sorts, chiefly connected with petty commerce and manufacture as well as the service sector; and state and commercial employees. But the leading roles were generally in the hands of professionals and merchants. Social position, therefore, did have some bearing on the internal stratification and hierarchies present in all of these groups. There was also a strong gender bias. The leadership was almost exclusively male, and quite often, women were excluded from the rank and file.

Thirdly, the leadership took great care in the organizational aspects of institutional life. Statutes and regulations established rules and procedures for the governing bodies, as well as the rights and duties of membership. The equality of all members, freedom of speech and deliberation, and the election of authorities through democratic procedures were the key principles upon which the associative creed rested.

Fourthly, this basic equality did not preclude the crystallization of hierarchies within each association, the formation of an elite or leading "class," and the eruption of conflicts among those who sought to occupy that position. The institutional leadership played a key role both in terms of the internal dynamics of every association as well as in public performance.

Finally, all of these institutions were at the very center of the public life of the city. They defined a shared space of initiatives and action; they established an ongoing dialogue and generated an intense inter-institutional exchange and circulation. Banquets, commemorations, festivities, protests, and social events crystallized this communion. At the same time, they mediated between civil society and the state and shared that particular role with another key actor in the public life of the city, the press.

The Press: "The First Instrument of Civilization"

"If anything reflects the progress of the Argentine Republic it is the present state of the press. . . . She should be proud; there is something extraordinary and wonderful in the rapid development that the press has experienced in the last years."[26] *La Tribuna* was highlighting a fact that contemporaries were well aware of: the great expansion of the press that had taken place in the country, and particularly in the city of Buenos Aires, after 1852. That same year, thirty periodicals were created, and although most of them were short-lived, a few—such as *El Nacional* and *Los Debates*—enjoyed prestige and continuity. From then on, the circulation of newspapers, magazines, journals, and other periodicals was always on the increase. Ernesto Quesada counted 83 of these publications in 1877 and 103 in 1882.[27]

The editions differed in size. In the early 1860s, important newspapers such as *La Tribuna* and *La Nación Argentina* published three to four thousand copies a day, a figure that rose abruptly in the following years. By 1887, the two papers with wider circulation, *La Nación* and *La Prensa*, printed eighteen thousand copies each. Although the rest were all well below those figures, the total circulation for seventeen of the twenty-four papers that were then published in the city reached one hundred thousand (one copy for every four persons).[28] The figure is quite impressive, and compares well with those available for other large contemporary cities.[29]

"Everybody reads the newspaper here . . . from the highest dignitary to the most humble porter." Quesada's perception may be exaggerated, but surely the reading public must have been quite large to consume all the periodicals published in the city.[30] It is hard to assess its scope, but it surely was not limited to the political and intellectual elites. Literacy rates were on the increase. Fifty percent of the men and forty-three percent of the women could read and write in 1869; those figures rose to sixty-four and fifty-seven percent, respectively, in 1887, well above the figures for the rest of the country.[31] The potential readership was, therefore, rising. But its actual growth depended mainly on the ability of the press to generate its own public by contributing to stage an arena for debates, information, and exchanges that attracted new readers.

In the 1850s, the expansion of the press was tightly linked to the renovated and vigorous political life of the city. Soon, to have a newspaper became almost a requisite for anyone aspiring to political influence. All leading Argentine politicians had their own papers or recruited the favor of one or more of the periodicals that circulated in Buenos Aires. In the late 1860s and in the 1870s, most papers still had ties with particular political leaders or groups (and with the government), but increasing autonomy became the rule. Also, a new press that did not originate in the political realm took shape. In 1875, *La Tribuna* observed:

Every social or political group has its own organ in the Buenos Aires press. The liberals, the reactionaries, the pro-government, the anarchists, the sensible and enlightened . . . everybody, absolutely everybody, even the different immigrant settlers have their own periodicals to represent their interests.[32]

By that time, any person or group that wished to become public, to press for a particular interest, to defend an opinion, or simply to have a voice in the city had to publish a newspaper.

Among all the different types of periodical publications edited in Buenos Aires, we shall concentrate upon those devoted to current political and economic affairs. They had the widest circulation and a key role in the public sphere.

A Newspaper "Mania"

The most renowned newspapers of these decades had originated in the political rivalries of the post-Rosas years.[33] Soon, however, they started to broaden their interests to include not only the partisan news and editorials but also international news and information on trade, commerce, and cultural events; editorials on topics of general interest; advertisements; and a feuilleton.[34] At the same time, new, independent (that is, nonpolitical) publications started to circulate widely in the city. The most important among them were those edited by immigrant groups with the double purpose of informing and representing their nationals.

Two of the main papers of the period were first published in the 1850s: *El Nacional* (1853–93), created by a prestigious member of the political establishment—Dalmacio Vélez Sársfield—which eventually became the organ of the followers of Domingo Faustino Sarmiento; and *La Tribuna* (1853–84), for many years under the control of the Varela brothers (Héctor and Mariano), which was always close to the Partido Autonomista.[35] Other, more ephemeral, periodicals were also published in those initial years of expansion.

The 1860s witnessed the creation of two newspapers that are still today in circulation: *La Nación Argentina* (1862–69) continued as *La Nación* from 1870 onward, mouthpiece of Bartolomé Mitre and his party; and *La Prensa*, founded in 1869 by José C. Paz, which had a more independent political position.[36] Another relatively autonomous political paper that started to appear in 1869 was *La República*, directed by Manuel Bilbao, which lasted until 1881.[37] Other, strictly partisan organs also circulated at the time, but had a shorter life, such as *La Presidencia* (1875–77), *mitrista;* and *La Política* (1872–75), *autonomista,* among many others.

Those were also the years of great expansion of a satirical press. *El Mosquito* (1863–93), directed by Enrique Stein, was the most renowned in its kind, and carried very elaborate cartoons and caricatures of the main political figures and events of the time.[38] But there were many others, such as *La Bruja* ("The Witch"), 1860; *El Diablo* ("The Devil"), 1864; *El Látigo* ("The Whip"), 1865; *El Sombrero de Don Adolfo* ("Don Adolfo's [Alsina] Hat"), 1875; *La Farsa Política* ("The Political Farse"), 1875; *Antón Perulero,* 1875–76; *El Bicho Colorado* ("The Red Beetle"), 1876; *El Fraile* ("The Friar"), 1878; *La Matraca* ("The Rattle"), 1878; *La Cotorra* ("The Parrot"), 1879–80.

The foreign language press was started by English and French editors. In the early sixties and after several failed attempts, two successful such papers came to being: *The Brazil and River Plate Mail,* continued by *The Standard* (1861–1900) and *Le Courier de la Plata* (1865–98). They provided updated information on trade and commerce, as well as on political and international affairs, and catered not only to their own nationals but also to a wider readership, particularly among the commercial and financial circles of the city.

Among the periodicals in a foreign language, the Italian papers soon became the most widely read.[39] The first efforts in that direction were made in the sixties, but it was only in the following decade that the Italian press acquired continuity and a wide circulation. The main organs were *L'Operaio Italiano,* created in 1872; *La Patria,* in 1877, which changed its name in 1881 to *La Patria Italiana;* and *L'Amico del Popolo,* in 1879. In 1887 the Italian papers printed twenty thousand copies per issue, half of which corresponded to *La Patria Italiana.*

Although the Spanish were not as successful as the Italians in this field, they also had their own papers. Their main organ was *El Correo Español* (1872–98), which started by printing one thousand copies and reached four thousand by 1887. The Germans, on their part, in spite of being a small community, also displayed a relatively intense editorial activity.

Other specific sectors besides immigrants also circulated their own organs. These included some craft unions, such as the hairdressers (*El Peluquero,* fortnightly periodical, 1877) and the typographers, as well as groups that promoted a particular ideological cause: the Masons, radical republicans, and some socialists published short-lived sheets and periodicals, such as *El Artesano,* 1863; *El Petróleo,* 1875; *Le Révolutionnaire,* 1875–76; and *El Descamisado. Periódico rojo* (1879). Women, who had a marginal presence in the press during most of the period, in the 1870s published *La Alborada Literaria* followed by *La Alborada Literaria del Plata.* Even the Church competed in this terrain, and its authorities supported several periodicals. Although they never reached a wide circulation, they succeeded in voicing the official opinion of that institution in the public arena.

Between Subordination and Autonomy

All these very different publications shared some common traits; above all, they were considered to be part of that "first instrument of civilization,"[40] the press. Halperin Donghi has made a compelling analysis of the press during the 1860s and 1870s. He has studied the "rules of the game" as they developed in those years of great expansion; the relations established between political leaders and newspaper editors and journalists; the financial difficulties of the various presses and their economic dependency vis-à-vis the government and the political parties, whose support was indispensable to sustain most of the newspapers.[41] These ties with the political realm notwithstanding, the press operated with an increasing level of autonomy. Except for a small number of generally ephemeral papers that were strictly party organs, the rest insisted more and more in presenting themselves as part of a "free press," representatives of an "independent opinion" that could show occasional sympathy toward a party or even support a particular candidate but were not subordinated to the government or political factions.[42] The pejorative label *prensa situacionista* was increasingly used to designate those newspapers considered to be actual organs of the current government.

The history of *La Nación* illustrates this passage to relative autonomy. The paper was founded in 1870 to replace *La Nación Argentina*, which had been a party and government organ par excellence. In the first issue of the new periodical, Bartolomé Mitre thus reformulated its purpose:

Today, the combat is over. . . .

Once the nation [*nacionalidad*] has been founded, it is necessary to propagate and defend the principles that have inspired it, the institutions upon which it is based, the security it has created for all, the practical ends it seeks, the moral and material means that have to be subservient to those ends.

Therefore, he concluded, while *La Nación Argentina* was a weapon for political combat, *La Nación* was to be a means of publicity, of "propaganda."[43] And although the paper continued to be tightly linked to Mitre's party, it became institutionally independent; broadened the scope of its interests to include national and international news, cultural information, and commercial advertisements; modernized its management; sought financial autonomy; and introduced technical improvements.

The Buenos Aires press soon defined a space of its own, with its internal rules, practices, and styles. The most important newspapers were printed in large format (around thirty-three inches long and twenty-five inches wide per page), had a uniform layout with columns of two to three inches wide, and a typography that used letters of different sizes and intensity but basically the same fonts. With the exception of the satirical press, which included cartoons, most papers carried no drawings or images. They were usually four pages long. The first page carried the international news, official documents, and the feuilleton; the second page, the editorials, opinion columns, and national and local news; and the last two pages, trade and maritime information, customshouse clearances, and numerous advertisements. The lesser papers were frequently printed in smaller format but could have more pages per issue. As for those edited by immigrant groups, they were generally written in their respective languages and paid special attention to news from the fatherland and that of the local immigrant community.

By the 1870s, publishing a large paper became a true business operation. Twenty years earlier, government funds had been the key to subsistence; although newspapers were usually sold by subscription, in order to cover their costs they had to obtain subsidies, or ensure large subscriptions, from the national or the provincial administrations. Later on, state support and subsidies from the political parties were maintained, but the editors explored other, more autonomous, ways of financing their businesses. The price of subscriptions was lowered, and the use of street vendors was successfully implemented by most large papers.[44] Some of them, like *La Tribuna*, produced an evening edition in addition to the regular morning one. Advertisements also became a source of income. In some cases, private shareholders contributed funds to the business. The most successful editing firms, particularly in the immigrant press, diversified their activities and introduced other operations, such as the printing and selling of other publications, money exchange, or the sale of transatlantic tickets.

Each paper had its own style, from the very formal rhetoric of *La Nación* to the irreverent one of the satirical press. Most of them shared a common, basic, republican liberalism, although with many variations that gave each its particular tone.

"The Fearsome Power of Journalism"

The press played different roles during this period—first among them in the political arena, where it became a key actor.[45] On the one hand, the papers were considered an instrument for the creation and development of a rational, enlightened, republican society. They were supposed to represent, and at the same time to shape, public opinion, one of the main pillars of a modern political system. Freedom of the press was highly praised and generally honored, although official control, censorship, and the closure of newspapers did occur on several occasions, most notably during the War of the Triple Alliance against Paraguay and the revolutions of 1874 and 1880.[46] On the other hand, the papers were one of the material sites where political discourse took place. The leaders and leaders-to-be wrote articles in the press, and a lot of the discussion and dialogue between them took place there. Thus the press helped to make politics a public matter, and through it, the word and the image of the politicians reached beyond the relatively few who were directly involved in the political game to a larger public.[47]

The papers were the mouthpieces and the *fora* for those involved in the political struggle, but they soon played the same role for anyone who wished to be heard or to have some influence in the city. The incipient leadership of immigrant groups rapidly perceived the importance of having their own press and proceeded to found many different papers. They had many things in common with the "national" press, but they also had their specific traits. The Spanish and Italian papers, in particular, were closely related to the immigrant associative movement. They both shared the same leadership, and they formed an interrelated institutional network that played a key role in the definition and construction of their respective communities.[48]

A Public Sphere

These networks were part of the larger web that included the whole associative movement and the press of Buenos Aires. Together they defined a space of shared initiatives and actions. All the important papers dedicated a daily space to information about their colleagues. They greeted or criticized the creation of new periodicals; lamented or celebrated their closure; reproduced, praised, or debated articles published by others; and so forth. They also included abundant information on the activities of the associations. The latter, in turn, paid attention to the papers, kept them informed about their programs, invited editors and journalists to their meetings, and sometimes produced their own publications. These institutions did not only represent, protect, and look after the interests and opinions of their actual and potential public; they also created a thick web of relations and exchanges.

They also played a central role in the mobilization of the urban public. The people of Buenos Aires were increasingly prone to collective action. The theaters, streets, and plazas were the favorite spots to meet for celebrations, protests, commemorations, and demonstrations. National patriotic holidays; the birthdays and the funerals of renowned public figures; the republican victories in Italy, France, or Spain; the inauguration of a statue, a hospital, a park, or a theater—there were plenty of opportunities to get together for banquets, ceremonies, and demonstrations. And the *porteños* seized upon those occasions to meet with increasing frequency. By the 1870s, every year there were numerous and varied public events.

In January 1878, for example, the Italians convened a "patriotic spontaneous demonstration" on account of the death of King Vittorio Emanuele II, and a few days later thousands of people joined in an "imposing march" that attracted around ten thousand people.[49] By the end of February, the city had commemorated the centennial of the birth of General San Martín.[50] The government organized the main celebrations, but dozens of associations (immigrant societies, cultural groups, scientific and cultural associations, Masonic lodges, various clubs, and so on) took part in them and paraded from the *Plaza de la Victoria* to *Plaza San Martín* and back, in perfect order, followed by "columns of citizens" and accompanied by musical bands and a carriage that carried a bust of the nation's founding father.[51] In March it was time for the inauguration of the statue of Mazzini, the republican hero of Italy. The caricature reproduced at the beginning of this chapter refers to that occasion. According to *El Nacional:* "[A]ll the associations that exist in Buenos Aires were present . . . : the Masonic lodges with their banners and symbols; Italian, French, Swiss, German, and other associations. . . . The musical bands played all the time. . . . All the people of Buenos Aires joined the meeting."[52]

Other, more restricted initiatives followed. There was a "patriotic banquet" that convened around three hundred Italians in the Café El Pasatiempo to commemorate the anniversary of the passing of the Italian constitution. A committee in favor of the erection of a statue of Adolfo Alsina (who had died the previous year) called for a subscription to that end. Another public subscription was organized "to help the family of [worker] Juan Solari who was killed . . . by a case with goods, which he was unloading from a cart."[53] And in December, two hundred bakers marched to the Municipal Building to voice their claims. The main demonstration of that year was also held in December, when thousands of people gathered to protest against a project, submitted by the provincial executive to the legislature, to tax the consumption of tobacco, playing cards, and liquor (see Chapter 7).

In those decades, Buenos Aires witnessed a true culture of mobilization. The press and the associations were key pieces of that culture. They formed an institutional system that operated as an organizational network that covered the city, generated linkages of various sorts among its members, and promoted collective action. They also defined a space of mediation with the state and the political realm, a public sphere. As the leading actors of a civil society in the making, they contributed to structure the population of Buenos Aires as a public. This public frequently addressed the authorities to voice an opinion, represent a claim, or place a demand in the name of the interests of the whole.

Those in power, in turn, were very attentive to the signals stemming from that public. The political elite of Buenos Aires was aware of the increasing visibility of civil institutions, and its members were particularly sympathetic to the urban public. Their attitude did not aim primarily at gaining votes, as the winning of elections followed a different direction (see chapters 3 to 6). They were, rather, motivated by their understanding of the role of public opinion as a key factor in the legitimization of political rule. Their attempts to influence, command, and even manipulate that powerful but elusive force did not preclude their being attentive to what the actual public had to say.[54] In this period, therefore, a fluid and persistent dialogue developed between the institutions of civil society and the political powers. That will be explored in Chapters 7 to 10.

3 On Election Days

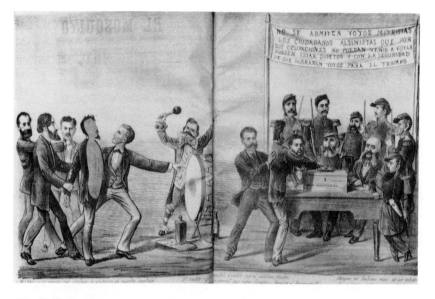

"Today's elections:

    Bilbao—Our party has to stop abstaining.

    Bartolo [Mitre]—It has to go on abstaining so as to follow the advice that says: 'Beware of the cheating.'

    Don Héctor [Varela]—Come on, people, come to vote for the noble Hector, the great orator of *ginebra y vermut* [in Spanish, *ginebra* means both 'Geneva' and 'gin'] who founded and ruined *El Americano!* Even if there were no more than one voter, the majority is secured."

The cartoon portrays a polling station on election day. On the left of the picture, a group of leading figures. The most prominent are Héctor Varela, with the drum, and Mitre and Bilbao, who are holding one half of a man whose jacket bears the word *pueblo* (people). The other half is casting the ballot on the right side of the picture. The men sitting at the table where the ballot box stands are well-known *autonomistas*—with Adolfo Alsina at the center. Armed men, presumably from the national guard, stand behind. The banner reads: "*Mitrista* ballots not admitted. *Alsinista* citizens who, due to their occupations, are unable to come and vote, stay calm; you may be sure that there will be a surplus of votes to win."

Solemn Agreement

[Celebrated at the Parish of La Piedad on occasion of the elections of February 1, 1874]

The committees of the two political factions of the Parish of La Piedad—formed on the one side by Don Juan J. Lanusse, D. José M. Huergo, D. Juan J. Castro, D. Antonio Lanusse, and D. Gregorio Gallegos, designated by the Club of the Party of General Mitre; on the other, by Coronel D. Alvaro Barros, D. Mariano Marcó, D. Marcos Paz, D. Luis N. Basail, and D. Manuel J. Sanabria, designated by the Club that sustains the candidature of Dr. Adolfo Alsina—met in session and in compliance with their mandate have agreed to the following:

Art. 1—Men from one and the other side will cast their ballots alternatively, three at a time, until two o'clock in the afternoon.

Art. 2—Draw lots to decide which three citizens are going to vote first.

Art. 3—Name a committee of two members from both parties, which will stay in the atrium or wherever they think most convenient to classify the voters and solve any doubts and difficulties that may arise in that respect.

Art. 4—The ballots will be received by the polling authorities as they are being cast.

Art. 5—The representatives of the two parties are obliged to make the individuals who have cast their ballots leave toward their respective Clubs.

Art. 6—After two o'clock, the ballots will be received according to the proportion of voters left on each side; that is to say, if there be one hundred on the one side and fifty on the other, two will vote from the first group and one from the second, previous classification of them all.

Art. 7—The classification will be started half an hour before the voting begins; if any of the sides are late in sending their classified voters, the Committee will command the others to continue.

Art. 8—When the voting ends, the members of each side will leave the place toward their respective clubs, and dissolve in opposite directions.

Art. 9—The scrutiny will be done only in the presence of the Committee mentioned in article three, which will be designated by the respective clubs and the presidents and vice presidents of each.

Art. 10—The purpose of this agreement being that the elections take place peacefully and honorably as it fits the civilized state of the country, we solemnly bind ourselves by all means available, to preserve order and see to it that the law is loyally and severely observed. In proof of this pledge, we sign the present pact in Buenos Aires, on January thirty-first, eighteen hundred and seventy-four.

Juan José Lanusse, José María Huergo, Manuel I. Sanabria, Marcos Paz, Antonio Lanusse, Mariano Marcó, Alvaro Barros, Luis N. Basail, Juan José Castro, Gregorio Gallegos

—*La Tribuna*, February 1, 1874

Why Vote?

In the years between 1860 and 1880, competition and rivalry between the parties that struggled for power was a constant feature in the political life of Buenos Aires. That confrontation reached one of its highest points in the electoral field. Elections were held regularly to choose national and provincial representatives (*diputados*), members of the electoral colleges that had to select the president and vice president, and municipal board members. It was not unusual to have five, six, or even more elections per year.[1]

To win an election it was necessary to gain votes. At the same time, the exercise of the right to vote was essential to the representative system established by the constitution. Elections were, therefore, a key element in the relationship between "the many and the few." In Buenos Aires, the former had enjoyed the right to vote since 1821, when universal suffrage for all native and naturalized men was instituted for good. There were no qualifications in terms of income, property, or literacy—none whatsoever. Yet in spite of the amplitude of the franchise, few people actually voted. Why?

As mentioned in the Introduction, some interpretations refer to a restricted citizenship and to the existence of limitations on the right to vote. They also mention the massive presence of immigrants who chose not to naturalize and could not, therefore, enjoy that right. Presumably, it has been argued, they were indifferent to politics, more interested in pursuing their private interests than in getting involved in public affairs. Yet the native Argentines, who by law were entitled to vote, very often chose to abstain. Why?

Maybe we should turn around the question and ask: Why did those who voted choose to do so? And what was the meaning of voting in Buenos Aires? Or, to return to my initial question: What was the role of suffrage and elections from the point of view of the actual relationship between "the many and the few"?

The Electoral Rules

In Buenos Aires, elections operated under regulations that had local, provincial, and national scope.[2] The provincial law of 1821 was still in force in 1862, the date of national unification. After that year, the federal laws of 1863, 1873, and 1877, and the provincial laws of 1864 and 1876, ruled the electoral life of the city. These demarcated the electoral districts and sections, established the requisites and the methods for registering, regulated the organization of the polls, and fixed the procedures for counting, validating, and annulling ballots. These were all fundamental aspects of the electoral system.

The city was always divided into sections or wards, which corresponded to different *parroquias*.[3] There were twelve sections in the 1860s: Balvanera, Barracas al Norte or Santa Lucía, Catedral al Norte or La Merced, Catedral al Sur, Concepción, Monserrat, Piedad, Pilar, San Miguel, San Nicolás, San Telmo, and El Socorro. Two more were added in the 1870s: San Cristóbal and San Juan Evangelista (see Map 1).

The polling stations were set up in the atriums of the corresponding parish churches, so that "the citizens meet their electoral obligation under God's supreme protection."[4] The polling authorities were in charge of controlling the whole procedure. Their composition was established by law. Before the passing of the federal law of 1863, the authorities were selected by the neighbors present when the polls were opened. After that year, each section was presided over by a justice of the peace, who worked together with two neighbors designated by the provincial legislature and four neighbors who were drafted by lots among those present at the polls. By the law of 1873, this composition was changed. From then on, each station was in charge of five citizens (and five substitutes), designated in advance by lots among twenty chosen from the registry by a special board formed by the president of the provincial legislature, the Supreme Court of Justice, and the section's federal judge. The role of the justice of the peace was restricted to handing the register to the authorities. The political parties were authorized to name observers at the polls.

As for the voters, the provincial constitution of 1854 established that "popular suffrage is a right and a duty inherent to every Argentine citizen" (Art. 48). The federal and provincial laws granted the right to vote to all adult men (over seventeen or eighteen years of age, depending on the law), born or naturalized Argentine, with the exception of "the insane," "felons who committed infamous crimes," clergymen, soldiers, and the deaf who did not read or write. Foreigners could vote in municipal elections, but they had to fulfill certain property and literacy qualifications that were not required of Argentines.

Before 1863, there was no register. Citizens who wished to vote simply presented themselves to the authorities in charge of the polling station, who decided on the acceptability of the voter. Besides the above-mentioned requisites, voters had to meet residence requirements and show proof of having fulfilled their military obligations (having been inscribed in the militia or *Guardia Nacional*, a requisite that was abolished by law only in 1877). Those whose credentials were accepted proceeded to vote publicly, viva voce, and the vote was registered in two different written records. The federal law of 1863 for the first time established a civic register, to enroll the voters-to-be in advance of the polls. In each section the register was in the charge of a qualifying board, formed by the justice of the peace and two neighbors designated by the executive. The register included the names of the resident citizens who had chosen to enroll and were accepted by the board. The act of registering was, therefore, a personal and voluntary one.

The ballot box was introduced in 1873, but the vote remained public. The voter produced his ballot in "white paper . . . expressing his name, his inscription number, and the name of the persons for whom he was voting" (Art. 24). The ballot was handed to the president of the polling station, who deposited it in the box. The counting was done at four o'clock in the afternoon, when the polls closed. The authorities then read the results to the public and proceeded to send all the documents to the legislature, which had to decide on the validity of the polls and, finally, proclaim the winning candidates.

These were the basic regulations that constituted the legal framework for the polls. The increasing punctiliousness of the rules, the multiplication of prescriptions, and the attention paid by the legislation to matters of detail proved insufficient to change the main traits of the electoral life of the city, which showed an amazing continuity, as we shall see below.

On Election Days

On January 17, 1860, *La Tribuna* complained about "the calm that has prevailed during the municipal elections . . . very close to indifference."[5] In July of the same year, the paper remarked: "[T]he elections for representatives were scarcely animated. Only in five parishes was it possible to go ahead with the polls."[6] This lack of animation on election days was frequent in Buenos Aires. On many occasions it was impossible to open the polling stations in over half of the parishes due to the absence either of the authorities or of citizens ready to vote. Such was the case in the elections for national representatives in December 1860, March 1867, January 1868, June 1869, and January 1872; for provincial representatives in June 1860, August 1868, and June 1870; for municipal electors in May 1869, November and December 1870, and December 1871. In 1871 and 1872, it was necessary to convene the citizens to elect the members of the constitutional convention seven times, because in the majority of the parishes the people did not show up.[7]

This picture could vary drastically, and the calm and apathy of the polls be replaced by excitement and mobilization. The advent of an election day in February 1860 was announced by *La Tribuna* with these words: "Today has been keenly anticipated as the day when a great battle would take place. Finally, it has arrived." A month later, after an election, the paper was again very eloquent: "Every parish became a true field of Agramante[8] during the last elections." The word "disorder" appeared once and again in newspapers, police reports, and other contemporary accounts when referring to the polling days. And next to it, the word "violence."

What happened on those exciting election days? The stories told by the contemporaries recur:

First scene. The place: the parish church of La Merced. The date: December 20, 1863. The occasion: the complementary municipal elections. The narrator: a contemporary witness, Félix Armesto:

One of the parties "owned" the polls and, with that force, it did not exclude any means—however fraudulent they might be—to win the election. . . .

The indignation of the vanquished was such that they tried to attack, a usual practice in those days; but the winners . . . had introduced their own party elements, and some in the church galleries and others on the roof retaliated by throwing rocks at the assailants.

The pistols and other portable firearms were monopolized by the rich, and so was the revolver, then very imperfect. The battle was therefore fought by means of the simple and primitive rock, as most of the fighting was done at a distance, and knives were reserved for face to face encounters.

The besiegers, more numerous than those within, used paving stones and brought piles of rocks from the Bajo [the riverside], while the latter tore apart the bricks from the walls and used anything that came to their hands; no tiles were left in the dome. . . .

[The neighboring buildings] were the refuge of the enemy forces and from there, as well as from the tower of the church, each party made accurate impact on the heads and eyes of the respective warriors. . . . Around the block, not one windowpane or glass remained in place, and not one of the combatants remained unharmed.[9]

Second scene. The place: the parishes of Buenos Aires. The date: March 27, 1864. The occasion: the election of provincial legislators. The narrator: the newspaper *La Tribuna*, March 29:

[In every *parroquia*] forbidden arms were displayed, and many of the nonforbidden ones were also used; there was uproar and scandal. . . . What happened?. . . . All the *parroquias* have been the theater of the same type of scandal. The stick, the rock, and the revolver have been the main *arguments* used by the clubs at the polls. To witness: the wounds suffered by Comandante Martínez y Orma, the knife taken by Mr. Blanco from a colored man named Posse, at the Parroquia de Monserrat.

Third scene. The place: the parish of Balvanera. The date: February 1, 1874. The occasion: the election for national representatives. The source: the report presented by the electoral board to the House of Representatives [*Cámara de Diputados de la Nación*] on April 10, the same year.[10]

[At] the time established by law, the polls opened . . . and the voters started to cast their ballots. Previously, there had been an agreement between the two sides, *mitristas* and *alsinistas,* to vote alternatively; that is, in turns, one from each side, on the condition that after twelve o'clock they would cease that alternate system, count the respective potential voters, and proceed with the casting of ballots, but now alternating the votes according to the proportion of potential voters present on each side.
     . . . [B]efore the appointed time, there was a great tumult that lasted for three quarters of an hour, with the result of several wounded and dead around the polling station and in the street, so that the polls were suspended.

La Tribuna was even more eloquent in the description of the same event:

At five minutes to twelve, the Comisario Estraordinario [Special Police Chief], Lieutenant Colonel D. Rodolfo Bunge, indicated that it was convenient for the two parties to divide into two different groups in order to proceed with the agreed recounting.
     It was done as indicated. . . . On the roof of the house right across the street from the church of Balvanera, there was a large group of people from the *mitrista* party, who started to shout at that very moment that they were being cheated. There followed a contest of shouts between those in the atrium and those on the roof, and a moment after the people at the polling table had stood up, three shots were heard, coming from the roof, followed by intense fire that went on uninterrupted for around fifteen minutes. The result of the combat was: three dead and ten wounded.[11]

Fourth scene. The place: the parish of Balvanera. The date: March 1877. The occasion: the election for provincial senators and representatives. The narrator: Leandro N. Alem (in a letter sent to the newspaper *El Nacional*):

At 8:20 in the morning, I was in the atrium of the church watching the organization of the polling tables, when I was told that two large groups, armed with Remingtons, were coming toward the church. In fact, around fifty people were coming down Piedad Street, and when they were a quarter-block from where I was, they spread out in guerrilla formation preparing their arms; another similar group, arms ready, was also coming down Azcuenaga

Street. Then a shot was heard. . . . The conflict started, and for five full minutes, the bullets crossed from one side to the other. The aggressors finally left,
and order and calm were resumed.[12]

Scenes like these were very frequent in Buenos Aires. Disorder,
turmoil, agitation, and violence were regular ingredients on election
days. Every "electoral assembly" resembled a combat where victory
was closely associated to armed conquest. Rather than referring to
ballots and votes, most accounts talk about rocks, knives, and revolvers. In those circumstances, the control of the territory was crucial.

"We know how to win elections," La Tribuna announced in 1864.
"Whoever has the strength, takes over the polling stations, and whoever takes over the polling stations, wins the election."[13] To take over a
station it was necessary to gain control of the church atrium, and also
of its yard, dome, roof, and walls. This holy site thus lost its sacredness
for the occasion. The Catholic hierarchy was not too happy with this
situation. Contrary to what happened in other places of Latin America, the Church did not play an important role in the electoral life of
Buenos Aires. And parish priests were not a visible presence on polling
days.[14] More than once throughout this period, the ecclesiastical
authorities asked the government to change the location of the polls,
but the answer was always strongly negative, as shown in this government letter of 1874: "[A]ccording to the electoral law and to its interpretation by Congress, it is impossible to satisfy [accept] your demand."[15]

The church premises became the center of a larger area that included the neighboring buildings, streets, roofs, and balconies, where
the violent episodes took place. This was an organized violence. The
first act took place at the time of the opening of the polls, when the justice of the peace arrived to set up the polling station with the police officer in charge of keeping order. Quite often, as we have seen, it was
not possible to open the polls, because the people simply did not show
up. In such cases, elections were suspended. In highly contested elections, however, this was a crucial moment. It was the time of the first
battle, as the neighbors present had to choose the authorities.[16] After
1873 that conflictive element was removed from the site of the polls,
because the authorities were chosen beforehand and the struggle that
surrounded their designation took place elsewhere.[17]

Once the polls opened, the key players were the voters. After 1863
previous inscription in the register was required of voters, but forged
inscriptions and altered registers were frequent. Often, groups that
did not belong to the neighborhood intruded in order to obstruct the

proceedings. Let us look at the voters, both genuine and phony, in action.

In March 1864, during the elections for provincial legislators, for example,

. . . the navvies of the Western Railway put pressure at the opening of the polls on the parish of San Nicolas. Bunched in groups, they prevented the presence of the neighbors and faked an election to designate the polling authorities; at the corner of the same room, the Justice of the Peace drafted the record, and forged the results. Once the authorities were in place, the group that controlled the situation voted repeatedly and impeded the voting of their rivals.[18]

The municipal elections were not any calmer. In December 1866 the police officer in charge of the Parroquia de la Merced announced that "once the voting started . . . some sailors of the Port Authority tried to get hold of the polling table to break it."[19]

In 1869, La Tribuna anticipated the cheating they expected on the part of their rivals in the election for provincial senators:

[T]he Castristas . . . buy the ballots, not for the legal act of voting, but to assault the polling station. . . . To that effect, they have already appointed the attackers for Balvanera and San Telmo. To the former, they are sending Moreno, the head of the train station of 11 de Setiembre, with the railroad navvies, and people bought by Unzué. To the latter, the cart drivers of Mr. Casares.[20]

During the election of national representatives held in January 1873, also according to La Tribuna, "[T]here has been a scandal in Monserrat. . . . [T]he majority of the neighbors were defeated by false and regimented registered voters, who were kept in great disorder and provided with liquor."[21] In 1874, we have seen how, in Balvanera, mitristas and alsinistas were organized into groups to cast their ballots in turns till midday, and how they entered into a fight after that hour.

All these accounts portray the main actors of these encounters as collective forces, groups mobilized not only for the purpose of voting but also to take part in the violent struggles that were a usual feature of election days. These "troops" had their leaders, major or lesser caudillos who, in turn, responded to the city's political bosses. On polling days, each one of them deployed his men. Félix Armesto recalls: "Paz ordered Garmendia to bring his gang, a noun that he used to designate a group of seven or eight former soldiers of the Castro Battalion . . . who were led by corporal Leonardo Gómez."[22]

Young politicians, many of them related to the socially and culturally elite families of Buenos Aires, were frequently a visible presence among those troops. Armesto portrays some of them in action: "Some people still remember the arrogant figure of José C. Paz, standing on top of the wall . . . by the school of the orphans and the atrium of the church [La Merced], insulting the assailants on the one side, and encouraging his men on the other; always fearless and ignoring danger. . . . [S]everal shots were fired at him, not only from the street below but also from the balcony at the corner, where Miguel Martínez de Hoz, Juan Chassaing, and Manuel Argerich were stationed."[23] Courage, audacity, intrepidity—those were the attributes expected from these young men of class, who belonged to the political parties and joined in the avant-garde of the electoral troops. They also played that provocative role by writing pungent articles in the press and participating noisily in the sessions of Congress and the legislature. Many of them were officers of the prestigious local militia, the *Guardia Nacional*.

A meticulous organization was set in motion on election days. The rival forces deployed their voting troops, who had to be ready to act. Their leaders armed the men, commanded them, and secured their obedience. In 1874, *La Tribuna* observed: "As on the dawn of any great battle, the chiefs review their forces, and recount the *fighting men* available for combat."[24] And electoral combat could be likened to a war: the recruitment and mobilization of the men; the hierarchical organization; the favorable disposition toward violence; the courage and heroism displayed in the field; the loyalty among the men; the importance given to the control of the territory; the language used by the participants—all these evoked war. It was, however, a limited war. The space of the battle was confined to the churchyard and its surroundings; the purpose was to capture the polling station and intimidate the opposition; the participants were known beforehand, and the fight lasted for only one day. Violence was kept under control, and although casualties were common they were seldom fatal.

It was, moreover, a war devoid of drama, that had rather a game-like quality. For Félix Armesto, "those face to face fights, where assailants and defendants exchanged insults, recalled the legendary combats of the Middle Ages, where action was accompanied by words."[25] In was a game in which the participants were old acquaintances, the rules were known to and respected by everyone, and the results were predictable. *La Tribuna* spelled out those rules eloquently in this 1864 article:

From 1852 onward every single election was won due to the . . . ability of the parties to enter the field and fight.

If the Club del Pueblo had had the men, it would have captured the polling stations, and once in possession of those mysterious machines that *produce votes*, they would have produced them by the thousands. . . .

Because that Club has lost the elections.

Because, in spite of the support provided to them by the government forces, they were not able to capture the stations.

Because the Club Libertad has shown its numerical superiority, *La Nación* [the newspaper of the *mitristas* and the Club del Pueblo] cries out and talks about scandal. But against what? Against the same things that it promotes.[26]

On election days at the polls, the parties compared their forces. "Numerical superiority" was important, both to casting and to *producing* the ballots. Ability and organization were crucial. All parties used the same methods, which were part of a larger system of electoral machines devised to compete and struggle to win.

The efforts to control the electoral results started before the polling day and continued afterward. Some of the methods used to "prepare" the elections are well known. The parties involved had to secure the appointment of their own men in the key posts: the justices of the peace, the police officers, and the registering boards. They also had to work on the civic register, enrolling their followers in more than one parish, discriminating against their rivals, and inventing names or using those of the dead.

The militia enrollment papers were false. The register tickets were false. The names under which one individual voted up to seven times in the same parish, and then proceeded to do the same in the next, were false. And these registers, basically false, were forged and enlarged with others that were drawn up in the clubs. . . .
—Who cheated?
—Both did—mitristas and alsinistas.
From the very beginning, both parties participated in the fraud.[27]

La Tribuna was answering here the accusations that *La Nación* had published after one of the more fraudulent elections of the decade, that for national deputies held in February 1874. The partisan press always denounced the cheating committed by their rivals, but they often accepted that these sorts of practices were common to all parties involved.

All this manipulation preceding election day seldom sufficed to secure a particular result. Most of the time, as we have seen, the parties had to compete at the polls, deploying their forces to win. Yet who made up these forces?

Who Voted?

In Buenos Aires, very few people actually voted. Time and again elections were postponed because the people didn't show up at the polls. When they did, their names were registered in a voting record, and therefore it is possible to estimate the number of voters. That source is only partially reliable, however, as the falsification of names, the theft of ballot boxes, and other forms of fraud could produce alterations in the figures. Albeit questionable, these records nevertheless are the only systematic information available on voter turnout.

Throughout the 1860s the turnout seldom reached one thousand voters. On very special occasions, however, that figure doubled. The number of those registered to vote, in turn, fell from around thirty-six hundred in 1864 to twenty-five hundred in 1869, but rose to nine thousand in the recounts of the following decade (1873 and 1878). The voters, on their part, showed up only on special occasions. The turnout for most of the elections of the 1870s oscillated between one and two thousand, but for the National Congressional and presidential elections of 1874 and 1880 that number rose to about six thousand.[28]

The turnout continually fluctuated, with no gradual increase in the number of voters, nor any other distinctive pattern of enlargement. The figures are, moreover, similar to those from the first half of the nineteenth century. The greatest leap took place in the 1820s, when the turnout rose more than ten times, from the one to three hundred voters of the postrevolutionary decade to around two to three and sometimes four thousand voters after the passing of the electoral law of 1821. The figures remained almost the same during the Rosas regime.[29]

While the population rose from 55,000 in 1822 to 65,000 in 1836, and to 178,000 in 1869 and 433,000 in 1887, the average number of voters remained constant. As a proportion of those figures, the turnout, therefore, dropped. If we take the highest turnouts for each period, in the 1820s and 1830s they represented around 7 percent of the total population, while in 1874 they oscillated around 3 percent and in 1880 they barely reached 2 percent. In most of the elections held in the 1860s and 1870s, the percentages were even lower. The same drop is evident when considering the proportion of actual to potential voters (those qualified to vote, even if not registered). In the 1820s that figure was almost 40 percent, while between 1860 and 1880 it was generally around 10 percent, with leaps to 20 percent.[30]

The legislation allowed for a wide suffrage, yet participation was scant. Why? Who chose to vote, and who did not? It is not easy to find out, as the testimonies of contemporaries only partially match the data of the civic register and the electoral records.

Before each election, the press urged the citizen to the polls. The day after, however, his figure disappeared from the news, and others occupied the center stage. In the elections for the municipal board in November 1863, for example, "in the parish of San Nicolás the elections were won by the railway workers," while on another occasion that same year "the heroes of the day were the road-builders, the peons of the municipal slaughtering yards, the street-lighters." The following year, at the elections for the provincial legislature, the Club Libertad won the day when "the workers of the *Ferrocarril Oeste* [Western Railway Co., which was administered by the provincial government] violently broke in at the time of the opening of the polls." *La Tribuna*, in turn, accused the rival Club del Pueblo of recruiting "customshouse employees . . . and the sailors of the port authority, who, in spite of being Greek, Canarian, and Spanish, voted as citizens of La Merced."[31] These images were recurrent in the press. In election accounts, the railway workers, led by the renowned autonomist *caudillo* Luis Elordi, were always mentioned in the foreground. And close to them were the peons of the customshouse, the sailors who worked for the port authority, the cart drivers, the members of the paving crews, and the journeymen employed in the slaughter yards, the storage sheds, and the barracks. Voters are always described as part of a collective force, consisting of men defined in occupational terms who generally belonged to the lower sectors of the popular classes. They always appear behind their leaders, who occupy prominent places in most accounts.

These images were generally portrayed by the partisan press to criticize the voting procedures of their opponents and contrast them with the ideal of elections in a liberal republic. Such descriptions, therefore, should not be taken at face value as depicting the actual composition and organization of the voting forces. At the same time, in order to be credible, the accounts of voting scenes in the papers—as well as those included in police and government records—had to use images familiar to their readers. Their stories could not be entirely foreign to the electoral experience of their public. Furthermore, similar stories were told by partisan writers about their own electoral practices. The *autonomista* Julio A. Costa, for example, relates that "this great and noble party . . . mastered these electoral maneuvers . . . and did not hesitate to resort to the aid of the customshouse journeymen, the cleaning crews, or the chiefs of police."[32]

Those absent from the polls were also mentioned in the accounts. "Men of certain social position . . . do not attend the polls," lamented a representative in 1873, and he added, "[T]he weak of spirit do not attend, the old do not attend." A few months later, *La Tribuna* warned:

"The honest people, the serious people, . . . they will not attend the polls."[33]

The figures on electoral participation show that many of those qualified to vote chose not to do so. Contemporary accounts emphasize the presence of voters from the popular sectors and the absence of men from the middle and upper classes. The scant information available from electoral registers and reports only partly corroborates this picture. The only registers that include the name, profession, address, age, marital status, and literacy of those who signed up as potential voters are those of 1867 and 1878, and they are available for most, but not all of, the parishes.[34] Only about half of those registered to vote finally showed up at the polls. In addition, the introduction of false registers and the substitution of voters' names were common practices on election days, further distorting the picture. Through these data, therefore, we obtain only an approximation of the profile of actual voters.

TABLE 1

Citizens inscribed in the *Registro Cívico de la Ciudad de Buenos Aires*, 1864, 1867, 1869, 1873, and 1878 (totals by parish)

Parish/Year	1864	1867	1869	1873	1878
Balvanera	250	148	114	975	911
Catedral al Norte	246	86	207	765	N/D
Catedral al Sur	431	97	287	554	559
Concepción	334	N/D	332	1,071	1,159
Monserrat	359	229	178	793	N/D
Piedad	295	112	215	724	984
Pilar	339	N/D	285	564	797
San Cristóbal*	—	—	—	529	N/D
San Juan Evang*	—	—	—	192	201
San Miguel	257	33	158	415	440
San Nicolás	347	208	262	600	N/D
San Telmo	221	220	103	690	682
Santa Lucía	118	N/D	190	257	N/D
Socorro	445	58	125	701	758
TOTAL	3,642	(1,191)	2,456	8,830	(6,511)

SOURCES: Registro Cívico de 1864, *La Tribuna*, January 1864; Registro Cívico de 1867, *La Tribuna* and *El Nacional*, December 1867; Registro Cívico de 1869, 1873 y 1878, Archivo General de la Nación, Sala X, *Elecciones Nacionales (1864–92)*, 30-6-2, y *Elecciones. Padrones, Actas, Antecedentes*, 30-9-3, 31-1-1 y 31-1-3.
*These parishes were created around 1870.

TABLE 2

Citizens Inscribed in the *Registro Cívico* in Nine Parishes of
the City of Buenos Aires, Classified by Occupational
Groups, 1867 (percentages)

Parishes/ Occupational group	1	2	3.1	3.2	Total 3	Total
Balvanera	23	18	4	55	59	100
Catedral N.	30	28	21	21	42	100
Catedral S.	29	56	14	1	15	100
Monserrat	10	23	8	59	67	100
Piedad	5	51	21	23	44	100
San Miguel	36	36	22	6	28	100
San Nicolás	5	8	50	37	87	100
San Telmo	15	12	30	43	73	100
Socorro	16	38	22	24	46	100
Total 9 par.	15	24	23	38	61	100

SOURCE: Registro Cívico de 1867.

NOTE: Group 1 includes those registered as property owners, *hacendados*, military men, rentiers, professionals (lawyers, doctors, etc.), and students. In 1878, in most of the parishes, students constituted the largest subgroup within Group 1.

Group 2 includes all those registered as occupied in "commerce."

Group 3 includes those registered in occupations related to the laboring trades. Group 3.1 includes white-collar workers and skilled workers (clerks, typographers, carpenters, tailors, etc.). Group 3.2 includes journeymen, *peones*, servants, and other unskilled workers (masons, painters, etc.). In most parishes, journeymen and *peones* constituted the largest subgroup within Group 3.2.

TABLE 3

Citizens Inscribed in the *Registro Cívico* in Nine Parishes of
the City of Buenos Aires Classified by Occupational
Groups, 1878 (percentages)

Parishes/ Occupational group	1	2	3.1	3.2	Total 3	Total
Balvanera	12	18	30	40	70	100
Catedral S.	50	38	8	4	12	100
Concepción	23	15	36	26	62	100
Piedad	23	25	28	24	52	100
Pilar	13	8	29	50	79	100
San Juan E.	7	7	26	60	86	100
San Miguel	35	43	15	7	22	100
San Telmo	23	21	27	29	56	100
Socorro	19	15	38	28	66	100
Total 9 par.	22	20	29	29	58	100

SOURCE: Registro Cívico de 1878.
NOTE: Occupational groups as in Table 2.

TABLE 4

Citizens Inscribed in the *Registro Cívico* of the City of Buenos Aires,
Classified by Age Groups, 1867 and 1878 (percentages)

Parishes/ Age groups	1867			1878		
	17 to 29 years	30 to 49 years	50 years and +	17 to 29 years	30 to 49 years	50 years and +
Balvanera	33	44	23	52	36	12
Catedral N.	34	44	22	N/D	N/D	N/D
Catedral S.	39	44	17	61	26	13
Concepción	N/D	N/D	N/D	60	29	11
Monserrat	28	60	12	N/D	N/D	N/D
Piedad	41	49	10	N/D	N/D	N/D
Pilar	N/D	N/D	N/D	55	35	10
S. Cristóbal	N/D	N/D	N/D	N/D	N/D	N/D
San Juan E.	—	—	—	66	26	8
San Miguel	33	34	33	52	33	15
San Nicolás	35	45	15	N/D	N/D	N/D
San Telmo	41	47	12	62	28	10
Santa Lucía	—	—	—	N/D	N/D	N/D
Socorro	36	38	26	62	30	8

SOURCES: Same as Tables 2 and 3.

TABLE 5

Citizens Inscribed in the *Registro Cívico* of the City of
Buenos Aires, Classified by Literacy, 1867 and 1878
(percentages)

Parish/Literacy Condition	1867		1878	
	Literate	Illiterate	Literate	Illiterate
Balvanera	37	63	59	41
Catedral N.	78	22	N/D	N/D
Catedral S.	N/D	N/D	99	1
Concepción	N/D	N/D	78	22
Monserrat	56	44	N/D	N/D
Piedad	69	31	86	14
Pilar	N/D	N/D	41	59
San Cristóbal	N/D	N/D	N/D	N/D
San Juan E.	—	—	44	56
San Miguel	88	12	95	5
San Nicolás	30	70	N/D	N/D
San Telmo	43	57	69	31
Santa Lucía	—	—	N/D	N/D
Socorro	74	26	83	17

SOURCES: Same as Tables 2 and 3.

The occupational classification of Tables 1–5 says very little about the social composition of the electorate. Although in some cases the social status of these men could be inferred from their occupation, most of the time such deductions are risky. A person who declares that he works in "commerce," for example, may be the owner of a large import and export trade business, a small shopkeeper, a retail vendor, or even a casual street monger. "Employee" and "professional" also refer to people who may belong to very different social sectors. In order to have a better picture of the voters-to-be, the tables include data on the age and literacy of the registered citizens in several parishes of Buenos Aires.

Tables 2 and 3 show that the citizens who registered to vote came from a wide range of occupations. Both in 1867 and 1878, more than half of them were skilled and unskilled workers, among which the journeymen and *peones* were predominant. Those related to commerce came second, followed by the professionals (mostly lawyers) and the students, the *hacendados*, the rentiers, and the military. This last group had increased its participation by 1878, due mostly to the larger presence of students among the voters-to-be. In that year, more than half of the registered citizens were under thirty years of age, while in 1867 the older groups predominated (Table 4). The available data, albeit scant, suggest a drop in the proportion of illiterates in the register, although in some parishes their numbers were still significant (Table 5).[35]

These averages hide a great diversity among the different parishes. In Catedral al Sur and San Miguel, the participation of professionals, students, and men involved in commerce was the highest, while that of the workers was the lowest. The illiteracy rate was also comparatively low. A second group of parishes comprising Balvanera (1867 and 1878), Monserrat (1867), San Nicolás (1867), San Telmo (1867), Pilar (1867 and 1878), and San Juan Evangelista (1878) shows a high proportion of workers, particularly journeymen and peons, a low proportion of professionals and people involved in commerce, and a high rate of illiteracy. In the rest of the parishes—Piedad (1867 and 1878), Socorro (1867 and 1878), Catedral al Norte (1867), San Telmo (1878), and Concepción (1878)—the participation of the different groups in the register was more uniform.

This diversity was probably a consequence of the residential patterns of the neighborhoods. For the city as a whole, the occupational structure of the population inscribed in the *Registro Cívico* was actually quite similar to that of the class of potential voters (Argentine adult men). Some deviations are, however, visible: journeymen and *peones* were overrepresented, while domestic servants and skilled workers were underrepresented. Commercial occupations were overrepresented in San Miguel, Catedral al Sur, and Piedad but underrepresented in the rest of the parishes.[36]

According to this information, therefore, the first step of the electoral procedure, the register, attracted all occupational sectors almost evenly. Those citizens were a relatively small but representative sector of the potential voters. The young, illiterate men who belonged to the laboring trades were a majority not only of the voters-to-be but also of the total population. And although that group was slightly overrepresented among registered citizens, this bias did not preclude other groups from taking part in the elections.

These observations are, however, quite problematic. They are based entirely upon the information available in the electoral registers. This source is not only incomplete and unreliable; it also considers voters as individuals. The inscribed citizens are listed one by one, with their individual descriptions—name, age, place of birth, occupation, whether literate or illiterate. And we have used this information in the same manner, adding up and subtracting men to make up abstract statistical aggregates. The resulting image is misleading. Most of the voters belonged to specific groups that participated in the polls as collective forces mobilized for the occasion. In order to explore voting patterns and behaviors, therefore, it is important to go beyond the individuals and consider them as part of those electoral teams.

Voting involved collective actors. Most of the men who attended the polls were party elements, who belonged either to the rank and file, recruited and organized beforehand, or to the leadership in its different levels. Electoral participation was the result of careful organization in the hands of the political machines of Buenos Aires.

4 The Electoral Machines

This picture portrays the closed door of the registering office, guarded by men in arms. In front of the door are two *autonomista* leaders, Alsina and Cambaceres. Mitre arrives with his flock of sheep.

"Dn. Bartolo [Mitre]:—Open up, open up. I'm going to register my sheep!

Dn. Antonino [Cambaceres]:—I never thought that the *mitristas* were going to work for my candidature. If the register opens again, I'll take two hundred workers from the Railway and register them in Balvanera." [*El Mosquito*, July 8, 1877]

> *Nolli Me Tangere*
>
> [Secret electoral committee]
>
> *We, the subscribers of this document, solemnly bind ourselves to constitute a secret Committee with the purpose of sustaining, in the next immediate electoral campaign, the candidacy of citizen Dr. Don Manuel Quintana for Governor of the Province.*
>
> *This pact is dissolvable in regard to the name of the candidate only if:*
>
> *1. his acts or opinions contradict the ideas and government rules whose supremacy we seek by elevating him to the first executive authority of the Province;*

2. *by the unanimous vote of its members, the Committee, in view of its political interests, would resolve to substitute his candidacy for another one. If the vote were not unanimous, those who do not agree to the new name are free of all obligations.*

This pact is dissoluble in regard to those who sign it only if:

1. *other centers of electoral labors decide to substitute the candidacy of citizen Quintana, without the unanimous approval of the Committee, in which case the pact may hold for those who agree with the new combinations, but may be overlooked by those who reject them;*

2. *by looking for support beyond those groups organized by this Committee, the candidate were to jeopardize the objectives envisaged when his candidature was initially proposed.*

We hereby sign the present pact. Buenos Aires, August 1, 1871

[Signatures] *Lucio V. Mansilla, J. M. Estrada, Carlos Alfredo D'Amico,*
              A. del Valle, Gerónimo Uzal, Dardo Rocha, Pedro Bernet

Organization

1. *The Secret Committee will designate an influential neighbor in each parish to act as its deputy and organize a [parish] committee of twelve persons under his presidency.*

2. *Each one of the twelve members of the parish committees, or those more trusted by the Secret Committee, will be in charge of forming other committees with the same number of members, all of them under the same president.*

3. *The constitution of these committees will correspond in the best possible manner to the divisions in each parish, in order to carry out the following tasks:*

1. *promote the inscription in the Civic Register of all the citizens that support our program;*

2. *register those who, having inscribed their names, support us;*

3. *register those who, not having inscribed their names, sympathize with our cause;*

4. *estimate the number of citizens, whether or not they be inscribed, whose opinions are against our cause;*

5. *The parish comisarios [inspectors] will be in touch with the Secret Committee. They will participate in those deliberations that may affect the interests and labors of their respective parishes, and they will receive instructions from the said Committee;*

6. *The members of the Secret Committee will communicate with their candidate in relation to all matters pertaining to the electoral labors;*

7. *The same members will propose candidates for the role of comisario in each parish, according to the following list:*

D. Lucio V. Mansilla—parishes of San Cristóbal and Piedad
D. Dardo Rocha—San Nicolás and San Miguel
D. Gerónimo Uzal and D. Aristóbulo del Valle—San Telmo, San Juan, Santa Lucía, Monserrat, and Concepción
D. Carlos D'Amico—Colegio [San Ignacio] y Merced
D. Pedro Bernet and D. José M. Estrada—Socorro, Pilar, and Balbanera

*8. The Committee will designate a President and Vice President and will deliber-
ate. Its decisions will be mandatory for all its members, whichever the number of them
present after being convened in writing by the President.*

Buenos Aires, August 1, 1871

[Signatures] *L. V. Mansilla, Dardo Rocha, Carlos Alfredo D'Amico,
J. M. Estrada, A. del Valle, Gerónimo Uzal*

—*Archivo General de la Nación, Archivo y Colección Dardo Rocha, File 291*

The Production of the Suffrage

The recruitment and mobilization of voters was not an easy task. The
competition between parties was harsh. Different institutions took
part in the production of the vote, and old and new practices were put
to test. During the first half of the century, in Buenos Aires, the current
governments had always been very influential at the time of elections.
They had used the public administration to their own benefit.[1] After
1852, however, the control of the administration, albeit still important, was not enough to win an election. A new institution, relatively
autonomous from the government, soon took shape, the political club.
These clubs were networks that started operating in the provincial
political arena after the fall of Rosas.[2] When Buenos Aires became the
seat of the federal government, these organizations consolidated, first
under the umbrella of the Partido de la Libertad and later as electoral
machines of the different factions that competed for power in the city.
In those decades, both the clubs and the government took part in the
production of the suffrage, as we shall see.

The Political Clubs

To gain access to public office, the parties had to compete in the electoral arena. As seen in Chapter 1, nineteenth-century parties were
loose associations of political interests and figures. After 1862 they
achieved a certain degree of continuity, so that two main parties ran
for power in the city during the following two decades. Partisan competition was, however, highly criticized at the time, as elections were
considered a means to select the best men to embody the nation rather
than to represent different interests or sectors. Actual parties, therefore, called themselves "parties of principles" that sought "to express
all legitimate political aspirations,"[3] and they used the label "faction"

to qualify their rivals. While parties presumably avoided the contested terrain of electoral competition, they bred an institution to operate precisely in that field, the political club.

The clubs were first organized in the 1850s, when the political life of the city flourished after the fall of Rosas.[4] They originated as organizations to conduct "electoral labors" in favor of particular candidates and to "form opinion." In the words of *La Tribuna:* "When it is necessary to unify the opinion of the liberal party in a common center, through visible links, in a community of efforts toward unity, then the Club Libertad stands up." The paper explained the function of the clubs as follows:

The Club Libertad has finished its task. . . . It will not hold a new assembly until next year, when the law opens a new electoral period to the citizens. . . . Such is the sole purpose of the Club Libertad, a purely electoral purpose. . . . Everybody knows; when the electoral period is over, the club adjourns. No one can say that they have seen it meeting even once beyond that period or with other aims.[5]

As the sheer insistence of these words suggests, the actual clubs went well beyond their prescribed functions.

As a form of sociability, the club had a long history before it was adopted in Latin America. Associated to the Anglo-Saxon political culture of the eighteenth century, it gained international notoriety during the French Revolution. Clubs proliferated in post-Restoration France, and the movements of 1848 were the occasion for the foundation of numerous republican clubs throughout Europe. By the mid-nineteenth century, this form was adopted in most of the new Spanish American republics. There were many variants to the political club. In Chile, for example, clubs were very formal institutions, "basically bourgeois and mesocratic"; in Lima, they were more ephemeral organizations set up during electoral periods to connect the leadership with potential followers.[6]

In Buenos Aires, as we have seen, clubs were originally created for electoral purposes. Very soon, however, they became more permanent associations within the parties. In fact, the main schism within the Partido de la Libertad started with the foundation of two separate clubs led by Adolfo Alsina and Bartolomé Mitre, and culminated in 1862 with the final division of the party. On that occasion the conflict did not revolve around the candidacies. The main issue at stake was President Mitre's proposal to designate Buenos Aires as the federal capital of the country. Rivalries between the two groups had a longer history, but it was that proposal that triggered the final confrontation. The group led by Alsina firmly opposed the federalization of any piece of land that belonged to the province of Buenos Aires and consolidated the split. The two clubs—Alsina's Club Libertad and Mitre's Club del Pueblo—eventually became two different parties, Naciona- lista and Autonomista, which replaced the original Partido de la Li- bertad.

This sort of confrontation between different groups continued within the new parties. The *autonomistas* were prone to division, main- ly on occasion of the definition of candidacies. An important split took place, for example, in 1868, on account of the selection of the presiden- tial formula. In February, the directive committee of the Club Libertad (by then, entirely autonomist) convened "the people to a great meet- ing to be held on Sunday at twelve o'clock in order to proclaim the presidential candidate." The newspapers reported the following day that some two to three thousand people attended the meeting, which had taken place in a warehouse by the Plaza de Monserrat.

The club president, Mr. Félix Benítez, chaired the meeting. Mr. Rufino Varela, editor of the newspaper *La Tribuna*, proposed that the club should work for the formula Domingo Faustino Sarmiento– Adolfo Alsina. The following speaker, the young Pastor Obligado, "in [a] lively and energetic speech" nominated Alsina in the first place, as presidential candidate. After a second speech by Varela, the president called for a vote. An extremely confusing episode followed, later re- ported by the press. *The Standard*, the paper of the British community, carried this ironic account of the meeting:

[The president] asked those who wished to vote for Sarmiento to stay on the other side of the well, which was the side of the sun, and a multitude went that way. . . . But when he asked those who voted for Alsina to go the opposite way, which was the side of the shade, many of the first group found the sun too strong and went toward the shade. That way of counting votes was, therefore, impracticable. . . . Everybody surrounded the presidential table, shouting and clapping.

Don Estanislao del Campo climbed the podium and succeeded in calming down the audience. . . . He said . . . [,] "I propose that the *alsinistas* go to the left and the *sarmientistas* to the right." . . . Once he finished, Florencio Varela . . . ran to the left, and few people followed who did not seem to understand the differ- ence between a proposal and its approval. [Then] someone proposed that each participant produce a written vote with the name of his candidate. On hearing this, Florencio Varela pronounced these memorable words: "I protest . . . be- cause the majority of the citizens of Buenos Aires are unable to write."

The excitement was tremendous. . . .

Mr. Benítez then said, "We haven't come here to play like kids or to have fun. . . . As the President of this meeting I order that those of you who are for Sarmiento go to the right, those of you who are for Alsina to the left, and the foreigners stay here with me." In less than two minutes the division was achieved. There was no doubt as to who had the majority.[7]

According to the official record of the proceedings, Sarmiento had obtained the majority of the votes. The followers of Alsina did not agree, protested the decision, and in April created a new club, the Popular. The founding document stated that "the proclamation of the formula Sarmiento-Alsina ... was not the expression of the majority of those who attended the February meeting." The new club would work to favor "Dr. Adolfo Alsina for the first place." The list of candidates for the electoral college was somewhat different from the one approved officially by the Club Libertad. When the election took place, on April 12, the *alsinistas* of the Club Popular won in almost all the parishes of the city.[8] The final national result was, however, favorable to the formula Sarmiento–Alsina.

In this case, the split was short-lived, but further divisions would affect the Partido Autonomista throughout the decade. In 1877, a group of dissident leaders created a new party, the Partido Republicano, that lasted only for a year but was successful in a couple of elections. Those leaders, among whom Leandro Alem and Aristóbulo del Valle were the most prominent, had consistently shown their differences from the official party line and had organized successive electoral clubs to compete with it: the Club Igualdad in 1868; 25 de Mayo in 1870; *Electoral* in 1873 and 1874; and *Guardia Nacional* in 1874 and 1875.[9] The Partido Nacionalista was, in turn, less inclined to divisions and had a more vertical leadership, with Bartolomé Mitre as its indisputable head. Nevertheless, on different occasions electoral clubs that dissented from the official line produced their own candidates.

All these clubs were institutions that operated in the electoral arena in behalf of the parties, but they also functioned as occasional political groupings within each party. They frequently organized minor branches and local parish chapters. The initial steps toward any particular election were taken at the time of the selection of the candidates (see Chapter 5). Once the lists had been produced, the clubs started the "electoral labors," working at different levels to attract and mobilize voters.

The main leaders rarely participated in those labors; they avoided the day-to-day operation of the electoral forces and tried to stay away from internal struggles. Eminent figures such as Bartolomé Mitre and Adolfo Alsina, who had started their political careers as club bosses, later became party leaders who seldom participated in the action. The electoral field was left to secondary figures, the true organizers of the voting mechanisms.

Each club acted as a centralized machine. Its directive committee met regularly and made the decisions. The main issues were frequently already agreed upon by a small group at the top. Many negotiations took place behind closed doors. This concentrated mechanism did not, however, prevent the clubs from discussing some very important questions in massive assemblies where different positions were displayed, debated, and voted. As the account of the February 1868 meeting shows, sometimes there was a public display of differences. The conflict among the heads was then acted out in tumultuous meetings in which the different levels of the leadership and the rank and file took an active part in the struggle. Deliberation and participation were, therefore, part of the life of every club, although it is not easy to ponder their relative weight.

The clubs were in the hands of a leadership that was bred in and by politics. They did not constitute a secret or tightly closed group, and their activity was highly visible. But they had a hierarchical structure, and a relatively stable group of figures occupied the leading places in party and club committees. Most of them were also among the candidates for the Senate, the House, and the provincial legislature, although not every one in those lists was a club man. Electoral bosses may be found among those figures, men such as Luis Elordi (see below), the police chief Enrique O'Gorman, the army commander Mateo Martínez, Tulio Méndez, Ventura Martínez, among others. Some of them, such as Leandro Alem and Dardo Rocha, later reached the higher levels of party and political life.

Besides the different levels of the leadership, there was also the rank and file—less conspicuous, more ephemeral in their visibility— who generally joined in the retinue of the more powerful. These were the militants who participated in the meetings and assemblies, where the leaders brought "their" men to action. On those occasions, it is easy to perceive hundreds or thousands of people cheering and clapping their own bosses and wooing the adversary.[10] These mobilizations were not too different from the ones that took place on polling days. Participation was carefully organized by the *caudillos*, who talked about their "elements" and "regiments."[11]

The clubs were, therefore, neither closed circles of friends—an accusation frequently made by contemporaries when referring to a rival group—nor democratic spaces of popular expression—the favorite self-image.[12] Rather, they constituted political networks that articulated the various levels of leadership and rank-and-file membership. *La Tribuna* described the Club Libertad, in 1869, as "a very important center of opinion, with great elements of action within its ranks."[13] Clubs became key links in the chain of institutions that gave life to political competition in Buenos Aires.

While in the clubs decision-making was centralized at the top, the best part of the action was decentralized and took place at the bottom, in the parishes. In the various neighborhoods of the city, another very important political institution developed: the parish club (*club parroquial*).

Parish Clubs

According to Carlos Heras, parish clubs first appeared in Buenos Aires in April 1852 and "consisted of an assembly of neighbors who, due to the absence of parties, met to unify their opinions relating to the candidates they would vote for in the elections."[14] A few years later the activity of these clubs was regulated, and their purpose was defined as follows: "to find out the true opinion of the majority of citizens" regarding the electoral candidacies. Every year, in each quarter of the city, the neighbors had to meet in assemblies of no fewer than thirty people in order to designate a directive committee formed by five fellow neighbor-citizens (president, vice president, secretary, and two other members). Once designated, all the committees of the city chose five among their members to form the Central Club.

When the time to propose candidates for any election arrived, each parish club convened the neighbors to an assembly to select (by plurality of votes) a list of potential candidates. The respective committees of all the parish clubs of the city then met at the Central Club to draft the final list, with the names of those most voted for in the different neighborhoods.[15] This complicated system was devised in order to ensure that the names of the candidates for elected posts spring from the bottom up, being proposed by the citizens of Buenos Aires. Also, it was supposed to "amalgamate wild spirits [and] conciliate different opinions."[16] The province had recently gone through the authoritarian experience of the Rosas regime, and those who aspired to lead the new political process introduced this original system, which spelled change at different levels. On the one hand, it made the elite-to-be look like the champions of the liberties recently recuperated from the hands of the tyrant. Their move also proved their trust in the citizens of the city. On the other, the parish clubs could become important centers of political sociability. Pilar González has suggested that neighborhood institutions could profit from the existing traditional social networks based upon "strong communitarian links."[17] As we shall see below, the parish clubs also provided politicians the opportunity of building new channels of political action that would prove more dynamic than the old ones.

The procedure presumed autonomous deliberation on the part of the citizens and their capacity to agree on a single list of the "best" names. Soon enough, however, the leadership of the political parties sought to operate at the local level in order to influence the choice. An incipient opposition—led by Bartolomé Mitre—accused the provincial government—headed by Pastor Obligado—of stepping into the parishes, and it created, in turn, its own "opinion clubs" to compete in the same terrain.[18] Their move was unsuccessful from the electoral point of view, but it contributed to shape new political networks and to stimulate electoral debate and competition in the city.

After 1857 a new alignment took place. The relationship with Urquiza and the confederation became the key issue of the cleavage between two main groups. All those who opposed negotiations with the government congregated under the leadership of the increasingly influential Mitre and formed the Club de la Libertad. The parish clubs gained new vigor, as many of the young politicians who had fought against their influence now joined them. New networks rapidly developed, and the political bosses "descended" to the parish level, where they recruited local *caudillos* who contributed their own clienteles to the political game.[19]

Although the parish clubs presumably represented the entire citizenry of the corresponding neighborhoods, they soon started to show internal divisions. As early as 1857, *La Tribuna* argued that "those defeated in the primary election had the right to create the Parish Club of the minority."[20] After 1862, the rivalry between *mitristas* and *alsinistas* was reproduced in the parishes, where clubs that corresponded both to the former and the latter were formed.[21] They now met to propose candidates for the lists of their respective clubs (del Pueblo and Libertad). And they also accused each other of manipulation of the nominations and betrayal of the neighborhood's true will.[22]

The importance of the parish clubs dwindled in the mid-sixties. In an article published in 1866, *La Nación* denounced the death of that institution, but added that "it is easy to bring it back to life and to reap [its] beneficial fruits." The *mitrista* paper urged neighbors to get together "spontaneously and with no waste of time" to organize the inscription in the electoral registers and designate the parish committees in order to take part in the Central Club. Finally, the paper criticized the permanent political clubs that "impede the harmonization of different opinions," and it accused the "hot-headed fraction of the Club Libertad of eliminating parish meetings from its by-laws in order to subject its members to the arbitrary will of certain bosses."[23]

In order to achieve control over parish clubs, the parties and electoral clubs favored the creation of branches in the various neighborhoods. Before any important election, these organizations—sometimes known as "popular clubs"—proliferated. They had their own

names and authorities. In 1864, for example, the following branches of
the Club Libertad were founded: de los Libres in Pilar; Rivadavia in
Balvanera; Buenos Aires in Catedral al Norte; Comandante Mateo
Martínez in Concepción; General Acha in San Nicolás; and Pavón in
La Piedad. The functions and actions of these popular clubs frequently
overlapped those of the parish clubs they were supposed to influence.
The *mitristas* criticized this duplication of institutions. In 1869 they
argued that "in order to have the blueprint of popularity," the electoral labors "ought to be public." They trusted the parish clubs and
believed that "the formation of the *popular Clubs* is not necessary."
The autonomist paper *La Tribuna* answered:

[In] a popular club, which meets spontaneously without coercion, and where
there is free access to every citizen, it is truly possible to study the opinion of the
people as to the candidates they will choose. . . . In the parish clubs, to the contrary, . . . the lists drafted are not the spontaneous expression of the neighborhood. . . . Half a dozen or a dozen men prepare these lists at home: *entre soi.*[24]

In spite of these seemingly strong opinions, both parties resorted to
every kind of electoral association at the parish level. In the 1870s the
mitristas founded numerous branches of their main club throughout
the city: General Belgrano in San Juan Evangelista; Nacionalista in
San Miguel; Constitucional in La Piedad; Coronel García in Balvanera;
General Garibaldi in San Nicolás, and many others. The *autonomistas*,
on their part, defended the parish clubs on several occasions.[25] With
the creation of the Republican Party in 1877, local electoral action
reached new heights. The party encouraged the mobilization of its
followers and organized colorful political meetings in most neighborhoods. The so-called *conciliados* (an alliance of *mitristas* and *alsinistas*)
also created their own local institutions, such as the Club General Belgrano in Balvanera. When convening a meeting in January 1878, that
club announced that "its members would march . . . through various
streets of the neighborhood, and then will go to salute the two parish
clubs of Balvanera."[26] The relationship between republicans and *conciliados* was not always peaceful. In November 1877, for example, the
republican *El Nacional* carried this piece of information:

The march [of the *conciliados*] took place yesterday in the parish of la Concepción. More or less one hundred people marched around the square, acclaiming
General Mitre. Some people who were sitting on the square benches and who
belong to the Republican Party acclaimed Dr. del Valle. The marchers then
pushed them, pulled out their revolvers, and fired. . . . The republicans left and
the *conciliados* confronted the police forces, led by Chief Manuel Dantas, of renowned republican sympathies.[27]

The Action in the Parishes

Electoral labors at the parish level were intense. Opinion clubs, parish clubs, political centers, *comités*, and other political groupings worked to produce candidacies, register voters, organize electoral forces on polling days, and protest or defend the electoral results when necessary. The newspapers regularly published party calls for the parish meetings to choose directive committees, to designate and proclaim candidates, and to "start the electoral labors." They also included information on the creation of opinion clubs and other political centers, on the assemblies, and on the composition of their respective boards and committees.

According to the legislation, the main function of the parish clubs was to select the list of candidates for electoral posts. This crucial step in the institutional life of the city was not, however, entirely resolved at that level. Rather, it was in the higher echelons of the parties that the candidacies were produced. The parish clubs were, on the other hand, the key site for "electoral labors." These started with the drafting of the register. The composition of the registration committees was not the prerogative of the parish clubs,[28] but theirs was the task of actively promoting the register of voters. They were also in charge of convening meetings and marches in favor of their candidates. The peak of their activity was reached on polling days, as they were in command of the voting. The gathering of the voters-to-be, the organization of the operations directed toward the control of the voting booths, the protection of the partisans, the attention to the wounded, the celebration of victories—all of these took place around the parish clubs.

On March 28, 1869, for example, on occasion of the election of provincial legislators, the "man in charge of the electoral labors" in one of the clubs of the parish of El Pilar rented two carriages to bring voters to the polling station. He also bought four demijohns of French wine, a cask of English beer, a heifer for barbecue, and fifty pesos' worth of bread for the celebration. He paid off the four inspectors of the parish elections with a dinner at "the Café across the street from the Cathedral."[29] Money was also frequently spent in invitations and posters, firecrackers, and paper balloons. Part of these expenses were met with contributions from the local members of the political clubs.[30]

At the parish level, party members of different ranks met and mingled. The rank and file came across the main public figures of the neighborhood and the city. Government officials, members of Congress and the legislature, newspaper editors, and occasionally the highest party leaders "descended" to the parishes. Just before the election of 1874, Adolfo Alsina toured the *autonomista* clubs of Concepción, San Cristóbal, and Balvanera and gave a speech in each of them. Leandro Alem did something very similar in 1877, when he campaigned in favor of Aristóbulo del Valle. In 1879, the newspaper *La Bola de Hierro* noted that "[t]he *mitrista* parish clubs are in such a state of disarray that Gral. Mitre himself finds it necessary to go to them personally to re-establish [party] discipline and prevent their disbandment."[31]

All this action did not actually produce any massive political mobilization in the parishes. The majority of the citizens seldom responded to the calls for meetings and assemblies.[32] It is hard to estimate the number of those who did, but the available data show very variable figures. When the press wished to underscore the success of a particular parish meeting, they mentioned from 60 to 150 participants in the 1860s, and from 200 to 300 in the following decade. At the highest point of political mobilization, in 1877, the numbers were higher, from 500 to 1,000.[33] Many names recur year after year. A relatively stable group of militants led the action in most parishes, although new recruits and occasional followers also took part in the game.

In the formal leading positions—the committees appointed year by year to represent each parish club at the Club Central—there was both continuity and change. Among the heads of the clubs enrolled in the *autonomismo*, some names were recurrent: Luis Elordi and Dardo Rocha in San Nicolás; the Dantas and Varela brothers in La Concepción, where León Orma and Cipriano Ballesteros also played leading roles; and the Uzal family (who had earlier belonged to the *mitrista* party) in San Telmo. Some of these men, such as Dardo Rocha, Héctor Varela, and Adolfo Saldías, would later become prominent public figures. The majority of them, however, belonged to the secondary rank of national politics. Their place as local *caudillos* resulted from their capacity to recruit and organize electoral clienteles: the young Dantas, as army and police officers; Don Luis Elordi, as manager of the Western Railway; and so on. Most of them were also officers of the militia, the *Guardia Nacional*. Not all the parishes, however, show the same pattern of recurrence, and in some cases new names appear with some frequency among those of leading local figures.

As to the rank-and-file members of the parish clubs, it is harder to individualize them in the historical sources. The information available for the 1870s shows that the social composition of club membership was similar to that of the voters. Journeymen, skilled and unskilled workers, and white-collar workers were predominant, but professionals, military men, retailers, merchants, and other tradesmen were also active in parish clubs. The latter were overrepresented in the directive committees, which also included workers. Young university students were highly visible in all ranks and played an active role in the electoral struggles.[34]

In the intermediate levels of parish activity, the so-called men of action were key figures. On polling days, they organized and commanded the electoral forces in the field. *La Tribuna* described one of these men, Guillermo Silva, who was killed in 1869, during an electoral skirmish: "[He] was one of the ardent members of the liberal-autonomist party. . . . A *caudillo* by nature, he guided and conducted the people of his locality [the parish of La Piedad] to those generous and bloody combats."[35]

Parish activism thus overlaps with electoral mobilization. The number of people involved and their social composition, as well as their style and forms of action, strongly suggest that we are dealing with the same collective actors. As we have seen in Chapter 3, these groups were shaped as a pyramid, with the leadership at the top, an intermediate level of *caudillos*, and a relatively wide but limited base of militants.

The relationships between the different links of this structure were probably very complex. What material and symbolic exchanges kept them together? What made someone join a particular clientele? In what follows, a relatively easier question will be addressed, that of the material bases for recruitment.

Recruitment

The parish was, as we have seen, a crucial arena of electoral action. Pilar González has argued that the traditional networks of local neighborhood sociability initially played an important role in the attraction of political followers for the parties. In the 1850s, the parish clubs were "a political association built upon old community links."[36] In that context, the "natural" leaders of the clubs were the notables of each neighborhood, including the priest, the justice of the peace, and other prominent residents. Their social connections were the key to their political power and their ability to recruit and mobilize voters. This situation, however, was short-lived, and a few years later the picture changed rapidly. The parishes became a field for political competition between the different groups. The traditional forms of leadership were replaced by new ones, while the old notables gave way to younger politicians.

These changes gained momentum after unification, when the city acquired national political prominence. From then on, Buenos Aires hosted the national, provincial, and municipal administrations, and though all of them were still relatively modest in size and budget, they became important places for the recruitment and support of political clienteles. The national guard, the army, the police forces, and the justices of the peace were also key pieces of the electoral machines of the parties.

Drawing on their control of one or more of the three levels of the administration, the parties recruited their followers among the workers employed in the government or in jobs related to public contracts, which included, among others, those signed with private entrepreneurs for the construction and upkeep of most public works and the provision of services. The group in power favored "political friends" both for jobs and for auctions and contracts. They, in turn, secured the votes of their employees down the line. The party in the opposition denounced that situation, as well as the persecution of its followers who happened to be employed in the administration. Already in 1864, *La Tribuna* accused the *mitristas* in power in harsh words: "Now also in Buenos Aires, the land of freedom, employees who do not obey their chiefs in matters foreign to their jobs are sent to Siberia." And as late as 1880, the same paper responded to the accusations made against the national government by the *mitristas*—who controlled the province but were in the opposition at the national level: "The present dismissals [at the national level] were provoked by a large list of resolutions of the same kind adopted by the government of [the province of] Buenos Aires. . . . Hundreds of dismissals have been made by the provincial administration."[37]

The control over one sphere of government or another gave the faction in charge the opportunity of turning employees into voters. Yet it was not simply a question of exchanging a job for a vote. A complex mechanism combined forms of leadership and control related both to electoral mobilization and labor organization. Foremen and overseers who were at the same time political bosses were a key link in the recruitment and supervision of the gangs of workers/voters. Frequently, the men hired were already part of an existing social web, based on family or neighborhood ties, on political allegiances, or on previous labor experience. But sometimes it was simply taking the job that led a worker to become part of a political network.

Not all government agencies played a role in electoral recruitment. Those that employed a relatively larger number of nonskilled workers were the favorite targets of partisan takeover. The customshouse was among the main agencies denounced by the press for discrimination against the opposition. In 1864 its manager, Bilbao La Vieja, was accused of being "a new electoral machine" who did not accept any worker that did not pledge allegiance to the *mitrista* Club del Pueblo.[38] His "men of action" were, among others, Don Esteban González and the foreman Gómez.[39] That same year, the Club Libertad was in turn accused of manipulating the voting register of San Nicolás through the inscription of 120 journeymen who worked for Western Railway and did not live in the neighborhood but were listed as residents of the Parque station. This was just one of the many charges against the railway and its manager, Don Luis Elordi, who soon became a true "electoral power."[40]

After a political exile followed by several years of traveling around the world, Elordi returned in 1857 to Buenos Aires. At thirty-eight he started working for the Western Railway as second to the manager. At first the company was a joint venture between private capitalists and the provincial government, but by 1862 the latter took over the whole business. Elordi continued as manager. He also organized a powerful electoral machine with headquarters at the Parque Station in the parish of San Nicolás. In 1869, when he supported a fraction of the *autonomistas* that joined the *mitristas* in favor of the candidate Emilio Castro for governor, his occasional adversary Héctor Varela made the following ironic comment on Elordi's electoral power:

The old women of the Parque district relate that late at night, when sleep with its belladonna wings shuts the eyelids of the male, female, and neutral inhabitants of that neighborhood, the shadow of D. Emilio Castro, dressed as governor, comes out mounted on a locomotive shaped like a broom . . . whistling in the air and scaring the owls. The station of the Western Railway becomes an enchanted palace that breeds voters in fantastic forms; the locomotives acquire human shape, and so do the wagons. Millions of electoral inscription slips fly in the air, and produce an infernal noise. The figure of D. Luis Elordi appears in the midst of a cloud of coal smoke.[41]

Elordi was an active member of the Club Libertad, where his electoral power made him quite influential in matters of party alignment and candidacies. He presided over several *autonomista* clubs and participated in party meetings and assemblies at different levels. His chief arena of electoral action was the district of San Nicolás, where he was frequently elected to the parish club directive committees and the Central Club. More than once he voiced his dissent and caused occasional party splits. He did not, however, join the group that provoked the main division of 1877.[42]

Elordi built a solid leadership based upon his managerial role in a prosperous company linked to the provincial government, his personal relationship with Adolfo Alsina, and his dedication to politics. "His men"—the railway workers but also the foremen and masters— followed him and acted as his devoted forces at parish meetings, in party struggles, and above all, in the electoral battles that took place on polling days. We do not know why these men followed Elordi or what sort of exchanges consolidated their relationship, but it worked for almost two decades.

Albeit not so visible as Elordi, other party bosses used similar mechanisms to gain political power. The sources mention Casares and his cart-drivers in the parish of El Socorro, in 1869; Biedma and the municipal public works crews in 1874; as well as less-known figures such as Mariano Beascochea and Romero, who worked for the municipal government and led their journeymen in the electoral struggles that took place in 1877 in San Cristóbal. These railway and customshouse journeymen, cart-drivers, municipal crews, and other workers, led by men such as Gómez, Beascochea, or Moreno, who in turn responded to party bosses such as Elordi, Casares, and Bilbao la Vieja, were the main collective actors on polling days.

Three state institutions also played an important role in the electoral game: the police, the army, and the national guard. The police were in charge of keeping order at the polls, and its officers used that function to favor their political friends. At the same time, the institution was a source of voters and electoral forces. Its employees could, and did, vote, and although active policemen were soon deprived of that right, on polling days they joined the partisan electoral armies under the leadership of their own officers. When the force was reorganized in 1872 under Chief Enrique O'Gorman, it employed eleven high-ranking officers and seventeen hundred sergeants, corporals, and policemen, distributed throughout the twenty city precincts.[43] The institution exerted territorial control over the whole town. Its members, particularly the officers, were active political organizers in their respective districts.[44] At the top of the force, the chief of police was appointed by the provincial executive, and during those decades all governments chose men of their own political sympathies.[45]

The army and the national guard also exerted an important electoral influence. These institutions constituted the land military forces that the country counted upon for its defense. The national guard was created in 1852 after the battle of Caseros, when the appointed temporary governor, Vicente López y Planes, dissolved the provincial militia that had been one of the bulwarks of Rosas's political and military structure. The organization of the new guard was similar to that of the former militia. All native adult men had to enroll. They received periodical military training and could be summoned by the government at any time to fulfill their duty. General Urquiza revoked the governor's decision, but after the September 1852 revolution, the province went ahead with the reorganization of its guard. Under the command of

Bartolomé Mitre, it played a crucial role in the defense of Buenos Aires during the siege imposed upon the city by the confederate forces. From then on, the guard was considered a heroic and glorious institution, a proud symbol of the autonomy of the province. In the 1860s, the young men of the upper classes made a point of having an active involvement in the national guard. They rejected the possibility of hiring a replacement—a procedure admitted by the law—and exhibited their militia records with pride. For anyone aspiring to political leadership, the guard became an almost inevitable station.[46]

After unification, in 1862, the new president, Bartolomé Mitre, resorted to the manpower of the Buenos Aires militia to organize a national army of ten thousand men. For two years this army participated in several successful military campaigns against the rebel forces of different provinces. In 1864, Mitre decided to reorganize the armed forces of the country. He created a permanent professional army of six thousand men and dismissed the guard. This last measure was resisted by the Buenos Aires provincial government, which finally succeeded in keeping its own militia. By that time the province was in the hands of the *alsinistas*, the political rivals of the *mitristas* who held national power.

The electoral influence of the guard was manifold. First, until 1877, enrollment in the militia was required of all citizens, and anyone registering to vote had to show his enlistment certificate signed by the guard commander of his regiment. The right to vote was, therefore, in the hands of the militia officers, who could eventually deny the certificate to their political adversaries. Also, they could "produce" false certificates, or grant them to whomever they pleased. Secondly, the guard itself was a mechanism for the organization and control of both people and territory, key resources in any electoral confrontation. Finally, it was also a place for the development and consolidation of political leadership. Alsina himself started his political career with a firm base in the *Guardia*, and when he broke up with Mitre in 1862 he resigned his post as commander of the Fourth Regiment. Several officers followed him, and there was talk of the demoralization of the men in his unit caused by "the sympathies of the citizens who were part of the Regiment toward [its] commander."[47] Other, less visible political leaders also built their clienteles using their places as militia officers. In 1864, for example, the *mitrista* paper *La Nación Argentina* was pleased to note that "the national guard formed by the battalion of Commander Barros belongs entirely to the Club del Pueblo." *La Tribuna* disputed this statement, and pointed out that most of its officers were, in fact, members of the Club Libertad: León Orma, political leader in La Concepción; Adrián Sosa, active in Monserrat; Esteban Gar-

cía, from Balvanera; Gerónimo Uzal, from San Telmo—all of them officers of the guard and political bosses of the Club Libertad.[48] The government always sought to separate the men of the opposition from the
commanding posts of the militia. Thus, for example, in 1877, after a
particularly violent electoral episode, Governor Carlos Casares de-
posed Leandro Alem, the main opposition leader, from the command
of the Seventh Regiment.[49]

The army was also influential in political and electoral matters. In
the 1860s, most of its officers had belonged to the national guard of
Buenos Aires, and many of them continued as militia commanders for
some time. The army gradually consolidated as a national institution,
relatively autonomous from partisan strife. Its officers, however, continued to participate in the political forces and in electoral battles. All
parties had "their" military men, whose power was so evident that in
1873, President Sarmiento proposed to Congress a project of law
aimed at avoiding "the influence of army and navy officers and commanders in the elections." The law was never passed, partly due to the
opposition of the *mitristas*, who, according to the *autonomista La Tribuna*, "then had important officers in the army." Five years later, the
situation had changed, and it was the *mitristas* who spoke out "against
the intervention of the commanding officers."[50]

It is well known that, among state officials, justices of the peace
were the key figures on election days. The office was created in 1821,
when the *cabildos* were suppressed, to deal with minor offenses formerly attended to by the colonial municipal institution. In Buenos Aires, there were as many judicial districts as parishes, although their respective territorial jurisdictions did not strictly coincide. The electoral
laws established the duties of the justice of the peace. As described in
Chapter 3, those obligations changed with time, due to the increased
precautions against fraud. Yet the justices of the peace seldom respected the formal place allowed them by the regulations and acted
well beyond the law. They used their power throughout the electoral
process: in the drafting of the register, the appointment of electoral
authorities, the polling act, and ballot counting. As prominent and influential men in their respective districts, they also operated in the recruitment of voters. The press of the time abounds in denunciations of
the fraudulent and manipulative activities displayed by justices of the
peace.[51]

The government had powerful electoral tools in its hands, inasmuch as it had control over institutions and mechanisms that could
play an important part in the recruitment and organization of political and electoral clienteles. Yet gaining control of the administration
did not necessarily mean immediate command over all of its parts.

Furthermore, voter mobilization was based upon collective organization, which required forms of leadership that transcended administrative and labor relationships. Thus the links forged in government offices or in military posts turned into political bonds only when they developed in the context of the electoral machines set up by the parties. In that respect, the chief institution was the club (in its various forms), while the parish remained the principal arena of the electoral game.

5 The Elections

The caricature portrays Héctor Varela riding a donkey, and carrying a banner with an electoral list for senators and representatives that includes his name as the only candidate, repeated several times. At the back, on the left, the figure of Bartolomé Mitre, and on the right, that of Adolfo Alsina. The text reads:

"[Héctor Varela]:—Gentlemen, the *Autonomista* Party is about to die! I, alone, can save it! Nobody fail tomorrow to vote for this list. . . ! And don't forget that *El Porteño* [a newspaper edited by Varela] has the widest circulation and the largest number of ads. Dzinn, dzinn, boumm, babala-boumm!" [*El Mosquito*, March 25, 1877]

Revolutionary Pronouncement

[Given by Bartolomé Mitre on the eve of the revolution of September 1874]

As a public man of well-known antecedents, as a presidential candidate in the last election, and as a citizen that has, and accepts, the moral responsibility in front of the people, I owe my fellow citizens an explanation for the attitude that I am deliberately assuming, in the face of the present, solemn, circumstances. . . .

I—being away from the country—did not wish nor think about being a presidential candidate for the next constitutional period. . . . Yet I accepted the candidature on behalf of the freedom of the suffrage, which I saw in jeopardy, only aspiring to the victory of the popular vote. At the same time, I abstained from any participation—whether direct or indirect—in the electoral struggle, and accepted beforehand the verdict of the legal majority, whichever that might be.

In spite of the means used and the coercive action of the governments [gobiernos electores]; *in spite of the incredible and obvious frauds committed with the acquiescence of the official powers and the violence of the public force,* [after the election] *I disarmed those who, having honored me with their ballots, wished to enter the field of action. In the name of patriotism, I publicly declared that the worst legal election is better than the best of revolutions.*

This conciliatory declaration . . . was not accepted.

. . . [T]he government accepted the fraud and excluded the true representatives of the people, and accepted in their place, the representatives of an incredible falsification, denied by no one, confessed by everyone. The false powers that deprived the majority of the citizens of the right of suffrage were confirmed.

From that moment onward, the right of suffrage, source of all power and reason in democracy, was de facto suppressed. The renewal of the government officials [Poderes Públicos] *was no longer trusted to . . . the majority vote, but to the false register, the electoral fraud, the strength of the governments, and the efficacy of the official means. . . . From then onward, the revolution, until then stopped by patriotism, had its justification and its banner, and it penetrated deeply in the conscience of the people. . . .*

I was summoned to lead the revolutionary labors not only by those who had sustained my candidacy but also by those who had opposed it. I declined, but at the same time I declared that the revolution was a right, an obligation, and a need; that not launching it, whether with few or many followers, even if just for the sake of protesting, arms in hand, manfully, would be opprobrious—it would prove that we are incapable and unworthy of deserving and keeping the lost liberties. I declared, moreover, that once the event were launched, I would lead the Revolution throughout the Republic, to give it national meaning and cohesion.

—Bartolomé Mitre, *Arengas* (Buenos Aires, 1889), p. 490

Electoral Competition

Soon after the fall of the Rosas regime, elections in Buenos Aires became increasingly competitive.[1] Contemporaries liked to compare
their times with the "happy experience" of the early 1820s when—
they reckoned—political and electoral freedom had reigned unfet-
tered. Several factors, however, accounted for a visible difference between the two eras. The complexity of the political organization and
the enlargement of the elites that took place after unification introduced new arenas of competition and negotiation. The polls became a
decisive moment in the political life of the city. And although in some
elections there was no opposition, and in others the outcome could be
told beforehand, in most occasions the results were achieved at the
polls. There was generally more than one aspirant to each elective post
submitted to the popular vote. This was not, therefore, just a mechani-
cal act of confirmation of candidates decided previously in closed
caucus. The procedure for the nomination of the candidates had also
changed (see below). And both steps—nomination and election—
became matters of public debate and were discussed well beyond the
narrow limits of the political parties.

The Candidatures

The creation of the parish clubs in 1852 inverted the procedure followed for the nomination of candidates during the Rosas period, when
decisions were taken at the top. The new system established the starting point at the parish level, where neighbors had to meet to select the
precandidates in open assembly.[2] It was based upon the notion that
the representatives had to originate in public opinion. And although
the actual mechanisms for the nomination seldom operated from the
bottom up, that ideal was repeatedly voiced by the parties. The different clubs underscored their efforts toward "finding out the true will of
the majority of its members," while their rivals were depicted as "half
a dozen men, the orchestra directors, [who] meet, draft the list, and
impose it . . . on the [parish] clubs."[3]

Soon after their creation, the parish clubs experienced a double
process. On the one side, they were supposed to reinforce the traditional links between neighbors and the influence of local community
notables. Those results were partially achieved only in the first half of
the 1850s.[4] On the other side, however, the creation and expansion of a
deliberative arena in the neighborhoods offered a great opportunity
for the development of new political leaders. Starting in 1857, the lat-

ter would challenge the power of the old heads and compete with them for control of the parish clubs. From then on, the choice of candidates became a complex game of mutual pressures between the different echelons of the leadership: the top figures of the parties, who negotiated among themselves and sought to impose their names upon the rest; the middle-range bosses and *caudillos*, who had power at the parish level and could mobilize their retinue in meetings and at the polls to press for, or against, a particular candidate; and the "men of action," who commanded the electoral forces in the field and knew how to operate to voice their preferences. These procedures never took place in the open, but they somehow found their way to the public eye. The newspapers not only informed and gave their opinions about the negotiations; frequently, they also tried to influence the nominations. Thus the definition of the candidates entailed a certain degree of deliberation within the parties, and of publicity beyond them, all of which turned the process into a relevant moment in the political life of the city.

Quite often, the meetings of parish clubs and the assembly of political clubs for the nomination of candidates were pacific sessions for the confirmation of names proposed from above. Other times, however, those occasions generated heated, and even violent, debates. When the leaders did not reach an agreement beforehand, the majorities were conquered in the field, with the participation of the partisan forces. As on polling days, the *caudillos* deployed their clienteles to fight for a particular candidate or list of candidates within their own party. The description published by *The Standard* of the *autonomista* meeting of March 1868 (see Chapter 4) is an eloquent example of the struggle for a nomination—in this case, of a presidential formula: fifteen hundred people, the divided voice of the leadership, young politicians in action, the cheers and applause, the successive ballots, the "tremendous" agitation. The scene was familiar.

The young students, professionals, and newsmen who were starting a career in politics were the most aggressive actors at the club meetings. They appealed to strong words and heated attitudes to make their opinions heard by the leadership. In order to push through a particular candidate, they publicized the name through the friendly press, generated sympathy among part of the public, and finally broke into the assemblies with their electoral forces in order to impose it. Most of the time, these young politicians in the making were backed by politicians of a higher rank, but occasionally they acted on their own, and not always unsuccessfully.

All this activity around the promotion and definition of candidates involved basically the same party machines that operated during the polls. When there was competition within a party, the different sectors mobilized their electoral forces in order to impose their will. These internal struggles were always more intense among the *autonomistas* than among the *nacionalistas*. In neither party, however, did the competition bring too many surprises, as the roster of possible candidates involved a relatively small number of political leaders. Electoral life was limited to a small circle of people, yet their frequent, visible confrontations instilled some degree of uncertainty and emotion into the politics of Buenos Aires.

The Electoral Results

Elections were not always truly competitive. Sometimes there was no opposition, the opposition abstained from participating, or the elections were manipulated in such a way that their results were known beforehand. Most of the time, however, a genuine confrontation turned the polls into a decisive political moment.

In most elections, there were two lists of candidates. The law established that the citizens vote for individuals, but each voter had to cover the total number of places in dispute in the district. The clubs, on their part, distributed among their sympathizers written lists of candidates that they expected their members to vote for. Not always, however, did the latter follow party instructions. They could, and sometimes did, change one or more of the names on the official list. The substitution could be the result of a personal decision; more frequently, however, these modifications were prompted by leaders who dissented from the official line.

In the early 1860s, the lists of the two parties sometimes had names in common, but that practice was left aside as the rivalries between the clubs increased.[5] *Mitristas* or *nacionalistas* and *alsinistas* or *autonomistas* were the two main political constellations, but there were frequent exchanges between them, crossed alliances, overlappings, as well as splits and dissidence. Most of the time, however, these operations ended up in two major lists.[6]

To win the elections, the contending political forces—as we have already seen—had to set in motion a field operation with the purpose of controlling the polls in each one of the city parishes. In most districts, competition between them was intense. It is possible, however, to distinguish certain recurrent patterns of voting. Catedral al Norte, Catedral al Sur, San Miguel, San Telmo, and Santa Lucía were quite faithful to Mitre; while Balvanera, La Concepción, and to a lesser extent San Cristóbal and La Piedad were strongholds of the *alsinistas*.

These inclinations seldom produced a unanimous ballot; rather, they systematically favored one of the two competing lists. The rest of the parishes, in turn, had more random electoral behavior. This pattern shows a predominance of the *mitristas* in the downtown district and of the *alsinistas* in the more popular neighborhoods of the city. We should avoid, however, the temptation of jumping to rapid conclusions regarding the social composition of the respective constituencies. Both parties had a strong presence in every parish; the nationalists also controlled popular areas such as Santa Lucía and, late in the period, San Juan Evangelista (La Boca); the autonomists were strong in some of the residential parts of the city. At the same time, the parishes were far from uniform in their social and demographic composition, and the city's downtown, for example, housed very different social sectors. As we have seen in Chapters 3 and 4, moreover, all political groups who competed in the elections resorted to the same type of electoral machines and developed similar networks of followers.

The polls were a key step in the road to power, but not the last. The electoral results had to be revised by the legislative authorities. They could confirm, question, and even annul an election. When competition had been high at the polls, the losing party generally challenged the results by accusing the winning side of fraud and other irregularities. The debate took place in the press and the legislature. It was the occasion for a lavish display of republican and democratic rhetoric that deserves further inquiry.

Quite often the confrontation went beyond the exchange of words, and violence erupted. The legislature building and its neighboring areas became the main sites for the showdown. The battles could be quite virulent, as in the famous "April days" of 1864, when the provincial legislature had to decide upon the validity of the elections for representatives and senators held in March.[7] In a previous election for national representatives held in February, the *mitristas*—in control of the federal administration—had won over the *alsinistas,* in power at the provincial level. In March the latter won over the former. The parties accused each other of manipulation and fraud. When the time came for legislative validation of the ballot, the political situation was very tense, and both sides were determined to prevail. Just after the March elections, the newspaper *La Nacion Argentina* invited all *mitristas* to meet in their respective parishes and sign a petition asking for the annulment of the elections, which had taken place only in a few districts and under very irregular circumstances. The *alsinista El Nacional* accused its rival of inciting the people to a revolt. The *Club del Pueblo* convened an assembly; drafted a declaration stating that it would fail to recognize the new representatives and would consider all their legislative acts null and void; and urged its members to attend the meeting of the legislature on the day of the ballot debate. The *Club Libertad*, in turn, also invited its members to attend the debate, while one of the main autonomist papers, *La Tribuna*, threatened its political adversary: "If *La Nación* wants blood, there shall be blood." In spite of the efforts made by President Mitre and Governor Saavedra to reach an agreement before the day of the debate, violence erupted both in the streets and in the hall. On April 20 the discussion among the representatives was very heated, and once and again it was interrupted by cheers, applause, and tumult in the galleries. Because of the disorders, the session was postponed to allow for new negotiations. On April 22 the session was resumed; no agreement had been reached, however, and in an extremely heated atmosphere the legislators approved the elections.

In the streets, the violence mounted. The forces of the two electoral clubs repeatedly clashed. *La Nación* talked about "the white scarf conspiracy," in reference to the shawl the autonomists wore as a badge, and *La Tribuna* denounced "the revolt of the daggers," alluding to the slaughterhouse workers who presumably formed in the *mitrista* ranks. The action looked familiar enough. As on polling days, each club deployed and organized its forces for the occasion. According to *La Tribuna*: "A club has leaders to head it and members who obey,"[8] and that is precisely what happened on April 22 in the political battlefield. In this case, the situation reached peak levels of violence. There were many wounded and some dead, and order was restored only after the intervention of army troops led by the veteran General Hornos.

The political conflict, however, continued. The partisan press now added denunciation of the violence to the continued accusations of fraud and electoral manipulation. The approval of the provincial senatorial elections was still pending. These were finally annulled, and new elections were called for May 15. At the same time, the negotiations that had started during the "April days" continued. The tension still ran high. New disputes erupted within each party. *Mitrista* dissidents, led by the vice president of the Club del Pueblo, Juan Chassaing, marched through the city streets, protesting against the negotiations that were taking place with the *alsinistas*. This objection notwithstanding, the leadership gradually sealed an agreement that contributed to pacify the political life of the city. On May 18, *La Tribuna* published an article entitled "The Compromise Succeeds":

The bases for this compromise are honorable. They impose to the confronting parties none of those sacrifices to honor or dignity that would make the compromise unacceptable to honest men. . . . It puts an end to a struggle that has lasted too long, reached . . . dangerous proportions, and threatened to conclude in a terrible revolution.[9]

Ten years later that menace proved only too real, when the electoral struggle led to a true rebellion. In September 1874 the *mitristas* launched a national revolution against the federal government. They accused the administration of having committed fraud in the elections for national representatives held in February of that same year. The initial returns, favorable to the *mitrista* lists both in the city and the several counties of the rest of the province, had presumably been changed to the advantage of the *alsinistas*. The manipulation of electoral results was nothing new in Buenos Aires and had generally been accepted as part of the game between the parties. But by 1874 the general political situation was changing rapidly. The Partido Autonomista had found an ally in a new coalition of political forces from the interior provinces. Together they nominated Nicolás Avellaneda as their presidential candidate for the elections of April of that same year. On that occasion the *mitristas* prevailed—once again—in Buenos Aires but lost in the rest of the country. The winning alliance felt strong enough to push through Congress the approval of the fraudulent February returns. The defeated *mitristas* sensed their increasing marginality from power and resorted to armed rebellion.[10]

The uprising was explained in terms familiar to the republicanism that was dear to the political and intellectual elites of the times. In the face of despotism, the people rebelled. *La Nación* pointed out that the constitution itself established the obligation of the people to bear arms in defense of its provisions and principles. In his pronouncement, partially reproduced in the opening of this chapter, Bartolomé Mitre stated that "the revolution is a right, an obligation, and a need."[11] The official press had a similar position regarding the right of the people to bear arms. They distinguished, however, a revolution—"the people's uprising against a government that inflicts violence on their inclinations and aspirations"—from a civil war—when the rebels find no support on the part of the people—and they included the *mitrista* revolt in the latter category.[12]

A real war followed. Troops were deployed and bloody battles ensued. Some generals were victorious, others were beaten. Many soldiers died.[13] The fighting took place far from Buenos Aires. Within nine weeks, the federal government defeated the rebels, and the punishments imposed upon them were soon mitigated by a presidential amnesty. The episode, however, alarmed the country's political leadership. By 1874 the state had presumably achieved a monopoly on violence. The last provincial *caudillos* had been defeated, and the conflict of interests between different sectors of the elite had been solved in a "civilized" way. The *mitrista* revolution, therefore, seemed to have turned the clock backward. The government's response, however, had been rapid and effective, and it had demonstrated the capacity of the administration to exert immediate control over any subversive attempt, even when it originated in the powerful province of Buenos Aires.

The failure of the *mitristas* strengthened the image of an effective central power. In the words of *Le Courier de la Plata*: "The Argentine nation has won with this crisis. It has reinforced the institutions, and has demonstrated the impotence of the agitators, regardless of their position, enlightenment, and resources."[14] From a political point of view, the defeat weakened Mitre as a national figure. In the long run, however, Avellaneda had to reckon that his rival still enjoyed wide support both among Buenos Aires political groups and the *porteño* public. So after a period in which the main figures were in exile, the nationalist newspapers remained banned, and the party abstained from electoral struggles, the *mitristas* returned to the political arena. In 1877 they were invited by the president to participate in the cabinet and to draft common lists of candidates for the next elections, in a move known as "the conciliation." It was a means of avoiding the electoral confrontations that had reached a dangerous peak with the revolution. The candidatures could be negotiated at the top, thus eliminating the competition in the field that could turn the electoral battles into a true war. Avellaneda succeeded in attracting the main figures among the nationalists and autonomists. But dissident factions in both parties, and particularly among the latter, drafted their own lists of candidates and renewed the electoral struggle, thus frustrating the main object of the pact.

This episode shows that "electoral operations" could become truly problematic. Their consequences and repercussions frequently transcended the limited arena of the parties and clubs. The people of Buenos Aires were aware of their importance. In fact, large sectors of the population were attentive to the electoral game and its results.

The Public Repercussions

The elections had great public repercussions in Buenos Aires. Although few people actually voted, the polls were like a performance, with many more spectators than actors.

The press paid great attention to electoral events. On the one side, the partisan newspapers devoted many columns to politics. They provided detailed information on club meetings and assemblies, urged followers to register and participate in parish clubs, published accounts of what happened on polling days, and reported cases of fraud and manipulation—always perpetrated by the rivals.[15] This information was destined, in the first place, for the party followers. Very often the papers seemed largely devoted to insufflating a partisan spirit among the closed circle of their supporters. Yet they also addressed a larger public with the purpose not only of attracting new proselytes but also of influencing public opinion—that increasingly important factor in the political life of the city. On the other side, the independent press, which did not respond to the parties, also discussed politics, reported on electoral events, and frequently was quite explicit in their opinion about the candidates.

The newspapers not only disseminated the party news, kept the people informed, and gave their opinions about the electoral events; they also provided the public with an interpretation of what was going on. Above all, they contributed to bring politics to the people in a city where, although few voted, many were attracted by the elections.

On especially exciting occasions, no one escaped the thrill: "It is an issue [the electoral one] that interests everybody, young and old, men and women, to such an extent that if anyone mentions *the great issue*, everybody knows it means the elections." *La Tribuna* refers here to the mood that prevailed in July 1873. It goes on to say:

The young women today are annoyed by the light literature of the gossip columns. . . . They would rather read a large article on politics. . . . The same thing happens with kids at school. . . . The bootblacks and street urchins talk about electoral combinations. . . . A young man cannot visit a family without the girls of the house or their mother demanding he profess his political faith.[16]

Félix Armesto also notes that:

The social world, the families, and their most distinguished gatherings were duplicates of the electoral *comités*. . . . The [social] clubs El Progreso and del Plata were heated by the discussions, and their respective directive boards had to include in their bylaws a clause to forbid the discussion of political issues in the premises.[17]

This image has little in common with the prevailing one in much of the historiography, in which the Buenos Aires public is portrayed as basically indifferent to politics, and of the political life as limited to very restricted circles. The usual mood of the city was probably not as heated as these quotations suggest, as they refer to a very particular moment of great political uncertainty. But every electoral confrontation aroused a wide public awareness. In the 1870s, for example, the meetings called by the parties to proclaim their candidates or to protest against the frauds presumably committed by the rival group were attended by many more people than visited the polls. These political demonstrations resembled the other public mobilizations of the period (see Chapter 7). The people met in a closed place, generally a theater, and then marched through the streets and filled the open space of one of the central city squares. *Mitristas* and *alsinistas* also competed in this field. The newspapers were a key piece of the show. Before the meeting, they encouraged the people to participate, and after it they narrated the event.

During the second half of 1873, as we have seen, the political atmosphere was agitated and party meetings recurrent. The year 1874 started belligerently. Already by January there had been several political demonstrations, and these increased in number sharply after the February elections for representatives, just before the presidential election to be held in April. In March the *mitristas* organized a protest against the fraud committed in February:

The Variedades [theater] wasn't large enough to accommodate the multitude that met there. . . . The avenues around the theater were equally crowded by those who could not get in. The session was opened by Costa. . . . After [several speeches] . . . Mr. Costa adjourned the meeting and invited everyone to march to the Plaza del Retiro. . . . After ten minutes, the head of the column, which we calculate had six to seven thousand people, reached the Plaza . . . more than seven blocks literally filled with people![18]

The followers of Alsina and Avellaneda also demonstrated. According to *La Tribuna*, a meeting held at the beginning of May in the Plaza de la Victoria "occupied around five blocks."[19] *El Correo Español*, a Mitre sympathizer, reported the meeting of the rival party:

[At the established time,] while a musical band marched around the plaza, the parish clubs arrived in four separate groups with their [respective] banners. The blast of the firecrackers . . . animated the feast. By 12:45 the congregation had swollen considerably; a table was set up at the foot of the cathedral's stairs to serve as a podium. . . . [After two hours of speeches] the demonstrators marched, band at front, through the streets. . . . When they reached Dr. Alsina's house . . . they invaded—some on foot, some on horseback—the rooms of the house in the midst of boisterous cheers and enthusiastic ovations. . . . [After Alsina addressed the crowd] they continued their march . . . to Plaza Lorea, where it was meant to dissolve.[20]

Other demonstrations followed. On April 15, it was again the *mitristas*: "Three compact blocks full of people, and in each one thousands of citizens. The stores and terraces were open and illuminated,

the ladies waved their handkerchiefs and cheered, the foreign population shared everybody's feelings."[21] The following day, *La Tribuna* reported a meeting of the partisans of Avellaneda's candidacy:

At half-past seven, a group of one thousand distinguished persons left the
club, marching toward the Plaza de la Victoria. . . . Half an hour later,
around *seven thousand* citizens had gathered there. . . . With three musical
bands, ardently acclaiming Dr. Alsina and Dr. Avellaneda, they left the Plaza
de la Victoria in [perfect] order, something hard to achieve in this type of action. . . . Many young women, among the most distinguished of our society,
threw flowers when Dr. Alsina went by [their homes] and cheered his name
repeatedly.[22]

La Tribuna used very similar terms to describe a meeting of their
adversaries, the *mitristas*, held only a few days later. They met at the
theater Variedades, which at noon was already full. After the
speeches, they marched through the streets:

When they reached the [social] club Los Negros, its members threw flowers
and cheered General Mitre. . . . Some young women [also] threw flowers. . . .
When they reached Retiro, we calculated 6,500 to 7,000 people, including the
curious and the foreigners [who had joined the crowd].[23]

These narratives are found once and again in the papers during the
years that followed, both in the partisan and in the independent
newspapers. They portray a political and electoral awareness that
transcended the restricted circles of those who were directly involved
in the electoral game. The wider public is represented in these accounts by those who acclaimed the demonstrators, consumed the
press narratives, and eventually took part in the meetings and
marches. It included not just native adult men—who could vote but
frequently chose not to—but also women and the foreign-born, who
were deprived of the right of suffrage. The visibility of women in these
accounts confirms Armesto's comment that "not even the ladies refrained from politics. They were the main advocates of Mitre's candidacy, as they had great sympathy toward him." Lucio V. López also
mentions the "political fanaticism of the women" and their passion
for their "political idol," who was none other than Mitre.[24]

These examples illustrate how contemporaries measured the success or failure of a political mobilization. The size of the gathering was
the first fact that counted. Successful demonstrations convened more
people than most elections. The "quality" of the participants was the
second relevant fact. In the accounts of the meetings, the usual generic
mention of "the people" was followed by their qualification. Such
phrases as "distinguished persons," "the most distinguished men,"
"*gente decente*," or, more explicitly, "a distinguished attendance, of the

sort that does not participate in the polls" were used to enhance the significance of a meeting.[25] "Elements recruited from the lowest social spheres," "people brought in from the countryside," and police or government employees were mentioned to produce the opposite effect, that of invalidating the importance of a political assembly.[26] A third element was the response the demonstrators found among the rest of the urban public. The cheers, the applause, the flowers thrown to the crowd, were signs of a successful event.

Press accounts also described the meetings in great length. They portrayed the site of the gathering, summarized the contents of the speeches, reproduced the path followed by the march, and made a general evaluation of the atmosphere that prevailed during the event. Order, calm, and respectability were positive signs, while violence and unruly behavior were highly criticized and generally ascribed to adversaries.

The accounts and narratives of the press shed some light on the important place these public events had in the political life of Buenos Aires. For the leadership, these were a means to prove that they enjoyed the support of a larger, and better qualified, section of the population than the one they deployed at the polls. At the same time, these meetings and marches themselves contributed to the formation of the constituency of a particular leader or party, to its display and identification. These demonstrations were, therefore, the "civilized" counterpart to the battles at the polls.

Together, they defined the contours of the electoral game.

The Debate

The electoral life of Buenos Aires was a topic of public debate. The press played a key role in that respect, but the national and the provincial legislatures also witnessed important and sometimes very heated discussions on that aspect of the political life of the city. Whenever there were incidents at the polls, or accusations of fraud and manipulation, the polemic ensued. On these occasions, however, the arguments were generally tainted by the specific political circumstances. This bias was less visible in the periodic debates of the electoral laws, when the representatives not only discussed electoral practices but also displayed their arguments regarding other aspects of political representation.

In Argentina, universal male suffrage was implicitly established by the constitution of 1853. Its text, however, has no explicit provisions regarding the right to vote. And the proceedings of the Constitutional Congress have no record of discussions on the suffrage. The specifics of electoral rights and procedures were later regulated by federal and provincial laws.

The first congressional debates are registered in the proceedings of the 1857 sessions, when representatives passed the first national electoral law. Important modifications were introduced in 1863, 1873, and 1877, and minor changes in 1878 and 1881. In the province of Buenos Aires, the Constitution of 1854 established the right to vote for all citizens "born in the province and [for] the sons of the other provinces of the Republic, older than twenty" and for "those under that age who are enrolled in the national guard and for married men over eighteen" (Article 7). In the 1850s, the province ignored the federal laws established by the confederate government. In electoral matters, the provincial law of 1821 remained in force until the federal law of 1863 and a new provincial law of 1864 were passed. The provincial constitutional convention of 1870 to 1873, and the 1875 and 1876 legislatures also produced modifications to the existing electoral regulations.

Both in the press and in the legislative chambers, objections to the current system started with the fraud and violence at the polls. These offenses were committed by all parties, but they were always denounced by the losers. The accusations were generally answered by the winning party with the argument that those practices, albeit undesirable, had become a regular feature of electoral behavior. Thus, in 1878, Héctor Varela responded to Mitre's fraud allegations in the following terms:

Don Bartolo [Mitre] . . . writes column after column on the electoral frauds . . . and the next moment, he goes on to remind Dr. Tejedor: Do you remember, comrade, those times when we pulled some tricks as large as the Cathedral? Those were nice frauds indeed! From your own pen there is the memorable *Felipe Lotas!*

—*Ja!* answered Dr. Tejedor, and from your own pen, my friend Don Bartolo, is the no less memorable *Benito Cámelas.* How is it, then, . . . that these gentlemen are so shocked by the frauds?[27]

Yet every time the issue was brought up in the legislative arena, all sectors insisted on the need to end electoral corruption in order to guarantee the principle of popular sovereignty and the mechanisms of political representation and suffrage. To achieve those aims, the legislators and publicists proposed, and tried to carry forward, various initiatives throughout the period.

In the 1860s, the prevailing concern revolved around what contemporaries called "the freedom of the suffrage": how to secure the constitutional right of every citizen to vote if he so wished, and how to eliminate official coercion and the electoral power of governments. These questions led to discussion of the mechanisms and procedures for voting, such as the definition of electoral districts, the drafting of registers, the composition of registering committees, the selection of polling authorities, methods of scrutiny, and the control of polling stations on election day. In this context, the debate around the privacy of the vote took the center stage. A proposal to introduce the secret ballot had been already formulated in Buenos Aires during the previous decade, in the projects of law submitted in 1856 and 1857, but at the time other concerns had been more pressing and that clause was disregarded.[28]

During the legislative treatment of the federal electoral law of 1863, on the other hand, the issue was one of the three main points addressed by the Committee on Constitutional Affairs of the House of Representatives.[29] On October 24, 1863, in the name of the committee, Representative Zuviría stated that:

[It] is not strange that [the secret ballot] was much discussed in the committee, as even the highest minds do not agree on the most convenient way to express the vote. The committee . . . opted for the public vote; because even if the secret vote guarantees freedom, it is more appropriate that once the individuals have all the freedom [they need], they vote publicly. Besides, the public vote is more adequate to the rights and liberties of a republic . . . [as the vote] is not only a right but it also implies an obligation. . . . The secret vote . . . should be in force only in a dictatorship.[30]

These arguments must have convinced the representatives, because the clause was voted without further discussion both in the House and in the Senate. The same reasons were repeated once and again in the following years every time the public vote was advocated in Congress or the press.

The controversy increased. In 1864 the topic was raised in the provincial legislature, and it was considered "the most important aspect of the project of law under consideration."[31] The corresponding committee had produced a report favorable to the secret ballot, "the only means that provides the citizen with a guarantee for the exercise of the highest of his rights." When the report was presented to the House, however, the informant, Representative Varela, admitted that "[we], the supporters of the secret ballot, enter this debate in great disadvantage, since . . . [the important] newspaper El Nacional has systematically devoted [its pages] to opposing the voting system proposed by the committee." The paper sustained the public vote, while the other important autonomist paper, *La Tribuna*, defended the secret ballot. In the legislature, the latter was finally defeated by seventeen votes to eight.[32]

In spite of these legislative reverses, in the following decades the secret ballot remained an issue of public debate. In 1873, when the new federal electoral law was being discussed in Congress, it was once more included in the project presented by the corresponding committee to the House. In the ensuing debate, several *mitristas* argued in favor of the secret ballot, because, as Dr. Elizalde put forward: "The secret ballot is the one that truly represents the majority of the suffrage, the truth of the democratic system. A citizen that exercises the right to vote fulfills an obligation and a correlative right, and has to account for it to no one."[33] More practical points were also put forward: public voting was associated with coercion, fraud, and violence.

The autonomists expressed their total opposition to the project, and representatives Bernardo de Irigoyen, Dardo Rocha, Dionisio Vega, Vicente López, and Aristóbulo del Valle presented the arguments against the secret ballot.[34] Some arguments recall John Stuart Mill's defense of the public vote; others resorted to history. These were Irigoyen's words on the occasion:

I believe that to leave aside public voting, after so many years of having it in operation, is to abdicate from a worthy practice that in itself reveals the moral progress of the country and the development of the democratic spirit based on responsibility, which dignifies all human actions.[35]

He also posed the question: "What do we owe to the public vote?" and offered an answer: "We owe it all we have," and he traced back that tradition to the May revolution of 1810. In the debate, all parties resorted to examples from the past, from ancient Greece to contemporary France and United States, often misusing them for their own purposes.

The speeches by representatives were followed by cheers, applause, and disturbances in the galleries. The partisan press, in turn, repeated the arguments of the politicians. *La Nación* and *La Prensa* favored the secret ballot, while *El Nacional* stood for the public vote. *La Tribuna*, in spite of its autonomist inclinations, continued to support the former. In the end, Representative Leguizamón proposed a formula for compromise. He called for a secret but not anonymous ballot. His reasons were somewhat different from the ones previously displayed:

[M]ost of the thoughtful, serious individuals do not attend the polls. . . . [They are] the stage where violent scenes are played . . . and discourage . . . a great number of electors who, being conscious of the suffrage, do not want, however, to be the victims of the disorders and even insults and abuses that often take place at the scene of the elections.[36]

He proposed, therefore, that the vote be written on a slip of paper that would carry the name of the voter, and then be sealed and deposited in a ballot box. The formula satisfied no one, but it was finally adopted with slight changes as a middle-of-the-road solution. Each voter had to hand in the ballot to the president of the polling station, who had to "briefly reveal its contents." The following day, *La Tribuna* ironically observed: "The public vote has not been accepted, since it was impossible. The secret ballot has been rejected, which represents a deplorable aberration. The House has sanctioned a composite system that has the vices of both."[37]

The clause was so weak that it was eliminated by the Senate. The final text read: "[T]he vote of each citizen . . . shall be written on white slips of paper . . . and will contain the name of the voter, his inscription number, and the name of the persons for whom he is voting" (Article 24 of the electoral law passed on September 18, 1873).

Leguizamón's presentation not only offered a compromise to solve the problem; it also brought forward a new issue that would become a chief preoccupation of the 1870s: "the lack of public spirit." In 1873, representative Costa said, "[T]here is something that should concern us all, and that is [the need] to arouse the public spirit, so that all citizens participate with their vote in the formation of government."[38] The distinction made by Juan Bautista Alberdi between civic and political rights had produced a dangerous gap between a civil society in the making and the political system, and had engendered an "oligarchy" that was unfamiliar with the needs and claims of the society it was supposed to represent. That political "oligarchy" appealed to the vote of popular clienteles to solve its internal controversies, while those who should be involved in public life—the propertied classes— abstained from electoral participation and were only interested in their private affairs.[39] These topics were central to the debates of the provincial constitutional convention held between 1870 and 1873. The problem was no longer limited to how to secure the right to vote of any citizen who wished to do so. Now the question of who those voters should be had entered the agenda.

The issue of the scope of the suffrage was raised for the first time in decades. At the convention, the Committee on Legislative Power, formed by Luis Sáenz Peña, Emilio de Alvear, Eduardo Costa, and Eugenio Cambaceres, proposed to make voting compulsory for all citizens over eighteen. On the other hand, the Central Committee, consisting of Vicente F. López, Bartolomé Mitre, Osvaldo Garrigós, M. Languenheim, S. Villegas, and Dardo Rocha, made a rather vague presentation on the subject that read as follows: "[T]he attribution of popular suffrage is, according to this constitution, a right inherent to the quality of the Argentine citizen and an obligation that he will fulfill according to the corresponding law."[40]

Voting as a right or as an obligation and public duty: those were the basic terms of the debate. That opposition had already appeared when the discussion revolved around the secrecy of the vote. But in the new context, it was related to the question of who the actual voters were, and who the ideal ones should be. For those who considered the vote as the people's right, there was no question of establishing limits to the citizenry. The notion of "the people" did not admit internal distinctions or external borders, except for those already embedded in the cultural definition of the political body (which excluded women and children, among others). On the other hand, for those who understood the vote as an obligation, the problem of who should vote became a key matter of discussion.

The proposals formulated by the representatives could be quite drastic. Representative Marín, for example, recommended restricting "the exercise of sovereignty to the most intelligent and capable sectors of the province or the city" by establishing voting limitations based on property and literacy. Minister Costa retorted that "universal suffrage is at the basis of our institutions; it is the only one that has value and force throughout the world."[41]

For Sáenz Peña, in turn, all efforts would be vain if the vote were not made compulsory. To limit the suffrage, as suggested by Marín, would not ensure the participation of those reluctant to fulfill their public duties. Only mandatory voting could "raise the public spirit." Bartolomé Mitre responded to this argument:

The theory of compulsory suffrage is founded on [the notion that] . . . the suffrage is not a people's right but a public function entrusted to certain citizens; that it is not a right inherent to democracy but a privilege granted to certain men. . . . Therefore, to make this theory of the duty against the right prevail, it is necessary to eliminate the latter, and then [the suffrage] becomes just a duty inherent to every Argentine citizen.[42]

At the convention, most of the debate revolved around these two poles. In the end, Mitre's proposal of considering the suffrage both as a right *and* an obligation obtained the majority. The new provincial constitution did not introduce compulsory voting or qualifications to the suffrage. The preoccupation surrounding the "quality" of the actual voters, the absence of the propertied classes from the polls, and the formation of a "political oligarchy" were finally left aside from the new provisions on the right to vote.

Another issue that generated intense debate at the convention was related to the principle of majority rule. Several representatives challenged the prevailing system that prescribed the subordination of the minorities to the electoral majority and left no room for the former. The people were considered a totality, and in spite of the divided voting that prevailed in most elections, their electoral verdict was understood as unanimous. "The subjection of the minorities to the will of the legitimate majorities" had been considered a constitutive principle of a democratic republic.[43] But in the convention, new ideas came up. José Manuel Estrada, a militant Catholic who was well aware of the subordinate place that his group had in the political arena, declared that "[t]he evil lies not in the universal suffrage itself. . . . [T]he evil lies in that not all the wills, not all the rights, and not all the opinions are represented in the [legislative] bodies. . . . The representation of minorities will save the democratic system and the principles of freedom."[44]

Vicente López was more emphatic when he responded to Mitre:

The representative Mitre [was saying] . . . that the more sovereign a people, the more free and independent, but I say that the more sovereign a people, the less independence there is for the individuals, the less independence for the corporate groups. . . . On the other side, this entity called the people does not exist either. . . . [It] is a fictitious entity. . . . What really exists . . . are the classes, and these classes have their particular interests, their harmonic interests that not always are in accordance with the interests of the majority, which receive the name of sovereignty of the people.[45]

According to López, the formation of a political oligarchy could be explained by the "rule of the [greatest] numbers," which wiped out all other legitimate interests, among them, those of the conservative classes. "It is necessary that the sovereignty of the number find its limitation in reason," he said, and proposed that the Senate be turned into a body representative of property owners.[46] His idea of the social was very different from the previous one; it postulated the existence of social classes with different interests, opinions, and rationalities that could not be subsumed in the single category of "the people."

López's proposals did not prevail, but the discussions incorporated the problem of social diversity. The constitutional text, moreover, introduced the possibility of minority representation. Article 49 established that "[t]he proportionality of representation shall be the rule in all popular elections." This clause, together with Article 214, which instituted the cumulative vote, triggered passionate debates in the province. Finally, the electoral law of 1876 introduced a specific system of proportional representation for all provincial elections.[47]

No new issues came up in the debates of the federal law of 1877. The controversy around the suffrage as a right or as an obligation returned, and also the complaints regarding "public indifference," but the voting system of 1873 was left unchanged. The clause that required voters to prove their enrollment in the national guard was, on the other hand, eliminated. This move was adopted in the name of "freedom of the suffrage," but it also had other connotations. The motif of the citizen in arms was dear to the republican ideas that had prevailed in Buenos Aires in the 1850s and 1860s. In the 1870s, however, republicanism was giving way to other sets of ideas, and therefore the association between citizenship and the militia was losing ground. The discussions around the secret ballot, the sovereignty of the people, and minority representation were also symptoms of that ideological transformation.

The Buenos Aires press devoted many pages to these legislative and constitutional debates. The newspapers not only reported what happened during the sessions; they also published extensive comments on the various issues under debate and gave their opinion on each. The electoral theme was recurrent in the public agenda. The concern for politics transcended the narrow circle of the elite, and a wider public was involved in the debates generated around the elections. This involvement, however, did not increase the turnout at the polls.

6 Political Citizenship and the Suffrage

Elections constituted a key piece of the political systems that developed in the Americas after the independence of the colonies. In the territories that had formerly been part of the Spanish empire, the principle of popular sovereignty was established in the early nineteenth century. When the new nations finally took shape later in the century, their respective constitutions firmly established the representative system based on the suffrage, and defined the characteristics of, and the limits to, citizenship. As we have seen, Argentina was no exception to this pattern. The Constitution of 1853 determined that the nation was a "representative republic." From then on, elections for the national and provincial executive and for the legislature were held regularly. The suffrage, the contours of political citizenship, and the forms of representation became constant themes of political dispute and public debate.

These questions have been addressed by Argentine historiography. Until very recently, prevailing interpretations have tended to describe the Argentine case as a "restrictive republic" (see the Introduction). They have understood the low voter turnouts as an expression of a limited citizenship and regarded the electoral systems of the nineteenth century as corrupt and illegitimate. By conforming to the general model, these narratives failed to account, however, for the actual role of elections in the political life of the period and for the real, rather than presumed, process of construction of a citizenry. The following interpretation, based on the previous chapters concerning the electoral life of Buenos Aires in the 1860s and 1870s, addresses these questions and seeks to challenge some of the received views on the subject.

A restrictive republic relies on the principle of representation for the privileged few, who constitute a limited citizenry of those qualified by their capacity or their property to enjoy and exercise the right to vote. In the Buenos Aires of the second half of the nineteenth century, the suffrage was widely extended to all adult men, regardless of literacy or wealth. The model of the restrictive republic clearly does not apply. This evidence does not imply, however, the existence of a citizenry—unrestricted or otherwise—in Buenos Aires. By definition, the suffrage is a necessary condition for the development of political citizenship, but it is not a sufficient one. The mere expansion of the right to vote and the staging of regular elections does not necessarily produce a political citizenry—if the latter is understood as a community of equals who participate, directly or indirectly, in the exercise of political power.[1] In the case of Buenos Aires of the 1860s and 1870s, to equate the voters with such a body would, indeed, be misleading. The actual voters were—as we have seen—far removed from the image, prescribed by contemporary laws and prevailing ideas, of the free individual citizen in command of his political rights. Under such circumstances, it is of little use to engage in a controversy as to the scope of the citizenry. The concept was indeed very meaningful in the normative and ideological debates of the time, but the political practices of Buenos Aires revolved around other, more pragmatic bases.

From the legal point of view, the universal male suffrage established in Buenos Aires in 1821 and confirmed by the Constitution of 1853 meant that any adult man born or naturalized Argentine could vote. The legislation said no more. The vote was not mandatory, and there were no special qualifications, aside from age and sex. Within those broad boundaries, there was no definition of the ideal voter, nor any mention of the contours of the desirable citizenry. Those borders were clearly established in societies where the suffrage was restricted and the law determined with certain precision who the voters and the citizens should be. In Argentina, the indetermination was superseded only after the passage of the electoral law of 1912, which kept the suffrage universal for all adult men but made it secret and mandatory. By introducing a voting obligation, the law provided both a definition of who the citizens *should* be and a starting point for the construction of the political citizenry: *all* Argentine adult men were to form the politically sovereign body of the republic. But prior to that year the legislation was extremely vague, leaving open a vast field for political organizations and electoral machines. They were the producers of the actual voters.

The elections were a crucial step for all political groups or individuals in search of power, and they played a key role as a relatively peaceful system for choosing government officials. In Argentina, as in many other nineteenth-century Western nations, elections did not respond to the ideal model that portrayed them as the supreme moment when free citizens transfer their sovereignty to those who will represent them as individuals and as a nation. Here, the elections displayed the confrontation between the parties in competition for power and involved a very small fraction of the population. Rather than autonomous individual citizens, the voters belonged to partisan forces, mobilized to participate in the generally tumultuous, and often violent, polls.

Voting was not, therefore, an individual act, but a collective move. Those who attended the polls were part of hierarchically organized groups that operated in the various neighborhoods. In each parish, a political network articulated the leadership and the rank and file around the electoral game. The relations that cemented these clienteles were very complex. Protection, connections, employment, comradeship, action—all these were factors of attachment to a group. Furthermore, the political and electoral activities themselves contributed to the integration and cohesion of each circle, to the forging of loyalties among the members, and to the practice of shared rituals.

The political and parish clubs were the material incarnation of these networks. They were the main site for the display of electoral action, the organization of meetings, the gestation of candidatures, and the preparation of the "electoral labors." The party heads met there with the local bosses and their following. It was there, too, that the rank-and-file members had the opportunity to see, listen to, and get in touch with their leaders. The clubs nourished political identities and loyalties.

The electoral networks relied strongly on the control of the state apparatus. Employment in the public administration or in jobs otherwise connected to the government was important in the recruitment and preservation of clienteles. Furthermore, the police, the army, the national guard, and the justices of the peace were fundamental pieces of the electoral system. Control of the government did not suffice, however, to achieve electoral success, and the creation of unofficial political machines was indispensable to win at the polls.

Those who wished to succeed could not just rely on their appeal to potential voters. Organization was essential. The electoral machines were mounted to operate in the field. Their job was to obtain the majority. And that they did not only by recruiting and mobilizing voters but also by blocking the participation of rival forces at the polls. The party that had the most efficient machine won the day by "producing" the largest number of ballots.

This electoral game was played by a small percentage of the city's population, chiefly formed by young men from different social backgrounds, a significant proportion of whom belonged to the lower sectors of the popular classes. Most of the people who were qualified to vote chose not to do so. The reasons for this widespread reluctance to exercise the prescribed form of political freedom were probably many and complex. In countries where the suffrage was restricted by property or literacy qualifications, voting was a privilege enjoyed only by those who met the requisites. In Buenos Aires that was not the case, and most of the people did not think of voting as a privilege or as an effective means of representation. In fact, the modern concept of representation was too abstract; it had been initially imposed by the elites, and its incorporation to the prevailing political culture took place only after a long, contradictory, and probably quite contested social and cultural process.[2] Voting, moreover, as a collective action, highly controlled by the leadership and usually quite violent, discouraged free riders. Among the upper echelons of society, personal influence with and family ties to the politically powerful made electoral participation seem superfluous. Among the rest, as we shall see in Part III, other forms of participation in public life were more appealing than voting, and they probably seemed more effective.

What, then, was the role of elections? If we look just at the electoral action on polling days, we may conclude that voting was a practice very much internal to the dynamics of the political parties. It had little to do with the rest of the society and, therefore, with the relationships between the political and the social realms. At this level, elections were like a game, with rules defined and respected by the players, all of whom had been recruited beforehand. A relatively stable body of participants, which did not increase through time, took part in the political battles.

The leadership did not show any interest in expanding the electoral base. In many other nineteenth-century nations, manipulation, political patronage, and control played an important part in the operation of the electoral networks. In most of those cases, however, these mechanisms tended to expand the electorate. The parties of Buenos Aires, on the other hand, chose to fight the electoral battles without enlarging their effective forces. This decision was probably—and paradoxically—related to universal suffrage. The lack of property or literacy qualifications for voting made it possible for the parties to organize an efficient system based upon very reliable and loyal clienteles. But that same system was ill suited for attracting new followers, particularly among the middle and upper classes. To recruit a different type of voter would have required a change in the partisan ways of fighting the elections, with the consequent risk of loss of control on the part of the current leaderships. At the same time, and for the reasons mentioned above, there were no pressures "from below" to open up the electoral game. So it remained very much in the hands of the politically involved.

The elections allowed for a relatively "civilized" and controlled resolution of the frequent conflicts within the political elite. Armed confrontation had been a usual way of solving those struggles in the past, now replaced by the restrained and sportslike violence of the polls. The elections were the repeated enactment of a political game in which the actors knew and accepted the rules and played their parts. There was also an audience. Although most of the people did not care to vote, they were attentive to electoral events.

The elections were matter of public debate in Buenos Aires. They had a central place in the press. When the elections were highly contested, the city fell under the political spell. Demonstrations and meetings convened more people than did the polls. They were attended by many who did not, or could not, vote. Why support a candidate and abstain from voting for him? Voting meant participating in electoral forces and polling battles, being a piece of a "machine." Those who did not wish to get involved in the game refrained from voting. If they had political sympathies for a party, they trusted that its leaders would know how to operate and win, without their personal presence. This absence from the polls, therefore, did not mean that they were indifferent to politics; rather, it was related to the gap that existed between the electoral showdown and the more abstract process of representation.

There were, therefore, two sides to elections. The electoral action that culminated at the polls was a game internal to political groups and parties, a relatively peaceful dispute among them for access to governmental posts according to the principle of popular sovereignty established by the constitution. It involved a small sector of the population organized by the electoral machines. The rest of the people of Buenos Aires were not, however, indifferent to what happened on the electoral stage. The elections were a matter of public debate and mobilizations that included vast sectors of the population.

Political participation was not, therefore, strictly associated with voting, while the exercise of the right to vote was not necessarily tied to the abstract process of representation. It was a system based on universal suffrage, limited voting, and extensive albeit occasional participation. Also, it did not define the contours of a political citizenry, inasmuch as those who voted did not respond to the blueprint of the autonomous citizen, and those who acted politically as free individuals did not vote. The system was, nonetheless, considered legitimate by contemporaries. And for a while it was quite efficient.

In the 1870s, however, it started to falter. The contradiction between the liberal rhetoric of citizenship and representation and the actual electoral practices became increasingly obvious to some members of the political and intellectual elites. Although they had devised and profited from these practices, they gradually became more and more critical of a system that tended to solve the elite's problems by recourse to an increasingly marginal sector of the lower classes. The mounting violence of the electoral games was also denounced. Finally, the abstention of the well-to-do from the polls started to be considered a problem that had to be addressed by the leadership.

At the same time, the political system centered in Buenos Aires proved increasingly fragile. Its mechanisms had been considered efficient enough to maintain peace and order for some time. The Revolution of 1874, however, put an end to that certitude. From then on the power of the Buenos Aires elite dwindled, and its political ways lost prestige and force. President Avellaneda, after his military victory of 1874, sought to eliminate electoral competition by opening some government posts to members of the opposition and negotiating a joint list of candidates with the *mitristas*. The latter complied, but a strong dissidence sprang within the autonomist party itself. The new and short-lived Partido Republicano insisted on mounting and operating a partisan electoral machine that replayed the old game. They obtained several successes at the polls, but their style, albeit effective in Buenos Aires, was less and less acceptable at the national level. True violence erupted again in 1880, when a large part of the *porteño* elites opposed the transformation of the city into a federal capital. President Avellaneda and his successor, General Julio Roca, did not hesitate to crush the rebellion by force. The military defeat of Buenos Aires, the electoral victory of the Partido Autonomista Nacional, and the coming of Roca to the presidency inaugurated a new political era. The political ways of the new regime were quite different from those followed by the *mitristas* and *autonomistas* in the previous decades. Among other things, the electoral system changed and the elections came to play an entirely different role than the one we have explored above.[3]

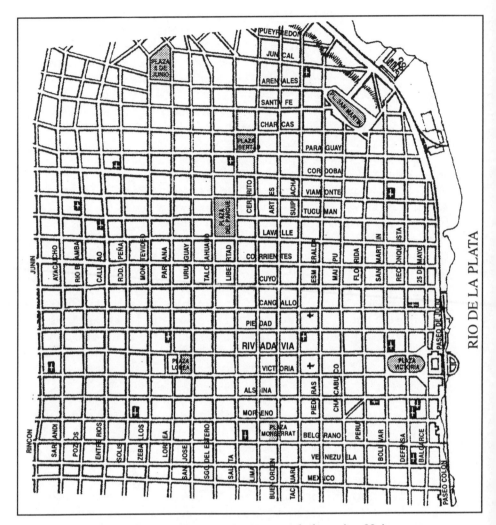

Downtown Buenos Aires—main streets and plazas (c. 1880).

PART III

7 The People Take to the Streets

Meeting against the taxes, December 18, 1878. [*El Mosquito*, December 22, 1878]

The People Demonstrate

Most residents of Buenos Aires did not care to participate in the electoral combats. Yet they were always ready to get together and take to the streets in order to express their opinion, press for their interests, or defend a particular cause. Far from being indifferent to public matters, they frequently mobilized and became involved in collective action. The image of massive public gatherings was familiar in Buenos Aires. As mentioned in Chapter 2, the *porteños* found plenty of opportunities to celebrate and demonstrate. Most of these demonstrations originated in civil society, but some of them were staged mainly to address the authorities and the actors of the political realm. This sort of mobilization was a key aspect of the development of a public sphere, and it will be the main topic of the present chapter.

In the 1860s and 1870s, the people of Buenos Aires often mobilized in order to encourage, protest, or otherwise influence government action. Important demonstrations were staged, for example, in 1864, to support Peru in its conflict with Spain; to support the War of the Triple Alliance against Paraguay in the following year; to sympathize with Cuba in 1869 and 1873; to oppose the death penalty when Pascual Castro Chavarría was sentenced to death in 1870; to object to the official organization mounted on occasion of the yellow fever epidemics of 1871; to protest the restitution of the church of San Ignacio to the original owners, the Jesuits, in 1875; to resist the law of 1878 that imposed an additional tax on liquor, tobacco, and playing cards; to demonstrate for peace in the face of the revolutionary events of 1880. These "causes" produced a massive response from the public. They were not the only ones, however, and lesser demonstrations frequently took place. The immigrant communities, for example, often produced their own mobilizations, triggered by their local claims or demands.

Until very recently, these forms of collective action were virtually ignored by the historiography of nineteenth-century Buenos Aires. The image of the people taking to the streets was not absent from the literature, but it was generally related to very specific events—such as the Revolution of 1890—considered to be exceptional moments of popular eruption. The people were portrayed as indifferent to, or absent from, the public scene. Only exceptionally and spontaneously did they resort to collective action as a form of rebellion against the established order.[1]

Contemporaries, however, had a very different image of the presence of "the people" in the streets of the city. Before 1890, public meetings and demonstrations were considered to be "a practice beneficial to the democratic institutions" that resulted from "the exercise of the right to assembly peacefully" established by the constitution and the laws of the republic.[2] It was understood to be a usual and welcome means of expression of public opinion compatible with peace and order. Revolutions were a different matter altogether, and they were associated with struggle between political factions rather than with the collective actions of the city's population.

There are plenty of references to the latter in the newspapers and other documents of those years. The press was particularly interested in the mobilization of the public and published detailed information on the organization, development, and results of every collective event. The absence of any reference to them in the literature cannot be explained, therefore, by a lack of information in the most usual and accessible historical sources. Rather, it probably has to do with the difficulty to see these events through the lens of traditional interpretations of the political life of the period. More recent works cast a new look at the relations between civil society and the state, and thus "discover" a whole new set of questions that require further exploration.

The following pages of this chapter, as well as Chapters 8 and 9, shall be devoted to analyzing the meetings and demonstrations of the 1860s and 1870s, considered as part of the development of the "culture of mobilization" characteristic of those decades of intense civic action. Chapter 10 explores the relationship between that culture and other forms of political participation, as well as its role in the construction of a national political order.

The Initiative

"To the People of Buenos Aires," "To the Youth," "Meeting of Commerce," "Demonstration," "Protest": these are some of the headlines of ads published in the city's newspapers to convene the people to meetings and demonstrations. The announcements were signed by the promoters of each event: sometimes a well-established association (such as Unione e Benevolenza or the University Club); at other times one or more newspapers. More often, however, the convener was an ad hoc committee formed by the leaders of several institutions, a few public figures, or one or more well-known politicians.

The invitation to meet usually came after intense institutional activity. The initiative generally originated within the dense network of institutions of the civil society. The promoters of a particular cause identified the issue, devised the strategy, and planned the mobilization scheme. The steps they followed defined a routine that was very similar in all cases. First, there was a meeting of the leaders of the institutions involved, who appointed an ad hoc committee. Secondly, the committee drafted a petition or a declaration and went about recruiting supporters for the cause. The third step was to convene a meeting that could be organized as a banquet in a club, a hotel, or a café, or as a public encounter in one of the city's theaters. And the last step was the organization of a massive street demonstration. Most mobilizations followed the same pattern, although not all of them included the full routine and culminated in the streets. The organization of these events improved with time. In the 1870s it was notoriously more careful and controlled than in the previous decade, when the institutional network had been weaker.

In 1864, for example, the mobilization in favor of Peru after the invasion of its Chincha Islands by the Spanish Navy had problems from the start. In May the Argentine newspapers wrote at great length and with a critical viewpoint about the occupation that had taken place the previous month. Soon, however, the progovernment paper *La Nación Argentina* observed: "The excitement produced in the public opinion by the events that are taking place in Peru has placed the issue on two false grounds: antagonism between America and Europe; war between republican and monarchical ideas."[3]

The newspaper rejected both oppositions, adopted a cautious attitude, and formulated the problem in terms of the defense of "the independence of the American republics." It suggested that it was important to wait for the official reaction of the Spanish government in the face of what the paper labeled "a unilateral action" on the part of an admiral of the fleet. This article responded individually to all of the arguments published in an earlier *El Nacional* column that had ended exhorting the government to act and prepare itself for "the contingencies to come."[4]

On May 31, *El Nacional* published an article cum announcement entitled "Grand Meeting" that invited the people of Buenos Aires to organize a demonstration in favor of Peru and against "the tyrants." It was signed by the young autonomist lawyer and journalist Pastor S. Obligado. Next to that article there was an invitation to a meeting held at the Café Garibaldi "to discuss the organization of the demonstration."[5] The meeting was held that same evening and, according to *La Nación Argentina*, it was attended by two hundred people. They proceeded to designate a committee. Colonel Emilio Conesa and Captain Lucio V. Mansilla[6] were appointed to "go see all the veterans of the independence wars [*guerreros de la Independencia*] living in Buenos Aires, from brigadier to colonel ... to inform them that they have been elected by the vote of a part of the people to integrate a committee" whose main purpose was to convene a larger meeting and deliberate on "the best way to carry out a solemn political demonstration in favor of the Republic of Peru."[7] This committee of veterans, "old patriots ... whose ages added up to one thousand four hundred years,"[8] met at Brigadier Zapiola's home and decided to convene the people at the Colon Theater for the following Sunday, to discuss "the way to organize a demonstration of sympathy in favor of Peru."[9]

Meanwhile, another group had come up with a different initiative. On June 2, the papers published an ad signed by the *mitrista* Club del

Pueblo that invited "all members of the association and all friends of the republican idea residing in Buenos Aires, regardless of nationality, to a meeting to be held on Sunday, June 5, at noon, at the foot of the statue of General San Martín," in the Plaza de Marte.[10] This unilateral move on the part of a political group was criticized by their opposition as well as by those who thought that public action in favor of Peru should not be tainted by partisan strife. The Club del Pueblo then asserted the universal spirit of its appeal; the cause was based upon "a thought shared by all republicans, that bears no relation with the ideas and facts that have produced the partisan divisions."[11] The encounter was successful, and the meeting convened by the committee of veterans was postponed for the following Sunday.

At the same time, a third initiative originated among the Italian immigrants of the Sociedad Republicana, of Mazzinian sympathies. They published a note in the papers inviting their fellow nationals to join a subscription in favor of the Peruvian cause, which is "the American cause."[12] Then they organized their own meeting at the Plaza del Parque, to be held also on Sunday, June 12.

In spite of the diversification of initiatives, the demonstrations were successful. A large public was present at the Plaza de Marte on June 5, attended the Colon Theater on June 12, and joined ranks that same day with those who had first gone to the meeting organized by the Italians at the Plaza del Parque. The action continued during the following weeks. University students published a declaration in favor of Peru and called for a new meeting. The American Union Society, created at the Colon and presided over by a "permanent committee" of the larger Committee of Veterans, organized a new demonstration. They also drafted a petition to be signed and submitted to Congress.[13] These proposals, however, were only partially successful. At that point, the government and the official party were operating to discourage any public action related to the Peruvian conflict.

In this example from 1864, the initiative to demonstrate originated in different quarters, but the political parties and the partisan press soon played a key role in the story. Some years later the direction of the mobilizations changed hands. Institutions such as mutual aid societies; professional, merchant, and workers associations; Masonic lodges; and the press, no longer mainly partisan, took the lead. The presence of these nonpolitical institutions was visible in the planning, organization, and display of the public actions.

The mobilization against the tax law of 1878, for example, involved a thick institutional web. Late that year, the governor of the province of Buenos Aires submitted to the legislature a bill establishing new taxes on the consumption of tobacco, cards, and liquor. The merchants of the city reacted immediately, presenting a petition against the measure, but to no avail. The law passed.[14] A society of retail merchants with branches in all the neighborhoods took the initiative and called a meeting. On December 14, an "assembly of grocers, bakers, inn-keepers, and cigar dealers" established a committee that convened a preparatory meeting to organize a public demonstration against the taxes. The meeting took place on the following day at the Café El Pasatiempo and was attended by "at least four thousand people," according to *La Nación*.[15] Three decisions were taken: to increase the number of committee members, in order to include the representatives of the various trades; to ask the governor to veto the law; and to call a popular meeting for December 18 in the Plaza Lorea.

There was no response from the governor. The committee, therefore, went ahead with the organization of the protest. On December 17, they issued a proclamation addressed "To the People. To the Shopkeepers and Consumers," inviting them to take part in the planned demonstration to ask the legislature to suspend the execution of the law. Newspapers published the announcement, which was also to be seen on walls and in shops throughout the city. *La Prensa* noted that "[a]gents were appointed in every quarter to advertise the meeting . . . and to advise the two hundred appointed deputies in charge of keeping order."[16]

Unlike the mobilizations of the previous decade, this initiative—and similar ones in the 1870s—originated entirely in the institutions of civil society. In spite of this difference, they all shared some common features: in the first place, their potential public. The preferred formula to head any proposal of collective action was to address it "To the People of Buenos Aires." Often the universality of the invitation was underlined by phrases such as "We do not appeal to any particular party," or "We are appealing to all men that. . . ."[17] The national and professional groups that participated in the organization of an event generally included their own local announcements. The university clubs addressed "the youth" or "the students"; immigrant associations appealed to their nationals ("To the Italians," "To the Spanish," and so on); and sometimes the associations that nucleated the trades and the professions added "To Commerce" or, more specifically, "To the Retailers," "To the Liquor Vendors," and so on.

The press was always the principal means of advertising the events. The papers took the initiative to inform their readers about them and published the ads and announcements on behalf of the organizing institutions. At the same time, printed advertisements appeared on walls and in shops; oral announcements were made at social or institutional gatherings; and, of course, the news got around by word of mouth. In the days previous to any mobilization, the information circulated widely in the city, creating expectation among the population, who awaited "the beloved meetings."[18]

Theaters, Streets, and Plazas

The people of Buenos Aires had their favorite spots for public demonstrations. The most massive ones generally included an assembly in a large theater followed by a march through the downtown streets that culminated in an open-air rally in one of the city's main squares. Lesser events could take place in the courtyard or ballroom of a café, restaurant, or club, and could always end up with a march and a rally.

The Teatro Colón, inaugurated in 1857, and the Variedades, open in 1872, were the preferred theaters for these events.[19] The public frequently was too numerous to fit inside and overflowed into the neighboring streets. The square, on the other hand, was an open space, and it became a favorite site for public demonstrations. The Plaza de la Victoria, in the heart of town, was the first choice, but not the only one. The streets, of course, offered a stage for marching in columns and the cheers and jeers of the spectators.

On the occasion of the demonstration in favor of Peru, in 1864, the first meeting took place in the Plaza de Marte. When it was over, "the large party, headed by two musical bands, marched toward the Plaza de la Victoria. . . . Colonel Arenas waited there, directing a musical piece composed by Italian patriots." The second meeting was held on the following Sunday. It started at the Teatro Colón. Later, "the six thousand people who occupied the immense theater left for the streets, headed by a musical band, and went toward President Mitre's house. . . . After [stopping there], they marched toward the [Plaza del] Parque in order to fraternize with the Italians, who had their own large meeting there."[20]

The demonstration organized to ask for the commutation of the death penalty imposed upon Castro Chavarría in 1870 started at 3:00 P.M. in the Plaza de la Victoria. Later, "the immense crowd left toward the seat of the provincial government."[21] The same square witnessed a meeting to organize the fight against yellow fever in 1871, a demonstration in favor of Cuban independence in 1873, and a rally against the Jesuits in 1875. On that occasion, "in the streets adjacent to the Plaza . . . a [group of] people ten times larger waited. . . . Those who had been in the Teatro de Variedades poured into the Plaza through the streets Victoria and Rivadavia."[22]

The display was even greater for the mobilization against taxes of 1878:

The grocers, bakeries, cigar shops, inns, restaurants, all closed at ten in the morning. A quarter of an hour later tramways full of people crossed the streets, and the sidewalks were filled with men of different trades who were going to the Plaza Lorea.[23]

The time set for the meeting was eleven o'clock. Half an hour later, the square was absolutely full. Groups of people were also occupying the [neighboring] streets.[24]

At twelve o'clock:

[t]he march set off . . . down Victoria Street. It occupied several blocks literally filled with people from wall to wall. On the way, groups joined in. . . . The crowd entered Maipu Street heading toward Plaza San Martín. After twenty minutes or so of marching, it entered the square.[25]

The newspapers described the scenes in great detail. In the press accounts, the city streets and squares are portrayed not just as the stage for public action; they appear also as characters in the story. The urban space is exalted; Buenos Aires itself becomes the protagonist. In fact, the city was not only the setting of public life; it was what made it possible. The urban structure, the form and location of the public spaces, were key elements in this respect. Buenos Aires of the 1860s and 1870s bore the marks of the urban transformations of the first half of the century. The modernizing project of the Rivadavia years brought about the regularization of the street grid, the multiplication of the plazas, the concentration of public buildings in the downtown area, the consolidation of that area as the privileged one for all government activity, and the use of republican patterns in the official architecture.[26] All these measures had contributed to define an urban structure that not only facilitated but also favored public action.

The People

Who made up the public? How many people took part in the mobilization? Who were they? These questions are not easily answered. Press accounts always emphasized the numbers in order to demonstrate the popularity or unpopularity of a cause.

From the very beginning, the papers expected the demonstration of 1864 in favor of Peru to be massive. Before the meeting, *El Pueblo* stated: "We don't doubt that tomorrow at twelve . . . a large attendance of foreigners and natives will be present at the Plaza de Marte." That prediction was later confirmed by *La Tribuna*: "A magnificent spectacle! Six thousand people surrounded the statue of the American

giant. Who were they? They were the sons of the universal republic."
The paper also noted that "hundreds of Italians fraternized with the
Argentine people."[27]

The numbers increased in the following decade. In the midst of the
yellow fever epidemics of 1871, the papers reported the presence of
eight thousand people—"citizens of different nations"—in the Plaza
de la Victoria.[28] In 1875 they wrote about the turnout during the first
stage of the mobilization against the Jesuits: "Buenos Aires had never
seen a larger and more determined meeting. The attendance was calculated at around twenty thousand."[29] According to *La Nación*, at the
demonstration against taxes of 1878, "at least thirty thousand people
met peacefully at the Plaza Lorea. . . . Without exaggerating we can
say that the retail trades were massively represented." The paper
added that "the demonstrators carried the flags of various nations;
there were two bands and several banners." *La Patria*, in turn, calculated "fifty thousand people of all races." *El Porteño* added that "[a]ll
the roofs, windows, balconies . . . were full of people who applauded
that splendid procession of forty thousand souls, and in many places,
threw flowers."[30]

As these examples—and there are many more—clearly show, the
press was particularly careful to underline both the magnitude and
the diversity of the public. A single yet heterogeneous people participated in the meetings. The accounts mention the presence of natives
and immigrants, men of all ages, occasionally women and children.
Sometimes they refer to students or the young, men of commerce or
the trades. The papers cast, however, a horizontal look; the distinctions they made within that "people" were seldom based on hierarchies. Only the top leadership merited special mention: the members
of the ad hoc committees, the men that marched at the head of the columns, the speakers in theaters and plazas. The rest were simply "the
public."

These images changed drastically when a paper wished to under-
rate an event. Then it emphasized the exiguous attendance, the absence of respectable leaders, and the socially marginal composition of
the participants. In spite of the bias of the press, their descriptions and
comments throw some light on the characteristics of the public.

First, the numbers. Even allowing for the exaggerations of the
newspaper accounts, the numbers are impressive. The demonstrations attracted a significant proportion of the urban population and
occupied central and visible areas of the city. The contrast with the
electoral participation is evident.

Secondly, the composition of the public. The announcements and
invitations made no reference to the social or class provenance of the

people they were addressing. They appealed to them just as "the people of Buenos Aires"; depending on the issue at stake they could also mention a particular group: "the consumers," "the Italians," "the shopkeepers and merchants," "the students," and so on. The reports and accounts of the meetings employed similar terms.[31] All this suggests that the people who participated in these events recognized themselves in those categories: both as members of a single "public" and as part of different subgroups. The latter were defined mainly on ethnic and occupational terms, but they did not include a class identification. From a social point of view, on the other hand, the diversity and characteristics of the institutions involved in the mobilizations also suggest that the participants belonged to a wide social spectrum.[32]

The constant reference to the presence of nonnationals in these events contradicts the image, widespread in the literature on the subject, of the immigrants as indifferent to public matters and concerned only with their private affairs. As to the women, in most available sources they are mentioned only as spectators, among those who cheered and applauded the demonstrators from a passive place on rooftops, balconies, and sidewalks. Some scattered references here and there suggest, however, a more active role of women in the culture of mobilization, a topic that deserves further inquiry.

Thirdly, the organization of the participants. In the 1860s, participation in public demonstrations had a certain degree of spontaneity. But in the following decade, the institutional presence was pervasive. The people marched behind the leadership and the banners of their respective associations. The latter not only organized each event; they also led and controlled its development. The single "public" unfolded in multiple parts; when the people formed according to their institutional affiliations, the undifferentiated citizens recovered their differences, their plurality. Each institution, furthermore, displayed its own internal hierarchies in the streets and plazas. The horizontal, nonhierarchical space evoked in the newspaper chronicles thus fades away. The institutional leaders, the band and the banners marched in front; the rank and file followed.

The Leaders

A global order presided over every mobilization. Certain figures clearly stood out; they were the promoters, the organizers, the speakers. Their public prestige enhanced the occasion. In newspaper accounts, the only names mentioned are those of the top leadership. Most names recur, and although in each demonstration some new ones appear, it is possible to identify a relatively stable cast of leaders. There were a variety of characters. A prevalent figure among them was the journalist-intellectual. We have already mentioned the importance of the press in Buenos Aires. In that context, journalists were key figures in the public sphere. Many of them became actively involved in the associative life of the city, in immigrant associations, Masonry, and clubs. In some cases, they also operated in the political realm.

Many of these characters were renowned in Buenos Aires. Héctor Varela (1832–91), for example, was a first choice to head public meetings, give speeches, sponsor carnival groups, and organize celebrations. He was one of the promoters of, and speakers at, the meetings of 1864 in favor of Peru. He also gave speeches during the demonstration against the sentence to death of Castro Chavarría in 1870, was the chief organizer of the meeting to create a popular commission during the yellow fever epidemics of 1871, and became its most powerful member. He stood out among the leaders of the march against taxes of 1878.

Born in Montevideo, Varela belonged to a family of *unitarios*, exiles from the Rosas regime. Héctor was twenty years old when he returned to Buenos Aires. A short time later, he and his brother Mariano founded the daily *La Tribuna*, which remained for many years the newspaper of widest circulation in the city. He belonged to the Partido Autonomista and participated in various electoral clubs. Although he was at some point elected as a representative in Congress, he always remained a secondary figure in the party. He also held public office in Uruguay. His travels through Europe and America kept him away from Argentina for extended periods.[33]

He was, nonetheless, a popular and well-known figure in Buenos Aires. His public presence, the flowery prose of his writings and speeches, and even his habits as a bon vivant were widely celebrated in the city. He was a Mason and a fervent republican. Garibaldi, Abraham Lincoln, and Benito Juárez were his heroes; "never . . . executioners, like the emperor of Russia."[34] In 1867, he participated in the Peace and Freedom Congress held in Geneva, "convened in that piece of land by democracy."[35] He boasted of his friendship with Garibaldi. *La Tribuna* reproduced an exchange of very brief notes between the two after the Italian hero had entered Rome in 1875.[36] That publication both sought to reveal the close nature of their relationship—Garibaldi's note was addressed to "My dear Varela"—and was a gesture of friendship toward Varela's republican friends of the Italian community in Buenos Aires. He addressed them in 1875, from Genoa: "Italians in the [River] Plate! I believe that I am indebted to you for what is happening to me: to you that there, in the bosom of my fatherland, which is also that of your children, so often made me the undeserving object of your great sympathy."[37]

He also cultivated a relationship with other immigrant communities. In 1870 he joined the cause of the French republicans and collaborated with the effort made by various committees of residents to collect funds. To that end, at the request of a group of "ladies from the French Committee," he organized a meeting at the Colon Theater. He also became a member of the Committee of Cosmopolitan Republicans, which, following an initiative of the Universal Republican Alliance (an organ of the Italians in Buenos Aires), convened a "demonstration in favor of the French Republic."[38]

Varela was always ready for public action. In addition to his above-mentioned commitments, he participated in various committees, among them those founded to fight the cholera epidemics of 1867, to assist the victims of an earthquake in Chile in 1868, and to organize the reception of the troops of the national guard in 1869.[39] His passion for associative life covered many fields and included a festive dimension. He was an enthusiastic mentor of the carnival groups (*comparsas*), a form of association that, in his mind, favored the development of the "public spirit" among the young.[40] He was named president of the *Comparsa Orión*, and in the carnival celebrations of 1868 and the following years he used *La Tribuna* to convene people to the masquerades and balls organized in the Plaza del Parque.[41] He participated actively in the feast, standing out as an energetic, vivacious, and fun-loving character.

Other men of the same generation as Varela, many of them his friends, such as Carlos Guido y Spano (1827–1918) and Lucio V. Mansilla (1831–1913), were also among the most visible leaders of the mobilization culture of Buenos Aires. Close to this first group, a second one was also visible. They came from the same social background as Varela and the like, but they were younger: students in their way to becoming politicians and intellectuals, most of them Masons, they were very active in public life. Adolfo Saldías (1849–1914), Matías Behety (1849–85), Pepe Paz (1842–1912), and others like them frequently played leading roles in the meetings and demonstrations of those decades.

A third group came from a different social and cultural milieu. Basilio Cittadini and Enrique Romero Giménez, for example, were immigrants, active organizers, and members of their respective communities, directors of newspapers, founders of associations. They were key figures in the creation of institutions and the promotion, preparation, and development of collective action, particularly in the 1870s.[42]

Among the Italian immigrants, the efforts to build and direct an Italian community in Buenos Aires led men like the above-mentioned Cittadini, as well as Gaetano and Felipe Pezzi, or Marino Froncini, to occupy a visible place in the public life of the city. Froncini and both Pezzis arrived in Buenos Aires in 1857–58, escaping political persecution in their homeland. Once settled in the new country, they continued to sustain and disseminate the republican ideas of the Mazzinian movement. To that end, together with a fellow countryman, Juan Bautista Cúneo, they opened a local branch of the Party of Action and entered the recently founded mutual aid society Unione e Benevolenza. The latter had been created in 1858 by young republican immigrants; two years later, Gaetano Pezzi was elected president. Unione soon established tight connections with members of the local elite, such as Bartolomé Mitre and Héctor Varela. The association rapidly stood out in the public arena; they organized meetings, banquets, the collection of funds, and other events mostly to help the cause of Italian unification and the republic.[43] The conflict between monarchists and republicans within the community triggered successive divisions in the Unione. Finally, the Pezzis founded a new association, the Società Republicana degli Operai Italiani, and shortly later renounced their former membership.

In the battle of Pavón (1861), both Pezzis sided with Mitre and the cause of Buenos Aires.[44] In 1864 they took part in the organization of the demonstrations in favor of Peru and spoke at the meetings in the Plazas del Parque and de Marte. Like his friend Héctor Varela, Gaetano was involved in various local committees. He also continued his republican militancy. In 1866, he became the president of the recently created Republican Alliance, later called Universal, and in 1868 he began writing for the new Italian paper *La Nazione Italiana*.

The daily had been founded by another Italian of republican affiliation, Basilio Cittadini. Soon after his arrival in Buenos Aires, he also became a visible presence in the public arena. In 1870 he was one of the leaders of the protest staged by the Italian community against the periodical *Los intereses argentinos*, an official organ of the Catholic Church. After the paper published an article attacking the immigrants of that origin, the various institutions of the community, leaving aside their differences, organized a multitudinous demonstration. On that occasion, Cittadini was the chief orator, while Pezzi and Froncini played only a secondary role.

That same year, however, both Cittadini and Pezzi, together with

Héctor Varela, headed the meeting in celebration of the fall of Napoleon III and the triumph of the French Republic. Later in 1870 they also celebrated the achievement of Italian unity. After Mazzini's death, in 1872, they initiated negotiations to erect a statue of the republican hero in Buenos Aires. Cittadini founded a new paper, *La Patria*, in 1876, while Pezzi and Froncini created an Italian Republican Center and the periodical *L'Amico del Popolo*. All of them were also active participants in public events of the city that were not directly concerned with the Italian community.[45]

Italian, Spanish, or Argentine—all of these figures belonged to a leadership that developed strong links among themselves. They cited each other in their respective newspaper articles and columns, shared banquets and celebrations, and exchanged places in boards and committees. They believed in the principles and practices of the associative movement, which they considered to be a pillar of a republican way of life. They were confident about their actions, and thus celebrated both their own initiatives and those of their friends and colleagues, exchanging congratulations and compliments. "*A Ettore Varela*" [to Héctor Varela] was the title of a long poem by Basilio Cittadini published in *La Nazione* in July 1870 in honor of "the great champion of the freedom of all peoples, a sincere democrat, a great tribune, and the enthusiastic friend of the Italians" on his birthday.[46] During the banquet organized for the occasion, speeches rich in republican tropes abounded. Agustín Alió, leader of the Spanish community, referred to the celebration as follows:

In brief, a magnificent feast, a delightful exercise in oratory directed to the noble emulation of revolution and liberalism, and a picture of beautiful colors to show the departing world the excellencies of the vigorous, coming new world, which arrives with a laurel branch in one hand and the torch of publicity on the other.[47]

And all this was possible, according to Alió, because "they lived in the classic country of the republic."

The front ranks of the leadership, who had a strong presence in the press and the institutions of civil society, were always mentioned in the accounts and reports of meetings and demonstrations. Other, less prominent leaders were, however, also important in the public life of Buenos Aires. They could be small merchants, shopkeepers, or members of the professions or the trades who were also strongly involved in the associative movement. The mutual aid societies, for example, counted a significant number of such figures within their leading ranks.

It was easy to distinguish the leadership in any mobilization. They occupied the most visible places: the stage in the theaters, the first rows in the marches, the central platforms in the plazas. The press accounts always mentioned such positions. Yet at the same time, they did not refer to these men as essentially different from the rest; rather, their role was that of primus inter pares, who stood out in the crowd but also belonged to "the people." That privileged place had to be ratified each time by the public in a lay ritual that connected the rank and file with the leaders and reached its climax at the time of the speeches.

The Liturgy

Once the people had come together in theaters or plazas, the main part of the function started. The newspaper chronicles for each occasion describe the ensuing actions as quite spontaneous, the unplanned result of the enthusiasm and commitment of the participants. The following examples, however, show a repeated pattern of collective behavior that suggests a careful organization.

On June 5, 1864, at the Plaza de Marte: "At two o'clock in the afternoon, the audience agreed to ask the gentlemen General Iriarte, Colonel Olazábal, citizen Alvaro Barros, soldiers of the Independence wars, to preside over the meeting. These gentlemen went up to the platform that had been improvised by the statue of the victor of Chacabuco and Maipu." In a preparatory meeting it had been agreed that the veterans would dress in civilian clothes and would not wear their medals or decorations "for reasons of republican equality."[48] General Iriarte read a declaration and won the applause of the public. The chair invited all who wished to speak to go up to the platform. Colonel Olazábal made a speech, and then "the people asked . . . Mr. Bilbao . . . to speak. And so he did." He concluded with the last sentence of the Argentine national anthem: "*Al gran pueblo argentino, salud!*" [Long live the great Argentine people]. Applause and cheers followed. "The people requested the words of gentlemen Mansilla, Chassaing, and [Héctor] Varela." When they had finished, each speech was followed by "prolonged applause," and other speakers came forward: Carlos Guido Spano, "the Spanish democrat Mr. García," and, finally, two Italians. All speeches centered around the republic, the "American fatherland," independence, and liberty.[49]

A week later, the meeting at the Colon brought together thousands of people. "A committee of old veterans of the Independence wars occupied the proscenium. Brigadier General Zapiola presided." The public sang the national anthems of Argentina and Peru "under the shade of the flags of both republics." Fifteen speeches followed. Some speakers "requested to speak, others were invited to do so by the people." Several resolutions were passed and approved by acclamation. The assembly decided to submit a petition to Congress asking the representatives to "authorize the national government to enter into offensive and defensive alliances with the [rest of] the American republics." Once more the public sang the two anthems, and "in the midst of cheers for Peru, American independence, the republic, democracy, and freedom, the six thousand people who crowded the theater went out to the street [and marched] with the band in front."[50]

In 1871, yellow fever was devastating the population of the city. Fear of the plague, however, did not prevent the people from expressing their enthusiasm in a public meeting convened to fight the epidemics. At midday, fireworks were detonated in the Plaza de la Victoria. The organizers of the event and their immediate following had left the editorial building of *La Tribuna*, marching toward the plaza. Once they reached it, Héctor Varela mounted on a chair and addressed the audience. He announced the creation of a Popular Committee on Public Health. "Each name pronounced by Varela was followed by a loud ovation approving its inclusion in the new . . . emergency organ." Manuel Argerich, Carlos Guido y Spano, and Basilio Cittadini made speeches. The meeting was adjourned and the committee went to the seat of the provincial government to inform Governor Castro of the resolutions adopted by the public meeting.[51]

Two years later, a demonstration in favor of the independence of Cuba followed a similar pattern. The people met at the Teatro Variedades, and there were speeches, banners, and resolutions voted by acclamation. The reading of an article against the Cuban cause, published by *El Correo Español*, aroused "a clamor of indignation." Attempts at calming down the audience were useless: "[It] was impossible to hear anything; a unanimous voice demanded 'To the plaza, to the plaza!'" The audience stood up violently, took with them the flags from the proscenium, and left for the plaza. Fortunately, no conflict erupted afterward."[52]

A similar clamor led the participants of the meeting of 1875 against the Jesuits to the Plaza de la Victoria. The event had started at the Variedades, where "an infinite number of flags and banners stood out everywhere. . . . The young president of the Student Committee [Adolfo Saldías] made a speech full of fire, of inspiration. . . . The applause, the cheers for the republic, and the repudiation of the Jesuits sounded like thunder. Gentlemen Zusini, Galleto, and Castro Boedo spoke in turn. The enthusiam turned into furor." Then the voices clamored, "To the plaza, to the Palace of the Archbishop."[53]

The demonstration against taxes in 1878 was kept under control.

Headed by Héctor Varela, Basilio Cittadini, José Ghigliassa [leader of the cigar-makers], and others, the crowd arrived at the Plaza San Martín, where:

[t]he table for the speakers was located in front of the statue of General San Martín. . . . Mr. José Ghigliassa, president of the committee, climbed on to the improvised tribune. . . . [He] announced that Mr. Daumas was going to read the petition to be handed to the president of the House of Representatives. . . . Once that reading was over . . . the committee left in two carriages for the legislature. . . . Some of the people followed them. . . . In the meantime, the popular tribune in Plaza San Martin was occupied by a young man called Vega and by the editor of *La Patria*, Basilio Cittadini. . . . Both spoke very well and received the applause of the audience.[54]

Meanwhile, the committee arrived at the legislature at 1:00 P.M., and Héctor Varela, himself a representative, handed in the petition and asked the House to study it. After a positive reply from the representatives, the committee returned to the square to inform the people of the results of their mission. The crowd answered with cheers and enthusiastic applause and proceeded to disperse quietly.

Examples of this sort abound in the historical sources. The rituals and symbols recur. There was the enthusiastic crowd, who detonated fireworks, carried flags and banners, and took an active part in the demonstration through their applause, cheers, and acclamations. There was the leadership, who climbed up to the stage, the platform, the improvised chair; gave the speeches; drafted the proposals; and read them to the public. Both parts interconnected tightly: the leaders sought the approval of the audience who, in turn, hoped to find in them the voice that might express their demands and assert their shared identities.

The atmosphere of most public events was what contemporaries would have called "respectable." The tone was set by the leadership: it was moderate, "civilized," proper. Violence was not on the agenda. Occasionally, however, the people pushed beyond those limits, and the specter of violence took shape. The fear of those excesses was never so strong as to overshadow the contemporaries' defense of the freedom of speech and reunion, as we shall see below (Chapter 8).

The Results

The practice of collective mobilization was highly cherished. Different combinations of republican and liberal ideas and principles nurtured that positive evaluation and gave the events both ideological legitimacy and political efficacy. The chief aim of most petitions, meetings, and demonstrations was to prove the popularity of a particular issue. Mobilizations were considered to be the materialization of "public opinion," and operated in three complementary directions.

Firstly, they addressed the authorities both directly—by submitting petitions, protests, proposals, and so forth—and indirectly—by displaying an issue or motif in the public arena—in order to influence their action. Secondly, by disseminating a cause, they attracted the support of many people not originally included among the promoters. And thirdly, they reinforced the collective will—and even the identity—of the promoters and their followers.

Success, however, was not secured beforehand. The capacity of the leadership and the magnitude of the following were important factors in this respect, but they were not the only ones. The political conjuncture at the time of each particular event had a great influence upon their outcome.

In 1864, the cause in favor of Peru had been formulated in the language of republicanism. The defense of the principles of freedom and independence against the attack of the old colonial monarchy constituted the chief motif in declarations and speeches. The rituals followed throughout the mobilization were highly symbolic, such as the designation of the veteran officers of the Independence wars as members of the organizing committee. Yet current political issues were not absent from the scene. During that same year of 1864, a virulent conflict between the two main *porteño* political groups erupted. At first, the public reaction in favor of Peru contributed to lower the tone of the partisan dispute. After several months of great tension, in May the clubs Libertad (led by Adolfo Alsina) and del Pueblo (headed by President Mitre) entered into a dialogue aimed at "saving the integrity of the province." They reached an agreement sealed by a banquet.[55] The defense of Peru appeared as an excellent opportunity to reinforce the rapprochement, although the *alsinistas* denounced the partisan spirit of their rivals' attitudes in the mobilizations.[56]

The settlement did not last. President Mitre wished to moderate the claims against the Spanish government. He was negotiating a bilateral treaty with Spain, and was very reticent to support a proposal to convene an "American Congress." The cause in favor of Peru was affected by the presidential withdrawal, and after the first enthusiastic moves it lost momentum. The Society for the American Union founded to support the cause failed in its attempt to organize a new demonstration, as well as in its drive to submit a signed petition to Congress. The fifteen hundred signatures obtained were considered insufficient. By mid-July, the daily *El Pueblo* complained because "the people of Buenos Aires betray the established hopes; abdicate from the first imposing attitude adopted when [the invasion] was announced."[57]

The political circumstances were different in 1871, when the Popular Committee on Public Health came to life. From the very beginning, the provincial government resented the mobilization to fight the yellow fever epidemics. On the one side, the people and their committee were treading a terrain that was supposed to be the responsibility of the administration. On the other, some of the leading figures of the public move, such as Héctor Varela, were members of the opposition. The organization to fight the plague entailed a critical attitude toward the official action. The committee in fact competed with the agencies created by the administration, and there was a constant tension between them that was tainted by political rivalries.[58] In spite of these short-circuits, the popular inititiave was quite successful and the provincial government had to accept it. This case clearly shows, however, the incidence of partisan strife in the public life of the city. Even in the extreme circumstances of the epidemics, the collective drive originated in civil society did not attain complete autonomy from the political.

In the revolt against taxes of 1878, the success of "public opinion" was—once more—firmly rooted in the political conjuncture. It had been a year of partisan realignments, in which the two traditional parties had experienced splits and renewed alliances. In this heated atmosphere, the popular mobilization had strong repercussions within the political circles of Buenos Aires. The various groups took sides, participated in various ways in the protest, and interpreted the whole episode through their press organs. The promoters of the public event, in turn, took advantage of this situation and placed their claims in the broader political context, thus giving a partisan twist to a demand that was initially apolitical. They asked Héctor Varela, recently elected national representative in the autonomist ticket, to oppose the project of law discussed in the House. He agreed to join the cause, and from then on he was a key actor in the events.

The city's press covered the protest extensively. Most papers did not miss the opportunity to relate the episode to the more general political issues, each one according to its sympathies and preferences. Those that opposed the provincial government, such as *La Prensa*, Héctor Varela's *El Porteño*, and Cittadini's *La Patria*, saw a good chance to ask for the resignation of the finance minister, or to undercut the aspirations of the governor to become a presidential candidate. Other papers, such as Mitre's *La Nación*, attacked the national government, while *La Tribuna*—at that point, an official organ directed by Mariano Varela—was all in favor of the provincial authorities and condemned the revolt in harsh terms.[59]

This display on the part of the local press shows how the tax episode acquired political relevance. Commercial interests generated a demand that was soon joined by a larger public. They displayed a great capacity to put pressure on the authorities, based upon their disposition to organize and their ability to mobilize important sectors of the urban population. The political moment was propitious, as the partisan strife provided a favorable context for the success of the protest. In the end, the government yielded to the public pressure, and the taxes were abolished.

The Limits

Most public mobilizations entailed a relationship with the political world. During these decades, however, these collective forms of expressing demands and opinions did not imply the contestation of government authority or political power. The issues raised were generally acceptable to the elite, although that does not mean that they were always accepted. When and why some claims were acknowledged and others rejected depended not only on what was being demanded but also on the political context.

Social conflict was also absent from these forms of public action. The people that participated came from very different social backgrounds and were not convened on a class basis. And the claims put forward through these means were presented as being the concern of the whole people, not the demand of any specific social sector.

Public mobilizations were praised for their moderation and nonviolence. The reference to order was recurrent in the press accounts of the period; they never failed to mention the "civilized" character of every event. Most chronicles convey an air of moderation, of celebration rather than of protest. Such insistence reveals the concern of contemporaries with order and the fear of violence.

For years on end, armed rebellions and intense partisan warfare had been the usual ingredients of Argentine political life. By the 1860s and 1870s, they had not yet been entirely eradicated. Law and order were a desideratum for the same political elites that made recurrent use of violence in their struggles for power. The orderly qualities of the public meetings and demonstrations were contrasted with the agitated atmosphere of the electoral battles. Violence at the polls, albeit mostly ritual, was nevertheless considered improper in a modern and civilized nation.

Contemporaries were also concerned about social conflict. After the days of the Paris commune of 1871, the specter of social violence haunted local elites. The expansion and modernization of the city, the massive presence of immigrants, and the increasing visibility of working-class men and women kindled an increasing feeling of apprehension among the propertied classes.

Order and moderation were, therefore, key targets for the promoters and organizers of public mobilizations. And in most cases, they met the standards. The one exception was the demonstration of 1875 against the Jesuits, when a crowd set fire to the Savior's College. This unexpected outcome alarmed contemporaries. The public action had gone beyond what was considered acceptable. The next chapter will explore that episode.

8 A Violent Episode

Si se descuida Nicolasito en lugar de la Iglesia libre en el estado libre
tendremos la iglesia libre en el estado esclavo.

Archbishop Federico Aneiros and President Nicolás Avellaneda [on a leash].
The text of the cartoon reads: "Little Nicholas, if you are not careful, instead
of having a free Church in a free state, we will have a free Church in an en-
slaved state." [*El Mosquito*, April 4, 1875]

Conversation

Interrogatory
—*Answer and tell the truth!* [says the Judge].
—*I'm ready, your honor.*
—*Were you present in the assault on the Savior's College?*
—*Actually, I was not present in the assault, but I saw the events from afar.*
—*Then, why is it that you had a silver crucifix in your pocket?*
—*I'll tell you. When the mess started, I was very ill in bed, so much so that
someone who thought I had exhaled my last breath put the crucifix that you now
have into my hands. I came back to the shouts of the* communards, *and I was so
curious [to see what was going on] that I ran toward the street. . . . and there you
have an explanation of why the crucifix was found in my pocket.*
—*La Nación*, March 14, 1875

February 28, 1875

It was a hot summer morning in Buenos Aires. Around eleven o'clock, people in increasing numbers poured into the downtown area. Men of different ages and social conditions approached the Teatro de Varie-dades. Most of them came by foot; some of them used the tramway. The great majority arrived in groups, marching in orderly clusters and carrying banners and flags that showed their national origins and their associative affiliations. Musical bands animated the scene. The theater was soon full, and the surrounding streets were occupied by thousands who could not make it into the building.

There was nothing new about this scene. At the time, as we have already seen, the people of Buenos Aires were increasingly prone to collective action. On this occasion they had met to protest the arch-bishop's decision to return a church that more than a century earlier had belonged to the order of the Jesuits to its former authorities. The order had been expelled from the Spanish colonial territories in 1768 and was still banned in Argentina in 1875. Jesuits, however, were al-lowed to settle in the country on an individual basis and were then making a comeback. In Buenos Aires they had established a private school for boys but kept, otherwise, a rather low profile.[1]

The meeting "against the Jesuits" followed the regular pattern. The public was excited and enthusiastic. Inside the theater the leaders made passionate speeches and the people warmly applauded and voiced their approval. Soon a single clamor rose from the assembly: To the Plaza de la Victoria! And off they all marched toward the central plaza, the site par excellence of public demonstrations. Argentine, Spanish, and Italian flags popped above the heads of the people, inter-spersed with banners that read "Down with the Jesuits," "For a Free State," and other anticlerical slogans.

The demonstrators entered the plaza. The excitement ran higher and higher. Soon enough, some of the men turned to the Palace of the Archbishop facing the plaza, started to throw stones at its windows, and went into the building, where they smashed some of the furniture. There was confusion among both the demonstrators and the specta-tors. The police reacted rather slowly. The crowd was mobilized by a new clamor: To the Savior's College! and, again, off they went, march-ing about twenty blocks through the city to the school run by the Jesu-its. Once there, they entered the building, forced the priests to leave, smashed windows and furniture, and left only when somehow a fire broke out that damaged a good part of the school. It was already five o'clock in the afternoon when the national guard, not the police, showed up and rapidly dispersed the remaining crowd.

The city was in shock. Not that collective violence was unfamiliar; it was a regular component of local political practice. But this unruly behavior typical of partisan strife was always contrasted with the peaceful and orderly qualities of public meetings and demonstrations. These regular events were considered an expression of a civic culture and were praised for their moderation and nonviolence. No one expected the meeting against the archbishop to be any different. So the incidents that culminated in the school fire came as a disturbing surprise for almost everybody. And almost everybody had something to say about them.

This situation is particularly fortunate for the historian. Yet in spite of the impact of the episode at the time, scholars have paid little attention to it. The most complete narrative of the events belongs to Guillermo Furlong, S.J., who wrote a history of the Savior's College based upon ecclesiastical sources. He reproduces the official interpretation that the Church made of the episode.[2] A more recent book by Carlos Brocato offers a vivid reconstruction of the facts based on the information provided by the contemporary press, and emphasizes the participation of the popular sectors in the second stage of the mobilization. The text is written as a parody of the liberal discourse and interpretation.[3] An unpublished paper by Leandro Gutiérrez offers a compelling version of the story that posits a radical break between the first and the second stages of the protest. The motivation for the latter was social, rather than religious or political: "it was an autonomous reaction of the popular sectors who protested violently" and thus staged a "primitive movement."[4] This chapter argues in a different direction. It approaches the episode by way of the opinions and versions that were voiced at the time, and offers an alternative interpretation that relates the protest to the civic and political culture of Buenos Aires.

The main voices in this case belong to the various actors involved in the drama, and are found in different sources. First and foremost, the press. As on other public occasions, the newspapers played a key role, not only informing about the events but also taking an active part in them. The Buenos Aires press, with the sole exception of the weekly *El Católico Argentino*,[5] was known for its liberal inclinations, and although the range of anticlericalism varied greatly, no lay paper failed to criticize the archbishop's move. The second source is the criminal proceedings against almost one hundred men accused of participating in the violent acts. They include the testimonies of the accused and the witnesses, the defense lawyers, the prosecutor, and the judges. All these are framed by the language imposed by judicial procedures, but they nonetheless convey to us various perspectives and opinions. A third set of voices comes from ecclesiastical sources. These include the above-mentioned Catholic weekly, the official statements that the Church made at the time, and fragments of a diary written by a Jesuit who witnessed the assault to the school, included in Furlong's book. Fourthly, we have a large number of official documents, produced by different branches and agencies of the national and the provincial governments.

"The Jesuits Have Nothing to Do among Us!"

In January 1875, the archbishop of Buenos Aires informed the national government of changes introduced in the organization of two of the central parishes in the city, among them the restitution of the churches to "their original masters."[6] Although he did not mention the Jesuits or the Order of Mercy by name, everybody knew to whom he was referring, and soon enough reactions against this decision sprung from various quarters.

The main newspapers launched a pungent verbal attack against the religious orders in general and the Jesuits in particular. *La Tribuna* asserted that "the tendency of modern civilization is to suppress the religious orders rather than to favor them. . . . [As] for the Jesuits, they are rejected everywhere."[7] The Order of Mercy, which was to receive back one of the parishes, was soon forgotten, and all the attacks were directed against the Jesuits. Thus *El Nacional* claimed that "[t]he people have the right to go to any limits, violent as they may be, if the convulsions of a tremendous cataclysm bring the Jesuits and with them, the social miasmas, to the surface."[8]

Petitions were signed by the well-to-do residents of the neighborhood where the church was located. The archbishop counterattacked with a declaration praising the order, but still without mentioning it by name.[9] The press raised the stakes. *La Prensa* and *La Nación* used relatively moderate language, but the rest of the newspapers were virulent. The Jesuits were called "vermin" and "assassins," while the archbishop was considered an ambitious schemer with a mediocre mind, "a midget." He was also portrayed in the most ridiculous cartoons.[10]

The national government was embarrassed by the whole exchange. The authorities had received the archbishop's note on the subject of the parishes and had produced a laconic answer: "No problem." But the press thought otherwise. There was an institutional side to the story, and the newspapers questioned the constitutional right of the national executive to decide in matters relating to the parishes (which fell in the orbit of the provincial government) and to the orders (which fell in the hands of the Congress).[11] Also, there were political implications, as the archbishop was a member of the ruling party and a representative in the House. He was also close to President Ave- llaneda, whose Catholic sympathies and close association with the Church irritated the *porteño* political leadership (see the cartoon at the beginning of this chapter). Aneiros was, therefore, an easy target for the opposition.[12] But even within the Church itself, his links to politics were objected to and his support dwindled.[13]

The debate on the role of the government in this conflict soon veered toward a larger and more controversial topic, the relations be- tween Church and state. The constitution prescribed that the federal government support the Catholic Church. Some liberal newspapers grasped the opportunity to denounce this provision. "All this is but the consequence of state religion," maintained *La Libertad*.[14] *La Tribuna* called the Catholic Church "an unproductive force, a sterile load" that the government used as "a political tool," while *La Política* pointed out that "in a cosmopolitan society like ours the state should not have a religion."[15] A constitutional reform to end the special rela- tionship was called for.[16] This last claim was resisted by the more mod- erate sectors of the press and the public, and the topic was not pursued any further. There was, however, a broad consensus on the need to stop "the advances made by the archbishop" and to convene a meet- ing to that effect.[17]

"Convene the People to a Grand Meeting"

On February 19, several papers published the first general invitation signed by a University Club to participate in a public meeting sched- uled for February 21. This was followed by articles supporting the ini- tiative and endorsement notes by different groups and individuals.[18] At the last minute, the meeting was postponed.[19]

On February 26, the formal announcement was made "To the Peo- ple." In the name of the young people of Buenos Aires, the University Club invited everyone to a meeting to be held on Sunday, February 28 at the Teatro Variedades, in order "to formulate a solemn protest against the aspirations of the Church, and the offenses committed against the . . . people of Buenos Aires." This meeting, they said, would be "peaceful, cultured, and elevated. . . . [It] will be the sublime expres- sion of what the society of Buenos Aires feels, thinks, and wants."[20] The invitation was rapidly endorsed by all the newspapers in the city ex-

cept the Catholic weekly, and many associations and clubs expressed
their support.

The Church responded immediately. Its weekly paper discussed
the arguments of the rest of the press and defended the Jesuits and the
archbishop. Processions were organized in various parishes. In one instance around one hundred women marched through the center of
town, and when they reached the University Club they fell on their
knees and started to pray. A rumor began to circulate: the archbishop
would excommunicate those who took part in the meeting. The ecclesiastical authorities and the Jesuits had conversations with the national and provincial authorities to try to prevent the protest, but they
were told not to worry, everything was going to run smoothly.[21] But as
we now know, things did not go so well, and the day after there was a
general outcry.

"A Barbarian Act"

Under the title "The Paris Commune" one of the more widely read
dailies exclaimed: "Never has the city witnessed a more barbarian act
than the one committed yesterday under the pretext of a demonstration against the Jesuits."[22] All the newspapers agreed in their outrage
and shock. They told the story in two acts. In the words of La Nación:
"The spectacle [of the meeting at the theater] was extremely pleasant
to the eyes." It went on to describe the enthusiasm of the people, the
enlightened speeches of the leaders, the colorful display of flags and
banners, the uniformity of the public sentiment, and the fervor that
led the people to the plaza. The demonstration "was an allegory that
represented the uniformity of human thought about the condemnation and expulsion of the Jesuits carried forward by that great states-
man [Bernardino Rivadavia]."[23]

At that point, the second act was about to start, and the accounts
shifted to a somber tone: "A menacing murmur could be heard
through the plaza, that grew to become a roaring thunder," reported
La Tribuna.[24] According to La Nación, when "all the persons of importance had left," groups of "unknown people" moved toward the Palace of the Archbishop, which faced the plaza. They shouted "Down
with the Jesuits!" "Down with [Archbishop] Aneiros!" "Down with
the Order of Mercy!" and threw stones at the building.[25] Confusion
reigned. The chief of police and other officers tried to stop the crowd,
to no avail. The latter responded with mud balls and more stones.
Windows were smashed. Some groups entered the palace and de-

stroyed part of the furniture. The Church of San Ignacio was also attacked, and then a new clamor rose: "To the Savior's College!" They
all marched toward the school.

In the words of *La Nación*: "The spectacle there could only have
been produced by a fanatic and enraged mob. . . . In the middle of the
street a bonfire was started, and all sorts of objects found in the school
were thrown into the fire."[26] The Jesuits ran away, the crowds attacked, and finally the school itself caught fire. "Like lightning, a
tongue of fire comes out of every window. Terrible scenes follow. . . .
Terror gets ahold of some, hatred of others, and the appetite for death
and extermination."[27]

No police forces were to be seen around the school. Only later, a
picket of forty-five soldiers of the national guard arrived. They fired
into the crowd, who ran away throwing stones. At five in the afternoon, the only men left at the scene were the firemen, doing their job.[28]

Condemnation was unanimous. The press, which had encouraged
the protest, was quick to express its repudiation. The University Club
produced a statement protesting the "savage acts of fanaticism" that
had taken place. Even the Supreme Council of the Masons condemned
the "barbarian excesses of the unbridled mob."[29]

The government also reacted promptly. There were statements by
the national and provincial legislatures, instructions by the executive
to prosecute the criminals, and a decree establishing a state of siege in
the province for a period of thirty days.[30] Confronted with all these re-
pudiations, the Catholic weekly observed with irony: "How odd! An
effect has been produced, but the cause is not visible. Everyone is sur-
prised, everyone is innocent, everyone washes his hands, everyone
protests."[31]

"The Savage Spirit of the Rabble"

No one seemed to assume responsibility for the events. Interpretations, however, abounded. Something radically different had occurred in a city that was proud of its civic spirit and of its capacity for
peaceful collective action. *La Tribuna* intoned: "The Paris commune
has arrived in the city. Buenos Aires did not protest yesterday; these
are not the events produced by a cultured and civilized people. No:
that was the savage spirit of the rabble."[32] Some newspaper accounts
insisted on the difference between the first and peaceful stage of the
demonstration and the second one, when the crowd took over.[33]

Yet who were in that crowd? Very soon, that question became the main issue of public debate. The first police accounts produced a version that would rapidly prove highly controversial: foreign immigrants prevailed among the violent demonstrators. After the peaceful meeting, the majority of the people left, and only fifteen hundred immigrants, most of them from Italy and Spain, took part in the criminal incidents that followed.[34] Some newspapers echoed that version and added an interpretation: the current agitated state of affairs should be attributed to "the agglomeration of immigrants in the capital and to the lack of controls to avoid the introduction into the country of elements that are contrary to progress, to social order."[35] Not all the press agreed on these matters, and several important papers argued in favor of the immigrants and of immigration in general.[36] Others pointed to the presence among the crowd of "the native elements that are used to electoral violence."[37]

They all agreed, however, in perceiving this episode as new and different. Rather than associating it with the familiar violence of partisan strife, they saw it as the menacing expression of a new problem, that of social conflict. The Paris Commune was the immediate reference. In the provincial legislature, a well-known senator drafted a declaration in which he mentioned not only the Commune but also the Socialist International, the communists, and the presence of "the collective mob of wage earners, all of them foreigners."[38] This language proved too inflammatory, however, and the senators finally passed a formal statement in which all those strong words were gone and only a general reference to the "criminal mob" remained.[39]

The specific actors were increasingly dissolving into the more abstract "multitude." Efforts to identify the leaders failed. Several of those who had called the meeting were arrested, but nothing could be proved. The responsibility of certain Masonic lodges and sects was mentioned at different points, but, again, to no avail.[40] Even an incipient and very small section of the Socialist International was accused and its members detained, only to learn that they had nothing to do with the events (see Chapter 9).

"The Moral Responsibility"

The days passed, and the image of the actual participants seemed to melt away. The debate around the ultimate responsibility, however, was heating up. The main accusations were pointed at the police, the press, and the archbishop himself.

The lack of response and action on the part of the police was mentioned by all involved. The provincial administration resisted the pressure for a few days but, in the end, the chief of police, Enrique Moreno, had to resign.[41] While the police were accused for what they had failed to do, the archbishop was criticized for what he did do. He was the "first provocateur," incapable, narrow-minded, and guilty for not having "soothed the passions." The opposition asked for his resignation, both as a Church dignitary and as a representative in the House. The latter resignation he finally submitted in May.[42]

The Church, in turn, saw the press, "with [its] impious propaganda, [its] senseless messages," as the main instigator, particularly *La Tribuna* and *El Nacional*.[43] The ecclesiastical sources also pointed to the provincial government as an accomplice, due to the known liberal inclinations of Governor Alvaro Barros. On the other hand, the liberal papers accused him of having been too lenient with "the pretensions of the Jesuits."[44] And the national government suspected the opposition.[45]

Thus, the merry-go-round of the presumed responsible expanded as the different public actors grasped the opportunity of choosing an enemy to blame for the incidents. At one point, the Jesuits themselves were accused of provoking the scandal.[46]

The Arrested

Meanwhile, the judiciary acted swiftly. During the first week in March, eighty-eight people were arrested and sent to jail.[47] They were all men, half of them native Argentines—a majority from the city and province of Buenos Aires—and half of them immigrants, most of them from different parts of Italy and Spain. Two-thirds of the arrested were under thirty; many of them were married.[48] Skilled workers and employees formed the largest group, followed by professionals and students, unskilled workers, and shopkeepers and merchants of different sorts (see Table 6). It was an assorted lot, and if we compare them with the total male population in the city, there was an over-representation of the native-born, the young and the professionals, teachers, and students. Unskilled workers and immigrants were actually underrepresented.[49]

The image of these men hardly fits that of the collective bunch of foreign laborers-cum-criminals that scared the elite and the press. Rather, they look very much like the regular members of the associations that proliferated in the city at the time. Their own depositions corroborate that first impression.

TABLE 6

Men arrested in March 1875 accused of participating in the events that
led to the fire of the Colegio del Salvador (distribution by occupational
groups, in total numbers and percentages)

Occupational groups	Number	Percentages
Group 1: Professional, teachers, military men, and students.	23	26
Group 2: Commerce	13	15
Group 3.1: Skilled and white-collar workers	33	37
Group 3.2: Unskilled workers	14	16
Group 3: Total of workers (3.1 plus 3.2)	47	53
No available data	5	6
TOTALS	88	100

SOURCE: Archivo General de la Nación, *Tribunal Criminal*, files P10 and P11, 1875.

Most of the men that were arrested confirmed their participation
in the demonstration of February 28 at the theater and the plaza;
some even accepted having marched toward the Jesuit school, but
none admitted taking part in the assault. Their initial depositions
and later pleas throw some light on how the actors perceived their
own deeds in face of the subsequent events. Although these declarations were formulated according to the juridical norms and language,
they nonetheless convey some of the attitudes and opinions of the arrested.

Several of the main leaders of the meeting at the Teatro Variedades
were among them. All of them refer to the peaceful character of that
assembly, and to what happened later at the plaza, before the meeting
was adjourned. Adolfo Saldías, a young, twenty-four-year-old *porteño*
lawyer, president of a Central Club of anti-Jesuit agitation, declared
that:

[as] the president of the Central Committee and of various other associations,
he had invited the students and the people in general to a meeting . . . to peacefully protest the request of the archbishop. . . . That once gathered there and
having left the place of the assembly, they went to the Plaza de la Victoria
where after a few moments they saw a multitude of people arriving and going
to the Palace of the Archbishop in a menacing attitude; that then the deponent,
both in order to stop the scandal and to avoid being mistaken for a member of
the mob, stood at the door of the palace . . . where the deponent was threatened; that then he went to the police station in the company of the president of
the University Club . . . and back to the Plaza de la Victoria, where he got . . . the
students and the other people that had gone with the deponent, to leave peacefully; that the rest of the people went to [one] corner of [the Plaza] where the
deponent left in the belief that everything had concluded.[50]

A few days later, another leader, Otto Schnyder, a twenty-three-year-old Swiss university teacher and member of the Committee of the Central Club, declared:

that the meeting [in the Variedades] was the exercise of a right and that it was not from there that the people who committed the offenses departed. . . . [Those people] were part of the Club General Belgrano, which he had seen entering the Palace of the Archbishop. That he also saw the Club Clemente XIV around the pyramid [at the center of the plaza], who were trying to reach the same palace, at which moment the deponent stopped the banner bearer and reproached him for what they were about to do. . . . That regarding the Club Belgrano, he believes it was they—although he does not know any of the members—because upon entering the palace they shouted "Long live the Club Belgrano," noting that among them a black man was carrying an Italian flag.[51]

Other leaders followed. All of them denied any responsibility for the violent events of the plaza. They did not even mention the march to the Savior's College and the fire, because they insisted on their having left the demonstration before the crowd started toward the school. In his deposition, Saldías mentioned "the multitude" but otherwise avoided more specific references. Schnyder, in turn, was more precise in his accusations, and mentioned two clubs as taking part in the violence at the plaza.

Among the men arrested, some belonged to those clubs, as well as to other associations. In their depositions, they spoke eloquently about the way in which they were mobilized. Gerónimo Freire, for example, a twenty-five-year-old shop clerk born in Montevideo, Uruguay, declared:

that . . . around half-past ten in the morning he left in the company of ten to twelve other persons from the house in Perú street . . . ; that the deponent took a flag with the inscription "Central Club, Down with the Jesuits"; that they were led by Don Juan Pentacochea . . . ; that they went down Belgrano Street to [the train station] "Once the Setiembre," where they were joined by the Club del Pilar, which had four flags and a blue banner with letters in gold. . . . That from there they went along Paraguay Street down to Paraná, in which way they were joined by two or three Italian flags.[52]

A Genoese shopkeeper, Santiago Ferro, told about the people coming from La Boca:

[He] left from La Boca with Eduardo Galeano, Armani, Serna, and three hundred other people and together they came to the Teatro de Variedades. . . . Some days earlier, several young men who said they belonged to the University Club had been there; they had gone to invite them to attend the demonstration; he was named vice president; the group left from the house of Don José Torres; the flag that the club carried was a banner with the portrait of

[Bernardino] Rivadavia; they also brought two Argentine flags, one French, and one Italian.[53]

Other deponents declared in a similar fashion. Their statements show that the great majority were affiliated with clubs and associations of different sorts, some of them created as a consequence of the protest against the Jesuits. The leaders belonged to the University Club, but many other smaller and more parochial groups also participated. Most of the men involved had heard of the meeting in their respective associations, where the arrangements for it were made. The morning of the February 28 they had left their neighborhoods in groups headed by their leaders and carrying various banners and flags. They marched together and joined other groups along the way, until they reached the theater. After the meeting, they all went to the plaza, but what happened there and how the march to the Savior's College developed is hardly inferable from their own depositions. None of the men accepted taking part in the violent episodes of that afternoon. Only the members of the Club Clemente XIV of the parish of El Pilar mentioned that they had gone by the Jesuit school. Their president, Miguel Sánchez—apothecary and medical student, born in Spain—pointed out that "they went by the Saviors' College only because it was on their way to the club."[54]

Only a handful of the arrested who were seen at the Jesuit school at the time of the fire declared that they had not attended the first part of the demonstration. Caught with objects taken from the Jesuit school in their hands, Giuseppe Bazani—a Genoese blacksmith of twenty-one— explained that he "had entered the school out of curiosity and took several objects [some silk handkerchiefs, two towels, two linen scarves] to save them from the fire," while Ignacio Salazar—an illiterate servant of eighteen—justified himself by saying that "he took those objects because they were being thrown into the bonfire that blazed in the street . . . and other people were also picking them up."[55]

The Witnesses, Defense Attorneys, and Judges

The witnesses also made their statements. The director of the school, a thirty-nine-year-old Spaniard, Esteban Salvadó, S.J., recounted

that around three in the afternoon . . . the college was invaded . . . by an unruly multitude that, having knocked down the doors, penetrated into the building, smashing portraits, books, furniture, and so forth and threatening and insulting and even injuring several of the priests that were present. . . . That he does not know any of the persons that were in, or led, the multitude but that . . . he could observe two persons who, according to their attire, belonged to the well-to-do and who attended, impassive, these deeds and far from stopping the crowd, they insulted the deponent.[56]

A younger Jesuit, Valentín Francote, also from Spain, added to a similar account that "all the time the mob threatened and insulted them," but "he was not wounded." He did not know any of the assailants, but he could recognize "a young man . . . who looked like a student, who told the deponent that everything there was their property, that is, the people's property."[57]

A Brazilian merchant with his wife and son were visiting the school at the time of the attack. He reported that they saw "a large multitude of people . . . penetrating the building"; then "two men who seemed to be leading the crowd helped the deponent out of the school." He added that "neither they nor their son suffered the least harm in their persons, nor were they in any sense offended."[58]

Many more witnesses came up to tell their stories, but they add little to the above. Some insisted on the bloody nature of the attack, others offered a more sober version of the events. Most of them, however, mention, on the one side, the presence of the leading figures, distinguished by their well-to-do aspect and their commanding attitude, and on the other the action of the rabble, the mob, the crowd.

The defense attorneys argued in favor of the accused. There were more than twenty lawyers, some of them young political activists, others well-known members of the bar; most of them were liberal.[59] They combined strictly juridical arguments with ideological and political comments, among them a very strong defense of public mobilizations and of the principles that sustained civic life. The constitutional rights to free speech, assembly, and association were a keynote in all the statements. The following text by Dr. Benigno Jardim, attorney to Andrés Andrade, is an eloquent example of the arguments put forward in favor of the associative movement:

The Club Clemente XIV and the others that constituted the meeting in the Variedades and the Plaza de la Victoria are not illicit associations organized in secret, tenebrously, with ignoble ends. . . . As *free men*, courageous and with dignity, they *convened in public* to conjure a common peril and agree on the means to formulate a protest, and *as free men they came out to the streets*, each one proceeding at *his own risk*. . . . Why, then, would it be considered a crime to belong to the Club Clemente XIV or any other?[60]

In this statement, an implicit contrast between associative life, free and public, and that of the religious orders, secret and confined, is used to emphasize the merits of the former. To belong to an association was not a crime; rather, it was an asset.

Freedom was another reiterated point. There are numerous references to the individual freedoms, and very strong ones to religious freedom, considered an essential feature of the modern, civilized world.

In order to explain the violent incidents of February 28, the figure of the anonymous multitude pops up again in the writings of the defense, now as the nonresponsible actor manipulated by others. "Electrified masses," "fanatical rabble," "ignorant crowd," yes, but not a guilty one. Also, this multitude was far less aggressive than the "populace of other countries," and a small police force could have easily prevented the assault. But the police were not there.[61]

By April, the prosecution found no cause to pursue a trial. Their arguments were similar to the ones formulated by the attorneys. The right to free speech, assembly, and association, the value of freedom, the anonymous quality of the crowd, the inefficiency of the police—all these were mentioned to back their recommendation in favor of the suspension of the trial. The Jesuits and the archbishop, on their part, did not want to formulate charges. Nevertheless, Judge Demaría, at the insistence of the federal court, decided to prosecute fifty of the initially accused with the argument that a dismissal without a sentence would give them freedom but would not protect their reputations. Twelve days later, however, he finally acquitted all of the accused. In two months, it was over.

The Last Echoes

By then, the initial public outrage had waned. Actually, very shortly after the episode, while the Church and the clerical organs insisted on their indignation, the rest of the press swiftly returned to their usual anticlerical mood.

A few days after the February events, a group of distinguished "friends of the Church" organized a Committee of Gentlemen to collect funds for the reconstruction of the Savior's College. They also asked the authorities to compensate the Jesuits for their losses.[62] On April 4, Archbishop Aneiros instructed his congregation that Sunday, April 18 would be devoted to repudiating the events and "right[ing] the wrongs." He established the rituals and ceremonies that were to take place in all parishes, and called for a "collection of alms destined to repair the damages." The liberal press reacted immediately. *La Pampa* published a long, critical article calling the archbishop's document "a bunch of thistle and nettle whereby the prelate scourges the wounds opened by the display of blood and fire that fanaticism, intolerance, and the lack of sense on the part of his Highness produced in February."[63]

Finally, the day of the reparation arrived. *El Católico Argentino* reported total success: twelve hundred people attended Mass at the cathedral, there was an "extraordinary communion" in the rest of the churches of the city, and congregations in all the "great temples and poor parishes" throughout the country. The paper emphasized the presence of "a large number of gentlemen" at a time when it was hard to convene "men, particularly in these public demonstrations of Christian piety"; of people of various classes and conditions; of schools, both private and municipal; of brotherhoods and confraternities. It also congratulated the congregation for the money collected, and gave ample coverage to the archbishop's sermon.

Other newspapers, in turn, talked about "a scant attendance," "meager alms," and the hypocrisy and stubbornness of the archbishop's words.[64] *La Tribuna* warned: "The memory of the excesses shall recede, sooner or later, but the protest against the advances of the Church will never die. Twenty years from now, the February scandals will be just a detail, and the people of Buenos Aires will feel proud to have protested in time."[65]

In May, Judge Demaría absolved the accused, who were set free. On May 12, most of the press celebrated the resignation of the archbishop from his seat in the House of Representatives. The Committee of Gentlemen insisted upon collecting funds for the reconstruction of the school. Their attempts were met, however, with poor results. In the end, most of the money for that purpose came from donations made by the federal government and loans granted by the Banco de la Provincia. Although the sum collected covered only part of the cost of the reconstruction, the school reopenend that same year "as if nothing had happened."[66] But the church of San Ignacio was never returned to the Jesuits. Thus, in two months everything went back to normal, and what occurred in February was left behind. But what did actually happen in February?

How Was It All Possible?

I have briefly displayed the different versions of the events that took place that Sunday in Buenos Aires. Rather than telling us what really happened, they talk to us about the images, concerns, and expectations regarding the present and the future that circulated at the time. They also reveal various forms of social practices, public action, and government procedures. Therefore, in what follows, rather than trying to find out what really happened that Sunday, I will venture an interpretation of how the whole story was possible, not only the violent action of the crowd but also the swift resolution of the episode with almost no visible consequences.

This case shows the importance achieved by associative life and the vigor of the mobilization practices in Buenos Aires of the 1870s. In that context (described above in Chapters 2 and 7), the initial demonstration against the decision of the archbishop was similar to all others. A group of young students and university graduates created a club for the purpose of organizing the protest. They recruited members and spread their cause through the friendly press and personal contacts with other institutions. New associations were created to the same end, and already existing ones joined the action. Political clubs and Masonic lodges also participated. Professionals, students, merchants and shopkeepers, workers, and people from various neighborhoods and social conditions were recruited. These institutions soon established their own hierarchies and developed symbols and rituals. Meanwhile, the press was very actively promoting the cause. The anticlerical and anti-Jesuit tone was virulent, and in spite of there being a large actively Catholic population, those involved in the organization of the event talked in the name of the general public, of the common good.

In this case, however, the enemy was visible and used similar means of action: a newspaper (only one), an institutional network of Catholic brotherhoods and guilds, petitions to the government, and processions through the streets of Buenos Aires. It also had its own territorial domains: the Palace of the Archbishop, the Jesuit school, the churches. It was quite clear, however, that clericalism could not claim to be the prevailing mood of the city—and this was true also among the elite—a fact that the Church admitted but fought to reverse.

The antagonism was not new. There were two main sides to it: the competition between church and state power in several contested grounds, such as education, and the opposition between the clerical and anticlerical worldviews. In both accounts, the conflict escalated to new heights in that summer of 1875. By the end of February, the atmosphere was electrified. The demonstration was massive, the language virulent, and the action excessive. The usual limits were ignored; the antagonist became an enemy, and violence ensued.

In this context, violence seems to have been the product of the events. The deep tension that ran through the city in matters pertaining to the Church was the fertile terrain upon which the events of that fateful day were nurtured. But the events themselves, the *evé-*

néments—the French word is more precise—attained their own momentum and pushed the action beyond its usual boundaries.

At first, contemporaries sought for explanations elsewhere. The protagonists of such reprehensible acts could not belong to the enlightened urban public, that epitome of all civic virtues. They had to be "others"—most probably, the "new elements" of this society that was in a rapid road to modernization. Their presence was increasingly visible in a city that was growing at a very fast pace. The population had doubled in ten years to reach almost 300,000 people, more than half of them immigrants from different parts of Europe. The deep transformations brought about by the vigorous expansion of a market economy were shattering many of the old ways. Social bonds and ranks were changing rapidly (see Chapter 1). An economic crisis that had erupted in 1874 aggravated the generalized sense of instability and uncertainty. It is not surprising, therefore, that contemporaries first trod the social ground in search of answers to the question of the *who* and the *why* of the February episode. Some interpretations were quite elaborate; they mentioned the "new moral and material needs of the Argentine society" and the existence of poverty, hunger, and unemployment.[67] Others, as we have seen, simply made reference to the immigrants, the communists, and the proletariat. After the first moments of consternation, however, these characters found their own advocates, even within the same press that had earlier been ready to condemn them. Their place was then occupied by a new motif, also associated with the modern city: the multitude. The relatively recent events of the Paris Commune made that specter very real.

Yet this image initially invoked by all sides, from the Masons to the Church, from the accusers to the accused, proved too far-fetched. The population of Buenos Aires was not at war—as the French had been in 1871—nor was its militia ready to take over the city and fight for the creation of an autonomous commune. One small picket of guards proved sufficient to disperse the crowd, and everybody thought that a timely police action could have avoided the whole incident. Beyond the rhetoric of the first reactions, contemporaries quickly saw that this was not the feared social revolt, nor were the actors revolutionary sans-culottes or proletarian activists. The blame then passed on to other, more visible, figures: the liberals blamed the archbishop; the clerical groups, the liberal press; the opposition attributed great responsibility to the government; the government, to the opposition. Other, more abstract causes were also cited: religious fanaticism, political intolerance, the conflict of beliefs.

Soon, everybody went back to the starting positions around the two poles, clerical and anticlerical, with the latter being by far the prevailing force. Even the archbishop spoke in the name of liberalism, as he denounced his opponents of using liberty—"the greatest of God's gifts"—to offend and disobey God.[68] For the anticlericals, however, the defense of liberty had to do with religious freedom and the right to free speech and association, both considered pillars of the liberal and republican order they were struggling to build. The February outburst should not cast any doubts as to the main causes of the mobilization. The assault on the school was only a detail, which should not obscure all the good aspects of the event. These, according to *La Epoca*, were to be found in:

1st. That the people have demonstrated with the undeniable eloquence of a colossal mobilization that Jesuitism is an institution incompatible with the aspirations of a society like ours; 2nd that the time has come to suppress those privileged classes that, with the pretext of being enrolled in the ranks of a religion, withdraw from the obligations that life imposes; and 3rd that the state must break up its marriage with the Church.[69]

Nor should violent incidents be used as an excuse to limit the freedoms guaranteed by the constitution. "Outraged by evil, should we deny the good? . . . Shall we not incorporate the great conquest to our present because a mere detail has come to disturb the severe outlines of the whole? No, decidedly not."[70]

This was the cultural atmosphere in which the judge's decision to acquit the men that had been arrested on the aftermath of the demonstration was arrived at. The elite and the institutional leadership had closed ranks to defend civic freedoms and practices. The specter of social revolt that was obviously haunting them did not prove strong enough to jeopardize their faith in the Buenos Aires public. Not that the presence of actual proletarians was not visible, as we shall see in Chapter 9. That new social reality notwithstanding, they continued to champion the public sphere, for reasons that will become apparent when this book is over.

Every time there was a demonstration, the city entered in a celebratory mood, and this was also the case in February 1875. The highly combative tone of the language used to protest against the Church did not seem excessive at the time, as that sort of verbal aggression and sarcasm was part of the public rhetoric of the age. No provisions were made by the authorities to police the meeting and the march across the city, as order in these events was generally enforced by the organizers and the people themselves. The ensuing tumult came as a shock to everybody—the government, the organizers, and even the participants. So the first reaction was one of outrage, followed by attempts to understand what was going on. And the specter of the social disorders typical of modernity was the first image that the leadership came up with. The authorities moved swiftly then to detain at least some of the protagonists. The evidence of any plot, whether communist, socialist, or of any other sort, was, however, close to nil. And the accused could hardly be identified as raging revolutionary proletariats. But more important than any evidence was the collective mood. Nobody seemed to wish the story of the Commune to be true—not the elite, not the institutional leadership, not even the minuscule cell of the Socialist International. The anticlerical sectors feared the power of the Church more than that of the working classes. The political groups, particularly those in the opposition, reacted against any move that could interfere with basic freedoms, such as the state of siege. The institutional leadership was concerned first and foremost with respect for the recently acquired freedoms of speech, association, and the press. And so forth. So the men that had been caught were set free, and the assault on the Jesuit school became a mere anecdote in a city that had other more immediate worries.

9 On the Margins

The caricature is entitled "The Four Plagues of the Republic. The *Mitristas* are Delighted." It portrays an Indian, a figure representing the Commune with a bucket of petroleum, Bartolomé Mitre with a stick that reads "opposition," and a woman with a locust on her head. [*El Mosquito*, November 21, 1875]

Citoyens

[Manifesto of the Association Internationale des Travailleurs, section française de Buenos Aires]

En présence de la misère qui pese déja sur une partie de la classe ouvrière et qui menace de s'étendre chaque jour, un certain nombre de travailleurs ont commencé a reconstituer l'association internationale et décidé de faire un appel a tous les citoyens démocrates, socialistes, sans distinction de nationalité.

Ce que désire l'Association internationale des travailleurs c'est l'union; ce qu'elle vent combattre, c'est la misère; ses seules armes sont ses instruments de travail; ses guides, la raison et le droit.

Venez donc a nous, travailleurs riches ou pauvres, nous prouverons que la fraternité n'est pas un vain mot, prendrons tous les moyens de combattre la funeste association internationale des parasites, c'est à dire, la classe que vit et jouit des fruits de la terre et de l'industrie aux dépens de ceux qui travaillent et qui souffrent.

Nous voulons, avant tout et par dessus tout, des hommes probes et inspirés par l'amour de la liberté, de l'égalité et de la fraternité; nous réjetons loin de nous l'égoisme, la cupidité, l'agiotage . . . et la prostitution.

Notre devise est celle-ci: Tous pour un, un pour tous.

Il sera donné ultérieurment un meeting *avec l'objet de faire connaître les principes de* l'Association International des Travailleurs.

Pour l'association.
Le président de la séance du 28 février 1875
Lourme

—Archivo General de la Nación,
Tribunal Criminal, L 1875, (7), p.1

"That Terrible Association"

Last Sunday at two in the afternoon Police Chief Dn. Eufemio Uballes caught by surprise an assembly of a Committee said to be part of the *International*, that terrible European association that turned the main buildings of Paris into rubble. The meeting was taking place in a room at the second *patio* of a tenement located in [the parish of] Monserrat. Several men are in jail.[1]

Three weeks after the fire at the Saviors College, this piece of news appeared in the main newspapers of the city. The association was thought to be connected with the events of February 28, although the formal cause for the detention of its members had been the lack of a permit for holding a meeting when the city was under state of siege.

The press reacted in various ways to the news of the existence, in Buenos Aires, of a workers' association that proclaimed its link to the

Socialist International, and to the trial that followed. Their reports and comments, as well as the proceedings of that trial and the records of the regular meetings held by the association, which were seized by the police and are now found among the trial documents, constitute a rich set of sources for exploring the different contemporary perspectives on the event.

Scholars of the Argentine labor movement consider the existence of that group a landmark in the history of the organization of the local proletariat along class lines. They have identified the association with a previous one, created in 1872, that started as a *Section française* in Buenos Aires of the *Association Internationale de Travailleurs* (AIT) and later added an Italian and a Spanish section. Each section had a Central Committee that sent delegates to a federal council chaired by A. Aubert. By 1873, they altogether grouped around three hundred members. The association held regular contacts with the London General Council of the International. Yet the difficulties for organizing a class-based movement in Argentina were many, as Raymond Wilmart, an envoy of the AIT in Buenos Aires, pointed out periodically in his letters to Marx.[2] And in the following year, these groups seem to disappear altogether from the public arena.

The irruption of the police into a Monserrat tenement in 1875 brought the International back to the scene. Yet the group that was meeting there that Sunday was not part of the association created back in 1872. It was a new organization, which had only indirect links with the former one, already dissolved. The recent creation was also, however, very ephemeral; the difficulties in sustaining such an enterprise being, as Wilmart lamented, indeed very great.

The International, Part Two

On Sunday, February 14, 1875, at three in the afternoon, eighteen people attended the first meeting of the group determined to constitute the second Buenos Aires section of the *Sociedad Internacional de los Trabajadores.*[3] The initiative belonged to French shoemaker Pablo Cuq and Belgian pastry cook Henri Brouvers, who convened some friends to a meeting held in the house of the former. When the session opened, the chairman, "Citizen Pourille[, referred] to . . . the object of [the] meeting and the causes that have impelled some citizens to constitute once more in Buenos Aires a section of the international workers' association." He added that it was his wish that "only be admitted into the society well-known citizens, who had given proof of being independent and honest workers, revolutionaries or liberal republicans." The member of the International should always be ready "to sacrifice himself for the social emancipation of the people or of the part of the people who want to get rid of the yolk of all tyranny, be it Mercantile, Religious, or Regal."

During this first session, it was established that the association would be "strictly a political entity." Their funds "should only be allocated to the dissemination of their social ideas, or the support of a trade union when on strike," and to cover the expenses of the section. With these provisions, they clearly discarded mutual aid from their ends, and thus distinguished themselves from the majority of the contemporary workers' associations (see Chapter 2). The participants also discussed whether atheism would be required from the members. The proposal was dismissed by the majority, because the International admitted "all classes of workers, of every race, nationality, and religion." They agreed, however, to advocate the separation of church and state. Finally, they named a committee of six members to draft the rules and regulations of the section.

On subsequent Sundays the group met again at Cuq's house, but the number of assistants went down to twelve. All the participants except two—an Italian and a Belgian—were French, and the records and the regulations were written in French. The topics of discussion were mostly related to institutional matters. On February 21, there was a heated debate around the proposed bylaws. These established that, in order to be admitted to the society, a person had to "demonstrate his worker's condition or present proof of his civic and social virtues." Those who "live on usury or the stock market," "belong to a religious order," or "keep a gambling house or a brothel" were excluded (Article 1). An information committee was created to see that those provisions were met. The bylaws also established the duties of the associates, regulated the assemblies and directive bodies, and made certain provisions for the administration of the group.

In the session of February 28, they decided to publish a manifesto announcing "to the class of workers that a French section of the International exists in Buenos Aires" (see this chapter's opening page). They convoked "all socialist democratic citizens" to join together in a society with the purpose of fighting poverty, and declared that "their only arms are the working tools; their guides, reason and the law"; their enemies, "the international society of parasites." Inspired "by the love of liberty, equality, and fraternity," they proclaimed their motto: *"All for one, one for all."* This manifesto was to be published in three languages—Spanish, Italian, and French—in three of the city's newspapers. This move was frustrated, however, by the state of siege.

The formal constitution of the "French section of Buenos Aires of the International Workers' Association" finally took place on March 7. Twelve members were present. In the same session, they appointed a "committee of initiatives" in charge of devising the formal organization of the section. Its members were Jules Auvergne (painter, forty-two years old, widower, with two years of residence in Argentina); Francois Duffour (baker, twenty-five years old, single, with seven years of residence); Paul Cuq (shoemaker, forty years old, married, fourteen months' residence); Henri Brouvers (pastry cook, thirty years old, single, Belgian with sixteen months' residence); Francesco Bocca (photographer, thirty-three years old, single, Italian with two and a half years' residence); Jules Duboin (clerk bookkeeper, twenty-five years old, single, one year's residence); and Desiré Job (cook, forty-seven years old, married, three years' residence, the only one who had participated in the previous French section of the Buenos Aires International). This group met every day from March 7 to March 12 to do their job.

The committee was also in charge of contacting Citizen Aubert, the last secretary of the Federal Council, because "it was an obligation of the Committee as well as of French courtesy to find out if the former Buenos Aires section exists, and in that case, to establish contacts with it," before doing it with the European headquarters. Aubert agreed to convene the members of the old council, but that meeting had not taken place at the time of the arrests.

The institutional arrangements, as we see, engaged the best part of the first month's sessions. Second in importance were matters pertaining to the day-to-day operation of the section. Desertions (several of the assistants to the first meeting never returned), repeated absences, and late arrivals were recurrent topics that concerned the assembly of members. In every session, they reprimanded and sanctioned those who had not followed the regulations.

On February 28, the day of the protest against the Jesuits, the section was to meet at the usual hour, which coincided with that of the demonstration. Some of them arrived in time, and they agreed to postpone for one hour the opening of the session to allow for the latecomers. The first resolution they passed that day, however, was a reprimand to Brouvers, in charge of drafting the order of the day, for "neglecting his duties and not being present in time for the discussion." The sanction was annulled after the man arrived and defended himself by "accounting for what he had seen and heard in the demonstration" and arguing that "there should be no slaves among us."

The group was obviously not involved in the events that took place that day. They neither participated in them nor paid too much attention to them later. They were even reluctant to step in in defense of other associations accused by the police or the press. At one point, one of the members, "citizen Bocca," proposed that the International respond to the attacks formulated by some newspapers against the Masons of La Boca, and claimed that "they strive for the same objective as we do." To that, Brouvers responded:

[t]hat the International does not have to worry about the Masons of La Boca or about any others; that, in the first place, we are not yet well organized to do that and, in the second place, that the principles of the Masons are not ours, that the Masons work in the shadows and we in daylight, and that if the Masons are scoffed at and attacked by the newspapers, it is none of our business.

In the discussion that followed, Bocca also mentioned the fact that the International itself had been mentioned by the press, and proposed the formation of a committee "to watch over the maneuvers of the government" and "to control what is going on in the city regarding us." This time the negative response was in charge of Job: "The International has nothing to do with the government; the association is not a secret society and it is exclusively political." Thus, the two more influential figures of the group, Brouvers and Job, insisted on keeping the section out of the affair that was troubling the city in those days.

The police, however, thought differently, and on Sunday, March 14, they broke into Cuq's room, arrested the eleven men present at the meeting, and confiscated all their documents and papers.

Counterpoint

Mr. Uballes, head of the Sixth Precinct, was in charge of the operation. Five police officers who were with him stayed behind, at the *patio*, while he entered the room and urged those present to surrender, which they did with no resistance. The chief of police, Manuel Rocha, ordered the transfer of the proceedings to the Seventh Precinct, in charge of Officer García. By March 22 the latter had finished taking the testimonies of the arrested. The material ended up in the hands of the province's minister of government, Dr. Aristóbulo del Valle, who asked the prosecution to act promptly. Meanwhile, the arrested remained in prison.

The press reported the story. By that time, mid-March, the alarm caused by the violent episodes of February 28 was already dying out (see Chapter 8). Most newspapers, therefore, were rather skeptical in their coverage of the International episode. At first, some of them seemed shocked by the revelation of the existence of a group of socialist workers. Soon enough, however, their tone changed. *La Prensa*, for example, first referred to the relations the detained kept with "that terrible European association," but on the following day, it introduced this ironical comment: "It would also be prudent to arrest the *alsinistas* who meet daily in the parishes."[4] A few days later, the same daily published a letter sent by the prisoners.[5]

La Tribuna cited the documents seized by the police, and recommended some of their words to the politicians: "[E]very government should emanate from the workers."[6] *La Libertad* went further. It did not find any reason to explain the detention of the group and warned:

What about Article 14 of the constitution that guarantees everyone the right to associate? They say this association is secret. Then, be logical and just: there are more than one hundred secret societies among us. . . . Why don't you proceed against all of them? . . . This is not the worst part, however. To put the right of assembly in the hands of the police is to blot out that right altogether.[7]

A few days later, *La Epoca* condemned the police operation, because "if there is a society whose doctrine is . . . in harmony with the theory of progress, that is . . . the International."[8]

Prosecutor Juan Fernández thought otherwise:

The purposes of this international association are subversive of the social order; they fight the property owners whom they call *International of Parasites*; and [subversive] of the political order, as they wish to make the government and the laws the exclusive patrimony of the working class, turning it into an oligarchy organized for its own benefit, into a privileged caste.[9]

He thus determined that the association did not meet the constitutional requirement of having "useful ends," and that its actions should be judged in court. The chief of police held similar views, and considered that "if [the group] were to succeed in attracting the working class they would produce serious damage to the country."[10]

The judge who received the proceedings sent it immediately to the criminal prosecutor.[11] The opinion of the latter diverged from that of his colleagues. Although he warned against "the aberrant ideas, both political and religious" of the accused, and of the need to teach them that "they are not to come here to mock our laws and produce inconvenience," he pondered that the whole story was "no more than an aberration of ideas or, at the most, of an imprudent project that has been discovered and failed in its first attempts." He therefore recommended that the arrested be set free, after a "severe warning."[12]

On April 20, Judge Hudson decided not to proceed with the trial and set the prisoners free. His verdict is eloquent. In the first place, he mentions the freedom of association established by the constitution, which does not admit of any limitations except in cases that imply "the purpose of disturbing the public order" or "the execution of a crime." Secondly, the judge refers to the liberty of conscience and of the written and spoken word, which "excludes the authority of the magistrates to proceed against those who express their individual or collective opinion." The accused, "whether or not they were wrong in their ideas," had limited their action to "declaring and discussing the doctrines and beliefs . . . that they profess" and that, according to the judge, did not constitute a crime.[13]

A few days later, *La Nación* praised the judge's decision on the grounds that it had correctly tackled a new issue: it was the first time that the members of an association were brought to court, and he had stuck to "the letter and the spirit of our laws . . . and saved one of the great principles upon which the republican system relies."[14]

This episode illustrates what was taking place on the margins of the Buenos Aires public arena. Those years witnessed the very first moves toward the organization of a class-based political activity, aimed at "emancipating the worker from the capitalist tyranny."[15] The initiatives in this direction were still few and rather weak. In the case of the International, the group was extremely small, its members had difficulties in observing their own regulations, and they did not fully agree on their ways of organization and action. In that first month of existence, they operated like an isolated cell, more concerned with their own internal problems than with their public performance. Their presence, however, did not go unnoticed by the authorities, and the police were finally called to act.

The images of the Paris Commune and the fear of social revolt were, again, a powerful force behind the reactions against the group. In this case, the fact that most of its members were French, and that some of them were said to have taken part in the Commune served as material proof of the dangerous connection. Soon, however, the revelation of the real magnitude of the association (twelve actual members); of their backgrounds (as the prosecutor observed, all of them artisans); and even of the contents of their documents was enough to dissolve the initial fears kindled by the press and the police. For the public, it was hard to believe that this group was dangerous, capable of producing social disorder or political turmoil. More harm could be brought about if the freedom of speech and association established by the constitution were ignored by the authorities.

As to the workers' group, it did not survive this experience of "pain and humiliation, tears and misery."[16] The repression they suffered, the return of some of the members to Europe, and the dissolution of their parent association, the International, decreed by their New York council, all contributed to put an end to this initial effort to organize the working classes.[17]

The First Strike

The frustrated second foundation of a Buenos Aires section of the International was among the first attempts at the political organization of labor. More successful ones would follow, but only in the subsequent decades. Still, the 1870s witnessed the first recorded strike staged by a workers' union in Argentina.

By the 1870s, various trades had succeeded in establishing mutual aid societies to succor their members (see Chapter 2). The Sociedad Tipográfica Bonaerense stood out among them, showed a sustained and very visible public life, and developed strong links with the political elite of the city. At the end of 1877, a group broke away from the association and founded the Sociedad Unión Tipográfica, soon to become the protagonist of the first strike in the history of the Argentine labor movement. Although there is some notice of earlier labor conflicts, the typographers' was the first to have public repercussions and coverage in the press.[18]

On August 21, 1878, the Typographical Union sent the owners of the printing presses a note, signed by its president, M. Gauthier, and vice president, Ginés Alvarez, informing them that: "[t]he typographers of Buenos Aires, congregated in great number . . . are persuaded of the convenience of adopting a new tariff [wage] that responds to the needs of the worker and the businessman."[19] They argued that the competition among the presses had led to the exploitation of the workers, which was unacceptable. They proposed a new wage scale and asked for a response before their next meeting scheduled for August 30.

On that occasion, four to five hundred typographers according to some sources—one thousand according to others—met at the Teatro Alegría. There were speeches by Ginés Alvarez, the vice president; Ramón Lozano, supervisor at the printing press of *El Nacional*; Merchante, manager at the printing house *El Porvenir*; Enrique Romero Giménez, director of the paper *El Correo Español*; and a few others. The speakers held different views as to the opportunity of taking steps toward forcing the businessmen to accept the new tariff. The meeting finally decided to form a committee "to gather information on the number of typographers who agreed with the society's aims"; to request once more a raise in the wage "from the newspaper directors and printing house managers"; and, if their demands were ignored, to convene a new meeting in order to call a strike.[20]

Only one day after these resolutions were approved, however, the society's leaders declared the strike. In view of such a measure, the directors of *La Nación* and *El Correo Español* promptly accepted the proposed tariff. *La Tribuna*, in turn, hired workers from Montevideo, while other papers, such as *La América del Sud* and *La Patria*, reduced their size. The latter apologized to its readers because *"il giornale esce un pó mutilato"* [the paper comes out somewhat mutilated].[21]

The decision to strike was strongly criticized by most of the press. With the exception of *La Nación* and *La Prensa*, which chose to ignore the event, and *El Correo Español*, which supported it, the city's main newspapers condemned the workers' procedure. "The strike is an ex- otic plant that cannot prosper in our soil, where the intelligent, moral, laborious worker is king not vassal" contended *La Libertad*.[22] Very similar arguments were voiced by the others. Strikes were reasonable in Europe, where the living and working conditions of labor con- demned them to poverty. But "here that does not happen: the worker earns more, lives better . . ."; "between capital and labor there is here no antagonism as in other places."[23] Therefore, if the workers had the right "to manage their interests as free men," and to ask for better wages, the strike was "a useless parody in Buenos Aires."[24] Workers should be cautious of "the trap set for them by restless spirits," and of the hands that "have come to introduce anarchy, sow disorder, and prepare for a harvest of dreary fruits."[25]

Meanwhile, the typographers insisted upon their demands. On September 3, they published a pamphlet named *El Tipógrafo* that in- cluded the text of some of the speeches made in the Teatro Alegría and information on the causes of the strike. A few days later the union called a new meeting for September 22. On that occasion they ap- pointed a new executive board and a committee to draft the bylaws.[26] Finally, in October, the workers obtained what they had demanded: a raise in wages, a reduction of their working hours, and the elimination of child labor.

In view of the success of the Unión Tipográfica, the original So- ciedad Tipográfica Bonaerense sought the reunification of both asso- ciations. A year later that step was finally taken, and the new union resumed its basically mutual aid character.

This whole episode occupies a salient place in the history of the la- bor movement as a significant attempt at labor organization and the first recorded strike. At the same time, it played only a marginal role in the contemporary political arena. The press, albeit being directly af- fected by the conflict, paid little attention to it. Other news filled the main columns, and the information regarding the typographers was relegated to the less visible spaces.[27] The tone used by the main papers to condemn the strike suggests that they did not believe the measure could spread to affect the mass of the working classes of Buenos Aires.

The workers' protest inaugurated a practice that would later prove quite disruptive for the social and political order. At the time, however, it did not seem to arouse the fears of the powerful. The typographical associations enjoyed great prestige in Buenos Aires. They developed a highly respected and "respectable" mutual aid effort and kept important political connections. The demands they put forward were circumscribed to their labor conditions, moreover, and were not part of any more ambitious or revolutionary political discourse. The strike introduced a disturbing novelty, but it was not yet perceived by the elite as fundamentally subversive of the established order.

For the workers, on the other hand, the strike was a radically new way of protesting, different from the other known forms of public action. Although at that particular moment the effects of the typographers' strike were limited, in the future the episode would become a landmark in the history of labor's struggles against capital.

10 A Culture of Mobilization

For almost twenty years partisan confrontation set the tone of the political life of Buenos Aires. During the same period, however, an intense public life developed that contemporaries considered to be beyond factional strife. The mobilizations studied in Part III bear witness to this process. They were seen as the material expression of the common will of the people, regardless of existing political divisions. Social, ethnic, gender, or cultural differences also melted away. In the streets and plazas, the variegated population became a single public unified behind a cause. That was the image portrayed in the discourse of the contemporary press and the institutional leadership, and most probably shared by the mass of the participants.

Collective action was always organized in the name of the people. No matter how specific the issue or how small the initial group, the mobilization had to appeal to the whole. Some causes could be considered, prima facie, of general interest, such as the fight against the plague or the protest against taxes. Any opposition to them had to be expressed in terms of opportunity rather than principle. Other issues, in turn, were obviously sectional, such as the protests and claims voiced by the various immigrant communities. Nevertheless, the organizers sought the support of a wider public than their own constituencies, and stressed the common interest of their cause. Even when unanimity was hardly possible among the *porteños*, the prevalent view was one of universal endorsement. On the occasion of republican or anticlerical demonstrations, for example, the majority of the press conveyed the image of a city completely captured by republican fervor in one case, or an anticlerical mood in the other. The papers unsympathetic to such ideas did not dispute the picture; rather, they accused their ideological rivals of exerting a pernicious influence among the people. Yet in Buenos Aires, monarchism was embraced by some sections of the population, particularly among the immigrant communities, and the Church had its strong following. Their existence, however, did not suffice to counteract the powerful ideological construct of unanimity upon which the civic culture of the city was built.

A second quality attributed to collective mobilizations was moderation. In fact, most of the demands raised in the public sphere conformed with the prevailing political and social order. As described in Chapter 7, these mobilizations very seldom challenged government authority or political power. The issues raised did not refer to strong political or social antagonisms. At the same time, most demonstrations were carried out in perfect order. Certain cultural, ideological, or partisan motifs, however, could sometimes heat up the atmosphere. Thus, in spite of the moderate tone of the demands and the orderly style of the collective action, some underlying tensions usually emerged. Firstly, these mobilizations were organized with the purpose of addressing the government and voicing a protest, claim, demand, or opinion. Therefore they included an element of resistance that could eventually develop into open antagonism. Secondly, the sheer display of thousands of people in the streets and plazas generated a collective excitement that could escalate and prove hard to control. To prevent excesses, the leadership paid special attention to the organization of the crowd; gave precise instructions to the participant institutions; and appointed inspectors to supervise the marches. After every demonstration that proved peaceful, the papers celebrated the orderly, "civilized" nature of the event.

During the 1860s and 1870s, only on very few occasions did public demonstrations go beyond those limits, when the demands put forward contested the existing order or the participants engaged in violent behavior and actions. The reaction to them was twofold. On the one side, there was official reprehension and repression, strong criticism and condemnation on the part of the press, and a great deal of concern and even alarm among the city's elites. On the other side, however, the same sectors (the authorities, the press, and the elites in general) in the end denied the disruptive potential or the criminal nature of the actions they had initially censured. In most cases, the empirical corroboration of the limited or the marginal nature of those actions proved sufficient to dispel the fears of social confrontation and violence that haunted the leadership. At the same time, they all shared a positive evaluation of civic life and public mobilizations that led them to close ranks in defense of the freedom of assembly, speech, and association, and to be ready both to avert and to dismiss any signals of conflict that could stem from the public sphere.

The practice of mobilization was also cherished by the rest of the people of Buenos Aires. Meetings and demonstrations offered a new way of participating in the public life of the city. A considerable section of the population considered them a significant means of political action. Many *porteños* probably thought them a more effective and direct way of political inclusion than electoral involvement, or understood them as a form of collective representation.[1] Also, they celebrated those occasions to get together, and most likely rejoiced "from the spectacle they give each other and from the perfect harmony of their hearts."[2]

In a short time, therefore, Buenos Aires witnessed the development and consolidation of a series of values and practices that I have encompassed within the term "culture of mobilization." In Chapter 7, I have identified repeated procedures, a common rhetoric, shared symbols and rituals, a secular liturgy, that were part of this culture. They also defined an increasingly elaborated repertory deployed when some institutions of civil society took the initiative to stage a demand in the public arena. Far from being spontaneous, collective action was carefully organized and monitored by the leadership. In the 1860s those institutions were weaker and the demonstrations less imposing than in the following decade. Organization increased with the consolidation of the institutional web. And the mobilization of the urban public turned massive.

From the very beginning, leadership proved essential. The men who inspired and directed the public action belonged to the educated circles of Buenos Aires. Some of them were part of the local social and political elites, others were immigrants with a personal background of political activism in their original countries. For all of them public life was a priority. Journalism—both partisan and independent—provided them with their own space of power and influence. Their associative involvement, in turn, allowed them to combine their social interests, political ideals, and civic concerns. In the 1870s, with the multiplication of the institutions of civil society, a second line of leaders became visible in the public arena. Most of them were important actors of the associative movement, and though not as renowned as the first group, they were a central link in the organizational chain of the mobilizations. Strong vertical and horizontal connections were established among the leadership, and between them and the rest of the actual or potential members of the Buenos Aires public.

In order to succeed, the organizers of any particular demonstration had to recruit a large and variegated following. Even if they could count on a more or less permanent circle of sympathizers, they always had to reach out to a larger public. And the people responded. They joined in collective action in increasing numbers. They did not act, however, as passive members of any closed retinue. In the first place, participation in any event of this sort was entirely voluntary and open to anyone. The appeal was always universal, and the spatial display horizontal and accessible. This is not to say that every participant was a free rider. In fact, most of them had an institutional affiliation, and probably some were related to the leaders by different types of clientelistic bonds. Secondly, the participants were, prima facie, "equals." In the streets, theaters, and plazas they came together around a common cause and left aside their differences in all other terrains. And although there was an institutional hierarchy and the public action itself generated internal differences (there were speakers and listeners, journalists and readers, organizers and followers), these were somehow put to the test in every public meeting.

The success of any such meeting depended very much on the number of people who showed up, as well as on their enthusiasm and "civic spirit." Diversity was also a key factor. The powerful image of a single public was generally obtained by addition. In contemporary accounts, the importance of any demonstration was measured by the number and variety of institutions that participated in it. The people are always portrayed marching with their respective associations, behind their banners and leaders. The spatial display of a great number of different groups somehow created the illusion of universality, while at the same time it did not preclude their being seen as undifferentiated parts of a single public.

Success also depended upon the response from the political realm. The efficacy of any particular mobilization depended not only upon the magnitude and scope of its own resources. The political circumstances at the time of each event had a decisive effect on the outcome as well. Although the institutions of civil society strove to stay away from partisan struggles, when the conflict ran high, such autonomy was hard to achieve; many public demonstrations were tainted by factious rivalry.

The *porteño* politicians were, in turn, particularly sympathetic toward the urban public, whom they courted in various ways. And the mobilizations staged in Buenos Aires materialized, and even "produced" that public. The political and government forces not only accepted such presence; they also encouraged public mobilizations, which they considered a genuine means of representation of the common interests of the people.

These mobilizations were, therefore, a key aspect in the complex relationship established between the political elite and larger sectors of the Buenos Aires population. And they were a central feature in the construction of the public sphere. By materializing *the people*, meetings and demonstrations operated as the visible incarnation of civil society and public opinion.

Epilogue

These pages have addressed the question of the political relations between the few and the many in Buenos Aires of the 1860s and 1870s. Two dimensions, we have argued, were decisive in this regard: electoral practices and public mobilizations. For those in government, who experienced politics at different levels, these two dimensions implied a direct relationship with the "governed." For the latter, in turn, the participation in elections and mobilizations involved the exercise of both their political and their civil rights, and an explicit relationship with the few.

Since the first decades of the nineteenth century, modern representation was the basic principle upon which political power rested. Electoral procedures and mechanisms were, therefore, not new in Buenos Aires, and it would be easy to trace the continuities between the ways inaugurated after unification in 1862 and those of the previous decades. The context, however, was entirely novel: on the one side, the national scope of the polity in the making; on the other, the political conditions created by the victory of the state of Buenos Aires over the confederate government and the rise to national power of the *porteño* elite, who came to life in the aftermath of the revolution of 1852. In this context, new and old ways combined; but the relations between the many and the few acquired a unique quality, different from those that had prevailed in former regimes and also in the one that would follow after 1880.

Electoral norms and political discourse presumed voters to be abstract, equal individuals, who enjoyed the right of suffrage. In theory, these citizens exercised their political freedom by choosing their representatives from among their peers. This could be done in different ways. In the city of Buenos Aires, the electoral system inaugurated immediately after the fall of the Rosas regime was meant to leave behind the previous one based on the imposition from above of the names of the candidates. The new leadership devised a mechanism whereby those names had to spring from the bottom up, proposed by the citizens. In practice, however, already by the early 1850s those who aspired to political power operated at the parish level in order to influence neighbors' choices. From then onward, the production of candidatures as well as their electoral success became one of the main concerns of a new institution, the political party.

In Buenos Aires, as we have seen, the first party—Partido de la Libertad—was not only an aggregation of political figures who shared an electoral interest. It also defined itself as a "party of principles," an enterprise that aspired to embody the collective values of the people. Its successors of the 1860s and 1870s—Autonomista and Nacionalista— each claimed to be the true heir of the original liberal party and also to represent the entirety of the good society, rather than any particular group or sector. At the same time, however, they had to organize as a group to compete in the electoral arena. To avoid descending directly into partisan competition, which was considered divisive and somehow pernicious to the nation, they gave birth to a separate institution that operated precisely in the electoral field, the political club. As we saw in Chapter 5, the clubs were organizations mounted for the purpose of producing and favoring candidatures, and of generating and directing electoral resources. Although they were conceived as ephemeral institutions, active only at election time, they soon became more permanent associations, some of which gave birth to new parties.

The tension between the aspiration to represent the people as a whole and the need to organize as a group in order to win at the polls was contained, as well as unfolded, within the party/club couple. The party/club convened "the people" but mobilized only a very small group of persons. They appealed to the civic spirit of the population but resorted to electoral forces composed of militants collectively organized for electoral battles. They invoked the free and autonomous citizen but formed their own clienteles linked to the leadership by paternalistic and deferential bonds. These political practices were common to many nineteenth-century societies. In Buenos Aires they combined with other, more specific features in what contemporaries labeled "la política criolla."

Three main aspects merit our attention. In the first place, the parties recruited their electoral bases among various social sectors but particularly among the lower classes. This was made possible by the wide franchise enjoyed by the population—in Argentina, all adult men born or naturalized citizens could vote—and gave the polls that plebeian atmosphere often denounced by contemporary observers. What attracted these people to the clubs? For the leadership, partisan politics was often an occupation, sometimes an entertainment, but above all it was the road to political power. As for the rank and file, party life offered connections, protection, a reference group, even an identity. The popular sectors were subject to the uncertainties and pressures brought about by the oscillations of the labor market, the contingencies of military recruitment, the varied forms of state control, and the everyday consequences of the swift social and cultural changes brought about by abrupt modernization. Partisan life protected them, or made them feel protected, from some such risks. At the same time, it included them in webs of sociability where the men could find friends, display their physical strength and courage, and share a masculine world of ritualized violence. These webs also connected the rank and file with the most prestigious political and public figures. Top leaders such as Mitre and Alsina, as well as secondary ones such as Leandro Alem or Dardo Rocha, were true *caudillos* of a vast following ready to fight, and even die, for their political masters. Most of the men were proud to exhibit their partisan credentials, of being *mitristas* or *alsinistas*. For all, politics meant action; in each election, their participants were, for a few hours at least, the main actors in the game of power.

Secondly, these bases constituted clienteles held together by multiple and often unequal exchanges among themselves and with the leadership. Generally, these links did not originate in the social realm; they resulted from political action. The prominence of most leaders was not a by-product of their economic fortune or social prestige, as in the case of the "notables" of other nineteenth-century societies. It was built up in the political realm. In Buenos Aires, parties and clubs strongly relied on their own political capital, as well as on state institutions and employment, while family links and economic or social relations established in the private sphere played a secondary role in the partisan world. Electoral activity was the key instance in the forging of that world. It was during the "electoral labors" that leaders and militants built up their mutual, vertical bonds, in a direct relationship that knew of no mediations. Rather than in any institutional structure, these relations emerged, developed, and were put to the test in the field of action.

This leads us to our third point, the weak institutional framework of the parties. We have mentioned that the clubs were created by the first parties to face that embarrassing aspect of their lives, electoral battles. By definition, clubs were supposed to be temporary organizations; in fact, as we have seen, they were the more visible and established structures within the parties. Electoral activity was the engine of party life. It was the most conspicuous function, and one that required a concrete following. Other party activities—in the legislature or the press, for example—relied entirely on the work of the leaders and a handful of secondary figures, who appealed to an ample and undifferentiated public, the single "people." The parties' only organizational drive, therefore, came from the clubs and was subordinated to electoral strategies. Their institutional structure was, therefore, very weak and did not respond to any prescriptive arrangement; rather, it was the outcome of transient but recurrent electoral needs and deeds.

These were the new political ways inaugurated in Buenos Aires after midcentury. They were far removed from the ideal model of a liberal or a democratic polity, but they were also different from the traditional forms of political action. The organization mounted to win at the polls mobilized human and economic resources both to make the elections possible and to control and manipulate their outcome. Relatively few people voted (or cared to vote), but they were strongly held together by symbolic and material bonds. Electoral practices became a device internal to the partisan game of politics, a game that was played by a small number but accepted as legitimate by the rest, who followed its ups and downs closely. It was, after all, quite a peaceful means of access to government posts, which both allowed for a controlled solution of the frequently violent struggles within the elite and was in accordance with the principle of popular sovereignty established by the constitution.

At the same time, large sectors of the population of Buenos Aires chose other forms of public involvement that seemed to fulfill their expectations of political participation better than the polls. They established voluntary associations, edited and read newspapers, and frequently mobilized to express their opinion, celebrate an event, put up a claim, or voice a protest. The press and the associations formed an institutional network that covered the city, defined a space of shared initiatives and actions, and generated linkages of various sorts among its people.

These institutions were presumably sites of modern sociability; they were organized on a voluntary basis to pursue an explicit end, and their members were considered prima facie equals. In practice, however, they defined a space that was not strictly egalitarian. Although those convened around a common cause or a shared identity became, in a sense, equals, they produced their own hierarchies: there were, as we have seen, speakers and listeners, journalists and readers, organizers and followers. Speakers, journalists, and organizers were usually the same people: a relatively small albeit open group who conducted the communication and organizational networks. This leadership showed a relatively broad social and national provenance that included a significant number of men from the middle strata of *porteño* society. All of them belonged, however, to the ranks of the educated (Chapters 2 and 7).

As for the rank and file, what motivated them to join the collective action? Although they came from different social and cultural backgrounds, they all shared the experience of living in a period of deep social transformations. The uncertainties and risks of a capitalist economy in the making; the tensions and conflicts brought about by the population increase, the influx of immigrants, and the definition of new social relations; the widening cultural cleavages—all these factors contributed, as we have seen, to shatter the old ways of *porteño* society. In that context, the material and symbolic benefits of participating in the webs of civil society were immediately visible to both natives and immigrants.

In the first place, associations rendered specific and much-needed services to their members, as defined in their founding charters and statutes. So did newspapers to their readers. Secondly, these institutions favored the development of human relations. In this space, just as in the partisan world, the people obtained protection, aid, and connections, and found a place in the world and built their own identities. The Catholic Church had traditionally played a similar role, and still did; but after the midcentury, the associative world took the lead. It was more egalitarian, participatory, and ideologically modern than the Church. In those decades, anticlericalism gained momentum in Buenos Aires. Enthusiastically proclaimed by the enlightened elites, it was also endorsed by large sectors of the population and became the dominant language in the public sphere. Thus, although the Church was still very influential and had its own mechanisms of collective action and gathering, in the field of associative practices it was successfully challenged by the institutions of civil society.

To most people, the latter were also more attractive than the partisan networks. Participation in the political and electoral machines demanded a strong militant commitment, clientelistic loyalty, and involvement in rough, often violent, actions. Women, children, and most immigrants were—prima facie—excluded. Active partisan engagement remained, therefore, a minority enterprise that did not really compete with associative practices for the favor of the *porteños*.

Thirdly, many people were willing to take part in the mobilization practices developed by the institutions of civil society. They understood meetings and demonstrations as an effective means of political participation and collective representation. On such occasions, they became a visible part of the community, which materialized in the streets and plazas of the city.

Finally, there existed a generalized positive valuation of the associative movement and collective practices. Echoes of Tocqueville, Mazzini, Fourier, and Saint-Simon resonated in the ideological atmosphere of the city. The people of Buenos Aires were proud of their own record in this respect, and therefore they responded favorably to the appeal of the leadership not only to join the associations or buy the papers but also to follow its many initiatives to petition, meet, and demonstrate as a public.

The institutions of a civil society in the making increasingly entered into a fluid and persistent dialogue with the state and the political realm and gradually shaped a public sphere. The construction of that sphere in Buenos Aires followed a road familiar from most studies of the process elsewhere. The place of that public sphere in the political system of Buenos Aires, however, appears less familiar. Theoretically and historically, participation in the public sphere has been associated with increasing participation in the electoral system, and both are seen as crucial to the construction of the political citizen. In this case, however, these two aspects were somehow dissociated. Electoral practices remained a game internal to the political realm, and involved a relatively small portion of the city's population. It is hard to associate these practices, however, with the exercise of political freedom, and to identify the participants with the ideal citizens presumed by the constitution or by theories then in vogue (Chapter 6). The public sphere, in turn, created a space of mediation between civil society and the state, through which expanding sectors of the people were involved in various forms of politically consequential public action. This participation implied the full use of their civil liberties; it did not lead, however, to the exercise of their political rights.

For some time, this combination worked and contributed to the relative consensus enjoyed by the political system for almost twenty years. The importance of the public sphere under formation was recognized by the political elite of Buenos Aires. Its leading figures developed an increasing sensitivity toward public opinion, and they worked hard to win over the new urban public. The voice of that public acquired a unique quality for a leadership who aspired to dominate the rest of the country. Not only was the city their own backyard; it was also the site of the more influential economic interests and of the representatives of foreign powers. Political leaders like Mitre or Alsina cultivated their civic image, and appealed to the larger public for support and endorsement.

Public opinion also played a part in the elite's effort to build and control a national polity. According to the ideological convictions most of them shared, the *"tribunal de la opinión"* constituted the most genuine expression of the collective interests of the nation. The institutions and practices of the public sphere embodied those interests. They always spoke in the name of the "common good" and acted as representatives of the whole. And they were seen at the time as the material manifestation of the body civic and the symbol of the unity of the republic, in contrast to the political world of parties and factions that was considered divisive and harmful to the nation.

The public sphere was the site for harmony. Yet the social order that was taking shape in those decades was anything but harmonious (see Chapter 2). The rifts and tensions that cut across that society, however, did not find their way to the public sphere. The institutions of civil society operated as horizontal and vertical networks that established connections and fostered communication among men and women of different social and cultural backgrounds. Collective action was always carried out in the name of the people, and it was not meant to reproduce or encourage conflict. Even those associations that may seem to have had an inbred class bias, such as the Sociedad Rural or the Sociedad Tipográfica, functioned along these lines. Street mobilizations were the favorite form of collective action probably because they materialized a single public. In the plaza, the multiple utterances of the heterogeneous population became "the voice of the people." Rather than displaying or reproducing the existing lines of tension, all these institutions and practices acted as a countervailing force that contributed to bridge some of the increasingly profound social gaps opened up by modernization.

At the time, this unanimity was frequently contrasted with the divisive world of politics. Collective mobilization was opposed to electoral manipulation; the open plaza to the club or the atrium; the citizen to the client; the ordered and civilized public to electoral forces made up of unruly, uneducated, and violent men; public leaders to the *caudillos* and bosses. Both terms of these oppositions may be seen, however, as belonging to the same ideological world, one that was nurtured by holistic, nonliberal notions of nation, republic, and "pueblo." In the political realm, the conflict was perceived as evil; the notion of "party" as the representative of specific interests or sectors was not readily accepted; the actual parties pretended to represent the whole, and called themselves "parties of principles." They lacked institutional structure, and resorted to a parallel, presumably ephemeral organization—the club—in order to descend to the electoral arena. The institutions of civil society, in turn, also acted in the name of all. While in other countries at the time the press and the associations represented different groups and sectors and displayed their interests and needs in the public sphere, in Argentina they embodied the common good.

Therefore social, ethnic, and cultural diversity was not acted out in the public sphere, nor was it represented in the political world of parties. Contemporaries privileged the unity of the body civic, and for two decades they succeeded in articulating a legitimate political order based on those two pillars. In the face of a past of civil wars and a present of uncertain and weak social and national bonds, of rapid modernization and abrupt change, the staging of unanimity assuaged the fear of dissolution that haunted the elite, as well as other groups and sectors of society. The pursuit of the common good, of strong republican resonance, was a topic present in various of the ideological perspectives that circulated in the city, and it became a shared aspiration of large sectors of the population. The image of a one and single people was realized in the political and public practices of those decades, and both the parties and the institutions of civil society contributed to stage unanimity and to discourage structural political diversity.

The peculiar combination of political and public life that we have described in this book, however, did not last long. The relationships established between the few and the many in those decades of the *Organización Nacional* in the context of the political regime shaped by the new elite of Buenos Aires was short-lived. By the 1880s, deep transformations in political and social structures, as well as in prevailing ideas, had changed the character and the role of the electoral game and the public sphere.

Already in the 1870s, the regime came under fire. On the one side, a new coalition of forces based on the interior provinces successfully challenged the power of the *porteños,* who were soon displaced from the main government posts. On the other, members of the political and intellectual elites became increasingly critical of the electoral practices upon which the system rested. As described in Chapter 5, there were numerous proposals to change the norms. The issue of the scope of the suffrage was raised for the first time in decades. The concept of a holistic people came into question, in the face of a new concern for the representation of different sectors of society. There were recommendations to restrict the vote on the basis of property and literacy, as well as to make voting compulsory in order to ensure the participation of those reluctant to fulfill their public duties, particularly among the well-to-do.

These discussions, however, did not alter the system, and the vote remained universal but noncompulsory for all men until 1912. The regime inaugurated in 1880 did not modify the suffrage laws in any significant way. It established, however, a different electoral dynamic, and based its strength in that field on the capacity of the provincial governments to produce the suffrage. The party in power became hegemonic, and, for some time, true competition almost disappeared from the scene. The notion of politics as civic engagement lost favor among the powerful. In this new political order, the electoral game in the city changed, and so did the relations between the *porteños* and the vote.

The Buenos Aires public sphere also played a different role after 1880. On the one side, civil society consolidated, and public opinion remained a key reference for legitimating political power. But the people of the city lost the privileged place they had held as the main actors of the public sphere during the years of *porteño* hegemony. On the other side, the social transformations already visible in the 1860s and 1870s consolidated. Buenos Aires turned decidedly modern, capitalistic, and—in the word of José Luis Romero—"bourgeois." Social conflicts erupted, and the public sphere lost the unified quality characteristic of the formative years.

Aspirations to unanimity, however, did not entirely die out. Actually, they would prove quite resistant to change, and may be identified in the ideas and practices of different political groups throughout Argentine history. The pretense of the large parties, such as the Radical and the Peronist, to represent the nation as a whole as well as the frequent negation of the political other as illegitimate enemy rather than legitimate rival have been among the most salient features of the political system well into the twentieth century. Still today, the word "pueblo" frequently evokes a single people. At the same time, the conception of politics as civic engagement remains deeply embedded in our political practices, while collective action and mobilization continue to enjoy popular favor. This is not to claim secular continuities with the past, but just to point to the persistence of certain particular motifs in the Argentine political landscape. In this sense, the short-lived *porteño* experiment of the 1860s and 1870s left some original and long-lasting marks in the ways of our democracy.

Notes

Introduction

1. David Hume, "Of the First Principles of Government," *Essays Moral, Political, and Literary* (Indianapolis: Liberty Classics, 1987). The original text is from 1758. I owe this reference to Margarita Costa.

2. Pierre Rosanvallon, *Le sacré du citoyen* (Paris: Gallimard, 1992); William H. Sewell, Jr., *A Rhetoric of Bourgeois Revolution: The Abbé Sieyes and "What Is the Third State?"* (Durham and London: Duke University Press, 1994).

3. See, among others, Giuseppe Duso, *La rappresentanza: un problema di filosofia politica* (Milan: Franco Angeli Libri, 1988); D. Pécaut and B. Sorj (eds.), *Métamorphoses de la répresentation politique* (Paris: Ed. du CNRS, 1991); Giovanni Sartori, *Elementi di teoria politica* (Bologna: Il Mulino, 1983); and the classic work by Hannah Pipkin, *The Concept of Representation* (Berkeley: University of California Press, 1967).

4. T. H. Marshall, "Citizenship and Social Classes," chapter 4 in *Class, Citizenship, and Social Development* (Westport, Conn.: Greenwood Press, 1973). The original text is from 1949.

5. According to this view, in Argentina the expansion of the suffrage and of the citizenry was achieved only after the passing of the electoral law of 1912, which is known as the "law of universal suffrage." That law did not actually extend the franchise, which since 1853 had been universal for all adult men. By introducing compulsory voting and the secret ballot, however, it brought about a significant increase in the turnout.

6. Rosanvallon, *Le sacré du citoyen*; Francois-Xavier Guerra, "La metamorfosis de la representación en el siglo XIX," Georges Couffignal (comp.), *Democracias posibles* (Buenos Aires: Fondo de Cultura Económica, 1993).

7. Although the Argentine constitution does not make any explicit reference to universal male suffrage, it has always been considered implicit in the constitutional text. In the case of immigrants, the requirements for naturalization were minimal: after two years' residence they could apply for citizenship, thus becoming potential voters. Nonnaturalized foreigners could vote in some municipal elections. See Hilda Sabato and Elías Palti, "¿Quién votaba en Buenos Aires?: práctica y teoría del sufragio, 1850–1880," *Desarrollo Económico* 30 (1990).

8. Luis V. Sommi, *La Revolución del 90* (Buenos Aires: Ed. Pueblos de América, 1957), pp. 89–90. This interpretation is found in many other works on Argentine political history.

9. Gino Germani, *Política y sociedad en una época de transición: de la sociedad tra-dicional a la sociedad de masas* (Buenos Aires: Paidós, 1968), p. 299.

10. This interpretation was eloquently suggested by José Luis Romero—and partially recuperated by Natalio Botana—but in reference to the regime installed after 1880. See José Luis Romero, *Las ideas políticas en la Argentina* (Mexico City: Fondo de Cultura Económica, 1946) and Natalio Botana, *El orden conservador: la política argentina entre 1880 y 1916* (Buenos Aires: Sudamericana, 1977).

11. See Edmund Morgan, *Inventing the People: The Rise of Popular Sovereignty in England and America* (London and New York: Norton, 1988); Francois-Xavier Guerra, *Modernidad e independencias* (Madrid: Mapfre, 1992).

12. In the last edition of his book *El orden conservador,* Botana has included a preliminary study that refers to the new political historiography on these sub-jects. Recent volumes on the electoral history of several Latin American countries include the special volume of the journal *Quaderni Storici,* nuova serie 69 (1988), edited by Antonio Annino and Raffaele Romanelli; Antonio Annino (comp.), *Historia de las elecciones en Iberoamérica, siglo XIX: de la formación del espacio político nacional* (Buenos Aires: Fondo de Cultura Económica, 1995); Eduardo Posada Carbó (ed.), *Elections before Democracy: The History of Elections in Europe and Latin America* (London: Macmillan, 1996); Carlos Malamud (comp.), *Partidos políticos y elecciones en América Latina y la Península Ibérica, 1830–1930* (Madrid: Instituto Universitario Ortega y Gasset, 1995); Hilda Sabato (coord.), *Ciudadanía política y formación de las naciones: perspectivas históricas de América Latina* (Mexico City: Fi-deicomiso de Historia de las Américas de El Colegio de México y Fondo de Cul-tura Económica, 1999).

13. This interpretation belongs to Marcela Ternavasio, "Nuevo régimen repre-sentativo y expansión de la frontera política: las elecciones en el Estado de Buenos Aires: 1820–1840," Annino (comp.), *Historia de las elecciones.* See also Tulio Halp-erin Donghi, *Revolución y guerra: formación de una elite dirigente en la Argentina criolla* (Buenos Aires: Siglo XXI, 1972).

14. Marcela Ternavasio, "Hacia un régimen de unanimidad: política y eleccio-nes en Buenos Aires, 1828–1850," Sabato (coord.), *Ciudadanía política y formación de las naciones.* Natalio Botana labeled this type of representation "inverted repre-sentation." Botana, *El orden conservador.*

15. José Luis Romero, "La ciudad patricia," José Luis Romero and Luis Al-berto Romero (dirs.), *Buenos Aires: historia de cuatro siglos* (Buenos Aires: Ed. Abril, 1983), vol. 1, p. 309.

16. The eighteen years of these three presidencies have been called the period of national organization (*Organización Nacional*). For the political affiliations and connections of each of them, see Chapter 1.

17. J. L. Romero, *Las ideas políticas,* pp. 163–68.

18. Ibid., p. 188.

19. Tulio Halperin Donghi, *Proyecto y construcción de una nación (Argentina, 1846–1880)* (Caracas: Biblioteca de Ayacucho, 1982), prologue, pp. lii ff.

20. Ibid., p. lvi.

21. For a synthesis of different conceptions of civil society, see Jean Cohen and Andrew Arato, *Civil Society and Political Theory* (Cambridge, Mass.: MIT Press, 1992).

22. Jurgen Habermas's book *Strukturwandel der Öffentlichkeit* was first published in German in 1962; in Italian, French, and Spanish in the 1970s and early 1980s; and in English only in 1989. There are numerous articles and books that discuss the concept of "public sphere" theorized in that work. See Arthur Strum, "A Bibliography on the Concept of *Öffentlichkeit*," *New German Critique*, no. 61 (1994): pp. 161–202.

23. Guerra, *Modernidad e independencias*, p. 89. See also Pilar González Bernaldo, *Civilité et politique aux origines de la Nation Argentine: les sociabilités à Buenos Aires, 1829–1862* (Paris: Publications de la Sorbonne, 1999).

24. Alexis de Tocqueville, *Democracy in America*, 2 vols. (New York: Vintage Books, 1945). The citation comes from volume 2, book 2, chapter 5, p. 115.

25. For the Latin American case, see, among others, Guerra, *Modernidad e independencias*; Carlos Forment, "La sociedad civil en el Perú del siglo XIX: democrática o disciplinaria," Sabato (coord.), *Ciudadanía Política y formación de las naciones*. For a somewhat different perspective, see José Murilo de Carvalho, *Os bestializados: O Rio de Janeiro e a república que não foi* (São Paulo: ed. Schwarcz, 1987).

26. The breach opened by modernity between private and public, as well as the differentiation between state and civil society, have generated many academic controversies. For a partial revision of these, see Arato and Cohen, *Civil Society and Political Theory*.

27. Habermas has defined the "bourgeois public sphere . . . above all as the sphere of private people come together as a public" for the purpose of engaging with the state "in a debate over the general rules governing relations in the basically privatized but publicly relevant sphere of commodity exchange and social labor." Historically, Habermas points to the formation of a public sphere as a key development in the construction of bourgeois societies. Theoretically, he presents the bourgeois public sphere as the space where citizens deliberate and interact discursively, and where the authority of the rational argument prevails over any other—for example, over the authority that can arise from social hierarchies. It is an arena in which people relate to each other as "equals," the criteria for admission being education and property ownership. Finally, it is—in the words of Nancy Fraser—"an institutional mechanism for 'rationalizing' political domination by rendering states accountable to (some of) the citizenry." Both Habermas's formulation and some of the critical responses provoked by his work provided a useful theoretical point of departure for my historical exploration of the configuration of institutions and practices originating in civil society that operated in Buenos Aires in the period under study. The citations are from the English edition of his book. Jurgen Habermas, *The Structural Transformation of the Public Sphere* (Cambridge, Mass.: 1989), p. 27. See also Nancy Fraser, "Rethinking the Public Sphere: A Contribution to the Critique of the Actually Existing Democracy," *Social Text* 25/26 (1990): p. 59. This article was later included in Craig Calhoun (ed.), *Habermas and the Public Sphere* (Cambridge, Mass.: 1992), together with several other articles that discuss the concept and its use.

28. Botana, *El orden conservador*, 4th ed., p. xvii.

29. PEHESA, "¿Dónde anida la democracia?" *Punto de Vista*, no. 15 (1982): pp. 6–10.

186 Notes to Introduction

30. The present English version of Chapter 8 was discussed at a seminar held in January 1999 at the Center for Advanced Study in the Behavioral Sciences, Stanford, California.

31. Ema Cibotti and Elías Palti collaborated with me in the elaboration of the following articles: Hilda Sabato and Ema Cibotti, "Inmigrantes y política: un problema pendiente," *Estudios Migratorios Latinoamericanos*, no. 4 (Dec. 1986): pp. 475–82 and *Historia em Cadernos* 4, no. 2; 5, no. 1 (July–Dec. 1986/Jan.–June 1987); and "Hacer política en Buenos Aires: los italianos en la escena pública porteña, 1860–1880," *Boletín del Instituto de Historia Argentina y Americana "Dr. E. Ravignani,"* Tercera Epoca, no. 2 (1990): pp. 7–46; Hilda Sabato and Elías Palti: "Quién votaba en Buenos Aires?: Práctica y teoría del sufragio, 1850–1880," *Desarrollo Económico*, no. 119 (Oct.–Dec. 1990): pp. 395–424. Partial results of this research are also found in my articles "Participación política y espacio público en Buenos Aires, 1860–1880: algunas hipótesis," *El reformismo en Contrapunto* (Montevideo: Centro Latinoamericano de Economía Humana/Ediciones de la Banda Oriental, 1989); "La Revolución del 90: prólogo o epílogo?" *Punto de Vista*, no. 39 (1990): pp. 27–31; "participación política y espacio público en Buenos Aires, 1850–1880: algunas hipótesis," Carlos Barbé (comp.), *Le ombre del passato: dimensioni culturali e psicosociali di un processo di democratizzazione* (Torino: Giappichelli Editore, 1992); "Citizenship, Political Participation and the Formation of the Public Sphere in Buenos Aires, 1850s–1880s," *Past and Present*, no. 136 (Aug. 1992): pp. 139–63; "Elecciones y prácticas electorales en Buenos Aires, 1860–1880: ¿sufragio universal sin ciudadanía política?" Antonio Annino (comp.), *Historia de las elecciones en Iberoamérica, siglo XIX: de la formación del espacio político nacional* (Buenos Aires: Fondo de Cultura Económica 1995); "Vida política y cultura de la movilización en Buenos Aires, 1860–1880," Marcello Carmagnani, Alicia Hernández Chávez, and Ruggiero Romano (coord.), *Para una historia de América: los nudos 2* (Mexico City: FCE, 1999); and "La vida pública en Buenos Aires," Marta Bonaudo (dir.), *Liberalismo, Estado y orden burgués (1852–1880): Nueva Historia Argentina*, vol. 4 (Buenos Aires: Sudamericana, 1999).

Chapter 1: Buenos Aires, a World in Transition

1. Xavier Marmier, *Buenos Aires y Montevideo en 1850* (Montevideo: Arca, 1967), p. 13.

2. Fernando Aliata, "La ciudad regular," Archivo di Stato di Reggio Emilia, *La memoria del futuro: Carlo Zucchi, ingeniero arquitecto,* 2d ed. Catálogo de la Muestra Realizada en el Museo de Bellas Artes de Buenos Aires, Abril 1996 (Buenos Aires, 1995); and "Cultura urbana y organización del territorio," Noemí Goldman (dir.), *Nueva Historia Argentina: Revolución, República y Confederación (1806–1852)* (Buenos Aires: Sudamericana, 1999).

3. Cf. Municipalidad de la Ciudad de Buenos Aires y Universidad Nacional de Buenos Aires, *La arquitectura de Buenos Aires (1850–1880)* (Buenos Aires: 1966); Francisco J. Bullrich, "La arquitectura: el clasicismo romántico," Romero and Romero (eds.), *Buenos Aires: Historia de Cuatro Siglos*, vol. 1; Margarita Gutman and Jorge E. Hardoy, *Buenos Aires* (Madrid: Mapfre, 1992); Adrián Gorelik, *La grilla y*

el parque: espacio público y cultura urbana en Buenos Aires, 1887–1936 (Bernal: Universidad Nacional de Quilmes, 1998).

4. On this topic, see Jorge F. Liernur, "La ciudad efímera: consideraciones sobre el aspecto material de Buenos Aires, 1870–1910," Jorge F. Liernur and Graciela Silvestri (eds.), *El umbral de la metrópolis* (Buenos Aires: Sudamericana, 1993).

5. Cf. James Scobie, *Buenos Aires: del centro a los barrios, 1870–1910* (Buenos Aires: Solar/Hachette, 1977); and Bullrich, "La arquitectura."

6. The names of the neighborhoods corresponded to those of the city parishes (*parroquias*). As we shall see, the electoral districts also had the same denomination.

7. Cf. Hilda Sabato and Luis Alberto Romero, *Los trabajadores de Buenos Aires: la experiencia del mercado: 1850–1880* (Buenos Aires: Sudamericana, 1992), table 10. The original figures in República Argentina, *Primer Censo de la República Argentina, 1869* (Buenos Aires, 1872); and Ciudad de Buenos Aires, *Censo General de Población, Edificación, Comercio e Industrias de la Ciudad de Buenos Aires, 1887* (Buenos Aires, 1889), vol. 2.

8. In 1869, 50,000 workers were employed in commerce, transportation, and the service sector, and 30,000 in manufacture and the construction trades. In 1887, the figures were 100,000 and 70,000, respectively. Cf. Sabato and Romero, *Los trabajadores de Buenos Aires,* tables 25 b and c.

9. José Luis Romero, *Latinoamérica: las ciudades y las ideas* (Buenos Aires: Siglo XXI, 1976), p. 171; and "La ciudad patricia," Romero and Romero, *Buenos Aires,* pp. 309–11.

10. This section summarizes the information and interpretations included in the main literature on nineteenth-century Argentine political history, and particularly in the following books: Botana, *El orden conservador*; Natalio Botana and Ezequiel Gallo, *De la república posible a la república verdadera (1880–1910)* (Buenos Aires: Ariel, 1997); José Carlos Chiaramonte, *Ciudades, provincias, estados: orígenes de la nación argentina (1800–1846)* (Buenos Aires: Ariel, 1997) and *Nacionalismo y liberalismo económicos en la Argentina, 1860–1880* (Buenos Aires: Solar/Hachette, 1971); Halperin Donghi, *Proyecto y construcción de una nación* and *Revolución y guerra.*

11. Halperin Donghi, *Proyecto y construcción de una nación,* p. xlv.

12. *La Prensa,* Sept. 23, 1874.

13. Halperin Donghi, *Proyecto y construcción de una nación,* p. xcv.

Chapter 2: The Institutions and Networks of Civil Society

1. Bernardino Rivadavia (1780–1845) was active in the political and institutional life of Buenos Aires from 1811 to the late 1820s. He is best known as an enlightened reformer. Particularly during his period as minister of government of the Province of Buenos Aires (1821 to 1824), he introduced path-breaking and highly controversial institutional reforms that aimed at the modernization of the postcolonial society. He reached the presidency of the United Provinces of the River Plate under the ill-fated Constitution of 1826 that was rejected by

most of the provinces. After his failure in attempting to organize and preside over a united polity, he left the country and lived abroad until his death. He and his modernizing program were celebrated in Buenos Aires during the period under consideration.

2. Here I use the concept of "civil society" in a restricted sense, which does not include political institutions such as the parties or Congress, sometimes considered to be a part of civil society. In this particular case, those political institutions were closely tied to the state, and may be understood as part of its sphere of action.

3. Guerra, *Modernidad e independencias*; Pilar González Bernaldo, "La Création d'une Nation: Histoire Politique Des nouvelles appartenances culturelles dans la ville de Buenos Aires entre 1829 et 1862," Thèse de Nouveau Doctorat, Université de Paris I, 1992, and *Civilité et politique aux origines de la Nation Argentine*; Jorge Myers, *Languages of Politics: A Study of Republican Discourse in Argentina from 1820 to 1852*. Unpublished Ph.D. dissertation (Stanford University, 1997) and *Orden y virtud: el discurso republicano en el régimen rosista* (Bernal: Universidad Nacional de Quilmes, 1995).

4. Cf., for example, Gino Germani, *Política y sociedad*, ch. viii; Samuel Baily, "Las sociedades de ayuda mutua y el desarrollo de una comunidad italiana en Buenos Aires, 1858–1918," *Desarrollo Económico* (Jan.–Mar. 1982): 84; Fernando Devoto, "Participación y conflictos en las sociedades italianas de socorros mutuos," Fernando Devoto and Gianfausto Rosoli (eds.), *Inmigración italiana en la Argentina* (Buenos Aires: Biblos, 1985); Ricardo Falcón, *Los orígenes del movimiento obrero (1857–1899)* (Buenos Aires: CEAL, 1984).

5. González Bernaldo, "La création d'une nation."

6. Sociedad Tipográfica Bonaerense, *Memoria de la Comisión Directiva* (Buenos Aires, 1862).

7. González Bernaldo, "La création d'une nation," pp. 438–39. Also cf. Germani, *Política y sociedad*; Falcón, *Los orígenes del movimiento obrero*, among others.

8. *Censo General de Población, Edificación, Comercio e Industrias de la Ciudad de Buenos Aires, 1887* (Buenos Aires: Compañía Sudamericana de Billetes de Banco, 1889). This publication leaves out a large number of institutions cited in other sources, such as the press and the local directories.

9. González Bernaldo, "La création d'une nation," p. 449.

10. This section on Italian associations is based on the information and interpretations found in Baily, "Las sociedades de ayuda mutua"; Ema Cibotti, "Mutualismo y política, un estudio de caso: la sociedad Unione e Benevolenza de Buenos Aires entre 1858 y 1865," Fernando Devoto and Gianfausto Rosoli (eds.), *L'Italia nella società argentina* (Roma: Centro Studi Emigrazione, 1988); Fernando Devoto, "Las sociedades italianas de ayuda mutua en Buenos Aires y Santa Fé: ideas y problemas," *Studi Emigrazione* 21 (1984); Devoto, "Participación y conflictos"; Fernando Devoto and Alejandro Fernández, "Asociacionismo, liderazgo y participación de dos grupos étnicos en áreas urbanas de la Argentina finisecular: un enfoque comparado," Devoto and Rosoli (eds.), *L'Italia nella società argentina*.

11. In 1861, after Garibaldi's victory in Sicily and Calabria, Vittorio Emma-

nuele became king of Italy, but it was only in 1870 that unification was completed. On September 20, 1870, Italian troops entered Rome and the city was designated capital of the new nation.

12. The basic argument and the quoted words are taken from Cibotti, "Mutualismo y política, un estudio de caso."

13. Sabato and Cibotti, "Hacer política en Buenos Aires."

14. Falcón, *Los orígenes del movimiento obrero*, p. 29.

15. The information on the Sociedad Tipográfica Bonaerense included here comes from the following: Silvia Badoza, "Typographical Workers and Their Mutualist Experience: The Case of the Sociedad Tipográfica Bonaerense, 1857–80," Jeremy Adelman (ed.), *Essays in Argentine Labour History, 1870–1930* (Houndmills and London: Macmillan, 1992); Falcón, *Los orígenes del movimiento obrero*; González Bernaldo, "La création d'une nation"; Sebastián Marotta, *El movimiento sindical argentino*, 2 vols. (Buenos Aires: Líbera, 1975); Félix de Ugarteche, *La imprenta argentina: sus orígenes y desarrollo* (Buenos Aires: Talleres Gráficos Canals, 1929).

16. Memoria de la Sociedad Tipográfica Bonaerense, presented in May 1864, cited in Ugarteche, *La imprenta argentina*, 441.

17. Marotta, *El movimiento sindical argentino*, vol. 1, p. 26. The foundation of the society was contemporary to that of similar institutions in Brazil and Chile.

18. Falcón, *Los orígenes del movimiento obrero*, pp. 105–6; Vicente Cutolo, *Nuevo diccionario biográfico argentino* (Buenos Aires: Ed. Elche, 1985).

19. Ugarteche, *La imprenta argentina*, p. 464.

20. Slavery was definitively abolished in Argentina by the Constitution of 1853.

21. Oscar Chamosa, "Asociaciones africanas de Buenos Aires, 1823–1880: introducción a la sociabilidad de una comunidad marginada," Tesis de licenciatura, Universidad de Luján, 1995 (unpublished); González Bernaldo, "La création d'une nation."

22. Ricardo González Leandri, "La Construcción Histórica de una Profesión: Asociaciones e Instituciones Médicas en Buenos Aires: 1852–1895." Unpublished Ph.D. thesis, Universidad Complutense de Madrid, 1997.

23. Enrique Puccia, *Breve historia del carnaval porteño* (Buenos Aires: Municipalidad de la Ciudad de Buenos Aires, 1974).

24. See Oscar Chamosa's excellent article "La 'sociabilidad festiva' a través de las asociaciones negras de Buenos Aires, 1850–1880," paper read at the symposium on "Poder político, sociabilidad y espacio simbólico en contextos latinoamericanos," Tandil, May 1996. Also his "Asociaciones africanas de Buenos Aires."

25. *La Broma*, Aug. 1, 1878, cited in Chamosa, "La 'sociabilidad festiva.'"

26. *La Tribuna*, Apr. 12, 1865.

27. Ernesto Quesada, "El Periodismo Argentino (1877–1883)," *Nueva Revista de Buenos Aires* 3 (1883): vol. 9, p. 87.

28. *Censo General de Población, Edificación, Comercio e Industrias de la Ciudad de Buenos Aires, 1887*, vol. 2, pp. 545 ff.

29. In 1880 Paris, for example, with a population of two million, the circulation reached 640,000 daily copies. See Philip Nord, *The Republican Moment:*

Struggles for Democracy in Nineteenth Century France (Cambridge, Mass.: Harvard University Press, 1995), p. 207.

30. Quesada, "El Periodismo Argentino," p. 75.

31. Cf. República Argentina, *Primer Censo de la República Argentina, 1869* (Buenos Aires, 1872); and *Censo General de Población, Edificación, Comercio e Industrias de la Ciudad de Buenos Aires, 1887.* In 1869, the percentage of the literate among the total adult population reached 62 percent (Sabato and Romero, *Los trabajadores de Buenos Aires).*

32. *La Tribuna,* Sept. 12, 1875.

33. "A Newspaper 'Mania'" corresponds to *La Tribuna,* June 14, 1864.

34. This section on the political press is based on the information available in: Quesada, "El periodismo argentino"; C. Galván Moreno, *El periodismo argentino* (Buenos Aires: Ed. Claridad, 1944); Guillermo Furlong, "El periodismo entre los años 1860 y 1930," Academia Nacional de la Historia, *Historia Argentina Contemporánea, 1862–1930,* vol. 2, 2d section (Buenos Aires: El Ateneo, 1966); Tulio Halperin Donghi, *José Hernández y sus mundos* (Buenos Aires: Sudamericana, 1985); *Censo General de Población, Edificación, Comercio e Industrias de la Ciudad de Buenos Aires, 1887.* An interesting outlook on the press edited by women is Francine Masiello (comp.), *La mujer y el espacio público: el periodismo femenino en la Argentina del siglo XIX* (Buenos Aires: Feminaria Editora, 1994).

35. Dalmacio Vélez Sársfield (1801–75) had a long and steady career both as a scholar and a government official. He served in various cabinet posts, was the author of the civil code, and collaborated in the code of commerce. Héctor Varela (1832–91) and his brother Mariano (1834–92) also had intense public lives. They were sons of a renowned writer and intellectual who lived in exile during the years of the Rosas regime and was assassinated by its partisans. Both of them belonged to the Partido Autonomista. Mariano reached high posts in various administrations, while Hector remained a secondary political figure but a very popular man among the Buenos Aires public (see Chapter 7).

36. José C. Paz (1842–1912) was an active member of the political circles of Buenos Aires.

37. Manuel Bilbao (1827–95) was a Chilean writer who lived many years in exile in Argentina.

38. On *El Mosquito,* see Ema Cibotti, "*El Mosquito* de Enrique Stein, un ejemplo de periodismo faccioso en la década del 80," paper read at the Cuartas Jornadas Interescuelas/Departamentos de Historia de las Universidades Nacionales, Mar del Plata, 1993.

39. The literature on immigration and immigrant groups includes many references to the newspapers published by those groups. The following is a select list of the works that have been particularly useful for our study: Samuel Baily, "The Role of Two Newspapers and the Assimilation of the Italians in Buenos Aires and São Paulo, 1893–1913," *International Migration Review* 12, no. 3 (1978); Ema Cibotti, "Periodismo político y política periodística: la construcción de una opinión italiana en el Buenos Aires finisecular," *Entrepasados,* no. 7 (1994) and "1880–1890: Una década de prensa italiana en Buenos Aires: liderazgo y trayectoria pública de sus principales hombres," Master's thesis, FLACSO, Buenos Aires, 1995; Beatriz Guaragna and Norma Trinchitella, "La revolución de 1880 según la

óptica de los periódicos de la colectividad italiana," paper read at the Jornadas Sobre Inmigración, Pluralismo e Integración, Buenos Aires, 1984; Alejandro and Fabián Herrero, "A propósito de la prensa española en Buenos Aires: el estudio de un caso: *El Correo Español (1872–1875),*" *Anuario de Estudios Americanos* 49, no. 1 (1992); Roberto Montes, "*El Correo Español* y las prácticas de intervención de la colonia española en la esfera pública porteña: Buenos Aires, 1872–1875," mimeo, Buenos Aires, 1993.

40. The expression comes from *Los Debates,* Apr. 1, 1852. Cited in José Campobassi, *Mitre y su Época* (Buenos Aires: EUDEBA, 1980), p. 63.

41. Halperin Donghi, *José Hernández y sus mundos.*

42. The quotes are from *La Nación,* Sept. 17, 1874, but similar expressions are found in other papers throughout that decade.

43. *La Nación,* Jan. 4, 1870. On the history of *La Nación,* I have followed the interpretation by Julio Ramos, *Desencuentros de la modernidad en América Latina: literatura y política en el siglo XIX* (Mexico City: Fondo de Cultura Económica, 1989). See also Ricardo Sidicaro, *La política mirada desde arriba: las ideas del diario* La Nación, *1909–1989* (Buenos Aires: Sudamericana, 1993).

44. Till 1867, the regular price for a monthly subscription to a daily was around $40 (*pesos moneda corriente*); one issue was $3.-. That year, *La República* introduced two innovations: street vendors who sold the paper at $1 per issue, and lower prices ($25 per monthly subscription). The other papers followed suit. (At the time, the average daily wage of an unskilled worker was between $20 and $30.)

45. The expression "The Fearsome Power of Journalism" belongs to Quesada, "El periodismo argentino," p. 74.

46. Tim Duncan, "La prensa política: 'Sudamérica,' 1884–1892," Gustavo Ferrari and Ezequiel Gallo (comps.), *La Argentina del Ochenta al Centenario* (Buenos Aires: Sudamericana, 1980); Ramos, *Desencuentros de la modernidad.* On press censorship, see Alberto Lettieri, "La construcción del consenso en los inicios del sistema político moderno argentino (1862–1868)," *Anuario de Estudios Americanos* 52, no. 2 (1995).

47. Duncan, "La Prensa Política"; Paula Alonso, "'En la primavera de la historia': el discurso político del roquismo en la década del ochenta a través de su prensa," *Boletín del Instituto de Historia Argentina y Americana, "Dr. Emilio Ravignani,"* no. 15 (1997); Halperin Donghi, *José Hernández y sus mundos.*

48. Cibotti, "Periodismo político y política periodística"; Montes, "*El Correo Español* y las prácticas."

49. *La Tribuna,* Feb. 2, 1878.

50. José de San Martín (1778–1850) was one of the two main military figures of the South American wars of independence against Spain (the other one being Simón Bolívar). He became one of Argentina's top national heroes.

51. *La Tribuna,* Feb. 24, 1878.

52. *El Nacional,* Mar. 3, 1878.

53. *La Tribuna,* Oct. 3, 1878.

54. Alberto Lettieri, *La formación del sistema político moderno: legitimidad, opinión pública y discurso parlamentario: Argentina, 1862–1868* (Buenos Aires: Cuadernos del Instituto Ravignani no. 8, 1995) and "La construcción del consenso."

Chapter 3: On Election Days

1. Every year, elections were held to choose municipal electors, provincial representatives, and senators. Every other year, half of the House was renewed; every three years there were indirect elections for senators, and every six, for president and vice president of the republic. Constitutional convention members were elected twice, in 1860 and 1870. Also, when an election was partially or totally invalidated, complementary elections were held. For example: in 1860, municipal electors were chosen in January, provincial representatives and senators in March, June, and July, convention members in August, substitute municipal electors in November and December, and national representatives also in December. Throughout the decade, between four and seven elections were held per year. In 1870, there were nine: to elect national representatives in January and again in June, provincial representatives and senators in May and again in July and August, convention members in April, and municipal electors in June, November, and December. For information on elections, see Archivo General de la Nacion, Sala X, *Elecciones. Actas, Padrones y Antecedentes* and *Elecciones Nacionales*, files for the corresponding years, and newspapers *La Tribuna* and *La Nación*.

2. The basic information in this section comes from Germán Tjarks, "Las elecciones salteñas de 1876 (un estudio del fraude electoral)," *Anuario del Departamento de Historia de la Facultad de Filosofía y Humanidades de la Universidad Nacional de Córdoba* 1, no. 1 (1963); and Ezequiel Ortega, *¿Quiera el pueblo votar? Historia electoral argentina desde la Revolución de Mayo a la Ley Sáenz Peña, 1810–1912* (Bahía Blanca: Giner editor, 1963).

3. These sections were integrated into a single district by the law of 1863, organized in four districts by the law of 1864, belonged to the larger provincial district by virtue of the laws of 1873 and 1877, or formed separate districts for municipal elections.

4. Cited in Tjarks, "Las elecciones salteñas," p. 425.

5. *La Tribuna*, Jan. 17, 1860.

6. Ibid., July 31, 1860.

7. The information comes from the electoral accounts available in the files of the Archivo General de la Nación, Sala X, *Elecciones: Padrones, Actas y Antecedentes*, Years 1864 to 1880 and *Elecciones. Policía.* 1854 to 1865 and 1866 to 1873.

8. *La Tribuna*, Feb. 14 and Mar. 29, 1864. The expression comes from Ariosto's *Orlando Furioso* and is used generally to denote tumultuous, confusing, and violent situations.

9. Félix Armesto, *Mitristas y alsinistas* (Buenos Aires: Ed. Sudestada, 1969), pp. 15 ff.

10. Archivo General de la Nación, Sala X, 30–10–6. *Elecciones: Padrones, Actas, Antecedentes.* 1874.

11. *La Tribuna*, Feb. 4, 1874.

12. *El Nacional*, Mar. 28, 1877.

13. *La Tribuna*, Mar. 1, 1864.

14. In Brazil, for example, the Church played an important role in the electoral life of this period. See Richard Graham, *Patronage and Politics in Nine-*

teenth-Century Brazil (Stanford: Stanford University Press, 1990). Pilar Gonzá-lez Bernaldo mentions the role of the parish priests in the political organization of the Buenos Aires *parroquias* between 1852 and 1862. I found no trace of this in the following decades. (González Bernaldo, "La création d'une nation.")

15. Archivo General de la Nación, Sala X, 30–10–6, *Elecciones: Padrones, Actas, Antecedentes, 1873–74*. Reply by the *ministro de gobierno*, Amancio Al-corta, to a letter addressed to him by the archbishop of Buenos Aires, Mons. Federico Aneiros, Jan. 24, 1874. As early as 1857, there is a similar request by Mons. Escalada to the provincial government, which was also denied. Cited by Carlos Heras, "El Proyecto de 1857 Estableciendo el voto secreto en la Pro-vincia de Buenos Aires," *Trabajos y Comunicaciones* (La Plata), no. 13 (1965): p. 111.

16. See, for example, Carlos Heras, "Las elecciones de legisladores provincia-les en marzo de 1864," *Trabajos y Comunicaciones* (La Plata), no. 5 (1955).

17. See, for example, *La Nación*, Apr. 4, 1874, and *La Tribuna*, Dec. 2, 1873, and Jan. 1, 1875.

18. Heras, "Las Elecciones de legisladores provinciales," p. 75.

19. Archivo General de la Nación, Sala 10, 32–6–3. *Policía: Elecciones 1866–1873*. Informe de Mateo Pacheco al Jefe del Depto. General de Policía, Don Cayetano Cazón.

20. *La Tribuna*, Mar. 19, 1869.

21. Ibid., Jan. 3, 1873.

22. Armesto, *Mitristas y alsinistas*, pp. 19–20.

23. Ibid. The persons named by Armesto were all young men of the proper-tied classes.

24. *La Tribuna*, Jan. 22, 1874.

25. Armesto, *Mitristas y alsinistas*, p. 17.

26. *La Tribuna*, Apr. 1, 1864.

27. Ibid., July 17, 1874.

28. These calculations are based on the information available in Archivo General de la Nación, Sala X, *Elecciones: Padrones, Actas, Antecedentes*, Years 1864 to 1880, and *Elecciones: Policía*, Years 1866–73 and 1854–65.

29. Cf. Ternavasio, "Nuevo régimen representativo y expansión de la fron-tera política," p. 67; "Hacia un régimen de unanimidad"; and "Política y Elecciones en Buenos Aires, 1820–1850." Tesis de doctorado, Facultad de Filo-sofía y Letras, Universidad de Buenos Aires, 1998.

30. The figures for the potential voters (native or naturalized adult men) have been estimated by interpolation from the census data for Buenos Aires in 1854, 1869, and 1887. The proportion of actual to potential voters in this case is generally lower that those available for other Latin American countries. See, among others, José Valenzuela, *Democratización vía reforma: la expansión del su-fragio en Chile* (Buenos Aires: Ed. del IDES, 1985); and Graham, *Patronage and Politics*.

31. Carlos Heras, "Un agitado proceso electoral en Buenos Aires," *Trabajos y Comunicaciones* (La Plata), no. 4 (1954): p. 80; and *La Tribuna*, Apr. 1, 1864.

32. Julio A. Costa: *Entre dos batallas* (Buenos Aires: Talleres Gráficos Mario, 1927), p. 192.

33. Cámara de Diputados de la Nación, *Diario de Sesiones, 1873*, Aug. 6, 1873; *La Tribuna*, Jan. 24, 1874.

34. Registers for other years during the period are available, but they have information regarding only name, address, and little more.

35. The literacy rates for the city as a whole were the following: In 1869, 50 percent of the men, 47 percent of the women, and 62 percent of all the adults (men and women) could read and write. By 1887, 64 percent of the men and 57 percent of the women were literate. See Chapter 2.

36. There is no information available on the occupational structure by parish, but the data regarding registered citizens may be compared with those of the occupational structure of the total native male population for 1869 and 1887. Although the categories are not the same, particularly for our Group 1, the information may be used to compare, for Groups 2 and 3, the occupational distribution among the citizens inscribed in the register and the total native adult men.

Chapter 4: The Electoral Machines

1. For the conflictive period from 1821 to 1835, as well as for the unanimity system implemented in the years of the Rosas regime, see Ternavasio, "Nuevo régimen representativo y expansión de la frontera política"; "Hacia un régimen de unanimidad."

2. On the political clubs in the period from 1852 to 1861, see Pilar González Bernaldo, "Los clubes electorales durante la secesión del Estado de Buenos Aires (1852–1861): La articulación de dos lógicas de representación política en el seno de la esfera pública porteña," Sabato (coord.), *ciudadanía política y formación de las naciones,* and her doctoral thesis, "La création d'une nation."

3. The expression belongs to Halperin Donghi, *Proyecto y construcción de una nación,* p. lii, and refers to the *Partido de la Libertad,* led by Bartolomé Mitre, during the late 1850s and early 1860s.

4. The initial purpose of the clubs was to exert electoral influence beyond the local struggle that took place in each parish. They were then called "opinion clubs." They played a key role in the elections of 1856/57, bringing together the various groups that rejected the influence of Urquiza and his followers in Buenos Aires. Cf., among others, González Bernaldo, "La création d'une nation," and "Los clubes electorales"; James Scobie, *La lucha por la consolidación de la nacionalidad argentina, 1852–62* (Buenos Aires: Hachette, 1964).

5. *La Tribuna*, Mar. 24, 1860.

6. Cristián Gazmuri, *El "48" Chileno: igualitarios, reformistas, radicales, masones y bomberos* (Santiago de Chile: Ed. Universitaria, 1992) and "La influencia del club republicano francés en las formas de sociabilidad política chilenas de la segunda mitad del siglo XIX," Maurice Agulhon, Bernardino Bravo Lira, et al., *Formas de sociabilidad en Chile, 1840–1940* (Santiago de Chile: Ed Vivaria, 1992); Carmen McEvoy, *La utopía republicana: ideales y realidades en la formación de la cultura política peruana, 1871–1919* (Lima: Pontificia Universidad Católica del Perú, 1997).

7. *El Nacional*, Feb. 17, 1862.

8. Scobie, *La lucha por la consolidación;* and Carlos Martínez, *Alsina y Alem: porteñismo y milicias* (Buenos Aires: Ediciones Culturales Argentinas, 1990). See also *El Nacional* and *La Tribuna,* first semester of 1862.

9. *The Standard,* quoted in *La Tribuna,* Feb. 5, 1868.

10. I have based this description on *La Tribuna* of February and March 1868; Bonifacio del Carril, *La combinación Urquiza/Alsina en las elecciones de 1868* (Buenos Aires: Emecé, 1982); Julio Costa, *Entre dos batallas;* and Olga Gamboni, *Adolfo Alsina: gobernador de la Provincia de Buenos Aires y conquistador del desierto* (La Plata: Imprenta de la Universidad Nacional de La Plata, 1989).

11. Leandro Alem (1842–96) and Aristóbulo del Valle (1847–96) had very visible political and public careers. They were several times elected to different government posts. As members of the Partido Autonomista, they were active in the electoral struggles of the 1860s and, particularly, the 1870s. They founded several clubs within the party, and finally split from it by creating the Partido Republicano. They both retreated from the front line during the years of the first of Roca's presidencies (1880–86) but came back in the late 1880s to oppose Roca's successor, Miguel Juárez Celman. They were among the main leaders of the revolution staged against him in 1890 and founders of the Unión Cívica Radical, a new party with a long life (today, it is one of the two largest parties in Argentina).

12. Accounts of other club meetings in *La Tribuna,* Mar. 6, 1860; Dec. 22, 1868; Jan. 1, Jan. 16, and Mar. 3, 1869; Mar. 11, Apr. 21, May 5, and Oct. 14, 1873; and Mar. 10, 1880; and in *El Nacional,* Mar. 12, Mar. 16, and Oct. 4, 1877, among others. Although the *mitristas* were less inclined to divisions than the *alsinistas,* they too had their own episodes of internal dissent. Cf. *La Nación,* Mar. 10 and 24, 1874.

13. These words were frequently used in the accounts made by the press of the club meetings, sometimes with positive, sometimes with negative undertones. See, for example, *La Tribuna,* Jan. 16 and Mar. 21, 1874.

14. Examples of these two different images of the clubs in *La Tribuna,* Jan. 22 and 23, 1864; Nov. 22, 1865; Apr. 21 and May 3, 1873. *La Nación* portrayed similar images.

15. *La Tribuna,* Jan. 16, 1869.

16. Carlos Heras, "Un agitado proceso electoral," p. 93.

17. *La Tribuna,* Mar. 25, 1855; and *El Nacional,* Jan. 10, 1860. See also Martínez, *Alsina y Alem,* pp. 28–29.

18. *La Tribuna,* Mar. 28, 1855.

19. González, "Los clubes electorales."

20. Bartolomé Mitre and Adolfo Alsina successively organized the clubs Constitucional, Argentino, and de Guardias Nacionales to fight against the old leadership, which—they denounced—"belong[s] to history." They rejected "the aristocracy of money made fatter by the blood of the people beheaded by Rosas" as well as the "hereditary patricians who fought against him." *La Tribuna,* Mar. 11, 1856, quoted in Martínez, *Alsina y Alem,* p. 35.

21. Thus the Club Libertad decided not to present its own centralized list of candidates; rather, it would operate in the parishes to favor certain names and then support the resulting lists. The Club increased the number of members of

the Directive Committee to twelve, one for each parish in which it hoped to gain electoral influence. Cf. Martínez, *Alsina y Alem*, ch. 4.

22. Quoted in Heras, "El Proyecto de 1857, pp. 112–13." In 1865 in Balvanera, several neighbors complained against one Ramón Rivas, who claimed to be the secretary of "the genuine parish club." They argued that "the parish may have the number of clubs it wishes." *La Tribuna*, Dec. 29, 1860.

23. The newspapers of the time bring many accounts of the foundation of different parish clubs in every neighborhood.

24. See, for example, *La Tribuna*, Jan. 22, 1864. Also Heras, "Las elecciones de legisladores provinciales," pp. 68–69.

25. *La Nación*, Jan. 11, 19, and 21, 1866.

26. *La Tribuna*, Nov. 21, 1869; and *La Nación*, Nov. 18, 1869.

27. See *La Nación*, Dec. 5, 12, and 14, 1869; and *La Tribuna*, Mar. 28, 1869.

28. *La Tribuna*, Jan. 20, 1878.

29. *El Nacional*, Nov. 19, 1877.

30. The national electoral law of 1863 established that, in each parish of the city, the committee in charge of drafting the register of potential voters had to be formed by the justice of the peace and two neighbors appointed by the executive. Every year, the committees worked on Sundays and holidays for a month and a half after the first Sunday of October. In 1873, a new regulation established that from then onward the neighbors to sit in the committee had to be appointed by the provincial legislature. This clause was changed again by the law of 1877: the neighbors were to be designated by lots, and the procedure would be overseen by the tribunal that was responsible for the ballot counting. Cf. Heras, "Un agitado proceso," pp. 70–71; and Tjarks, "Las elecciones salteñas, pp. 422–23.

31. Archivo General de La Nación, Archivo y Colección Dardo Rocha, Legajo 291.

32. See, for example, the accounts of the Club General Belgrano of Balvanera in *La Tribuna*, Jan. 31, 1878. The political clubs also organized fund collections among their members. See, for example, Archivo General de la Nación, Archivo y colección Dardo Rocha, Legajo 291.

33. *La Tribuna*, Apr. 12, 1874; *El Nacional*, Nov. 12, 1877; *La Bola de Hierro*, Mar. 19, 1879.

34. The newspapers of those decades abound in ads published by the parish clubs announcing the failure of a planned meeting and convening the members to a new one.

35. See, for example, *La Tribuna*, Jan. 12, 24, and 26, 1864, and Mar. 19 and Aug. 12, 1874; *El Nacional*, June 4 and Nov. 6 and 12, 1877.

36. I have made a partial reconstruction of the occupational and age composition and literacy of the participants in several parish club meetings in the years 1876 to 1878. The names of the assistants were found in the press of those years, and the information regarding each of them comes from the voting register of 1878.

37. *La Tribuna*, Apr. 16, 1869. In the voting register of 1867, Guillermo Silva is listed as being thirty-one years old, dedicated to "commerce," enrolled in the

First Regiment of the national guard. He was also a member of the registering committee of La Piedad. See Voting Register of La Piedad in *La Tribuna*, Feb. 19, 1867.

38. González, "Los clubes electorales," p. 145.

39. *La Tribuna*, Jan. 10, 1864, and Apr. 22, 1880. The newspapers of the time abound in denunciations of the manipulation of public employment on the part of the political parties. Each party accused its rival of the same practice. See, among others, *La Tribuna*, Jan. and Feb. 1864, and Feb. and Mar. 1869; *El Nacional*, Oct. and Dec. 1877; and *La Nación*, Apr. and Aug. 1874, and Mar. 1879. See also Heras, "Un agitado proceso electoral."

40. *La Tribuna*, Jan. 18, 1864. The accusation was included in a letter sent to the paper by a group of dismissed employees.

41. Ibid., Jan. 10 and Feb. 13, 1864.

42. Ibid., July 8, 1868. The expression belongs to Lucio V. Mansilla.

43. Ibid., Feb. 27, 1869. On election day, also in Balvanera, the journeymen of the Western Railway were present at the polls, led by the stationmaster (*La Tribuna*, Mar. 19, 1869).

44. The information on Elordi comes from different sources. In the biographical dictionaries presently in circulation he is briefly mentioned, but there is no reference to his political life. The newspapers of the time as well as the literature on political history include some data on his political career, which has been used here.

45. Adolfo Enrique Rodríguez, *Cuatrocientos años de policía en Buenos Aires* (Buenos Aires: Editorial Policial, 1981), p. 122.

46. See, for example, the denunciations published in *La Nación*, Mar. 8 and Aug. 2, 1874; and *La Tribuna*, Mar. 30, 1869 and July 31, 1873.

47. Between 1860 and 1880, the Buenos Aires chiefs of police were Cayetano Cazón (1861–67), Enrique O'Gorman (1867–74), Enrique B. Moreno (1874–75), Manuel Rocha (1875–77), Domingo Viejobueno (1877–79), José I. Garmendia (1879–80), and Julio S. Dantas (1880). Cf. Rodríguez, *Cuatrocientos años*, pp. 73–74.

48. Cf. Alberto Lettieri, *La República de la Opinión: política y sociedad civil en Buenos Aires entre 1852 y 1862* (Buenos Aires: Biblos, 1999).

49. Martínez, *Alsina y Alem*, pp. 67–68.

50. *La Nación Argentina*, Jan. 4, 1864; and *La Tribuna*, Jan. 10, 1864.

51. Martínez, *Alsina y Alem*, pp. 129–30.

52. *La Tribuna*, Apr. 10, 1873.

53. See, among others, the articles by Carlos Heras cited above.

Chapter 5: The Elections

1. During the long years of the Rosas regime, the elections in Buenos Aires were noncompetitive. There was one official list of candidates, dutifully voted by the people of the province. Cf. Ternavasio, "Hacia un régimen de unanimidad."

2. "Reglamento de los Clubes Parroquiales," Archivo General de la Nación, Archivo y Colección Dardo Rocha, Legajo 309, no date.

3. The citations are from *La Tribuna*, Jan. 21, 1864. Similar expressions may be found in the rest of the newspapers of the period.

4. González Bernaldo, "Los clubes electorales."

5. This practice had been typical of the electoral ways of the 1820s. Cf. Ternavasio, "Nuevo régimen representativo y expansión de la frontera política."

6. In 1864 and 1874, the lists responded strictly to the two parties. In the elections for national representatives of February 1864, the list presented by the Club del Pueblo (*mitrista*) defeated the list of the Club Libertad (*alsinista*). In February 1874, the *mitrista* Nationalist Party (represented by several electoral clubs) confronted the *alsinista* Autonomist Party, and the results were disputed. In 1866 the two opposing lists belonged to the *autonomismo* (split into two clubs); in 1869 and 1870, a group of *autonomistas* joined the *mitristas* against the rest of the party; in 1877, a coalition of both parties confronted a new party created by former *autonomistas*. These are just a few examples of a pattern that was recurrent throughout the period.

7. A detailed reconstruction of these events is in Heras, "Un agitado proceso electoral" and "Las elecciones de legisladores provinciales." The description that follows is based on those articles and in several accounts published by *La Nación Argentina* and *La Tribuna* of that year.

8. *La Tribuna*, Apr. 24, 1864.

9. Ibid., Aug. 18, 1864.

10. On the *mitrista* revolution of 1874, see, among others, Armesto, *Mitristas y alsinistas*; José C. Campobassi, *Mitre y su época* (Buenos Aires: EUDEBA, 1980); Julio A. Noble, *Cien años: dos vidas* (Buenos Aires: Bases, 1960); Ortega, *¿Quiera el pueblo votar?*; Adolfo Saldías, *Buenos Aires en el Centenario*, 3 vols. (Buenos Aires: Hyspamérica, 1988), vol. 3.

11. Bartolomé Mitre, *Arengas* (Buenos Aires: Ed. Carlos Casavalle, 1889), p. 490. The *mitrista* press abounds in arguments similar to those expressed by Mitre in his revolutionary pronouncement.

12. *La Tribuna*, Nov. 17, 1874.

13. According to Adolfo Saldías, the government forces amounted to 35,000 men, while the rebels had only 13,800 men. Cf. Saldías, *Buenos Aires en el Centenario*, vol. 3, p. 119.

14. Cited by *La Tribuna*, Dec. 5, 1874.

15. Cf. Halperin Donghi, *José Hernández y sus mundos*.

16. *La Tribuna*, July 27, 1873.

17. Armesto, *Mitristas y alsinistas*, p. 31.

18. *La Nación*, Mar. 10, 1874. On the same day, *La Tribuna* also reported that the meeting had a large attendance.

19. *La Tribuna*, Mar. 10, 1874.

20. *El Correo Español*, Mar. 10, 1874.

21. *La Nación*, Apr. 17, 1874.

22. *La Tribuna*, Apr. 17, 1874.

23. Ibid., Apr. 21, 1874.

24. Armesto, *Mitrisas y alsinistas*, p. 31; and Lucio V. López, *La gran aldea* (Buenos Aires: EUDEBA, 1960), p. 28. Armesto and López actually refer to the "most poshy ladies of Buenos Aires," but the presence of a wider social spectrum of fe-

male fans is visible in the accounts of the public demonstrations that took place every year on Mitre's birthday, and every time he returned to the city after a long trip.

25. See, for example, *La Tribuna*, Mar. and Apr. 1874; also Sept. 1873. See also Hebe Blasi, "Las elecciones presidenciales de 1874 a través del periodismo," *Trabajos y Comunicaciones* (La Plata), no. 20 (1970): p. 55.

26. See, for example, *La Nación*, Mar. 24, Apr. 18 and 23, 1874; and *La Tribuna*, Sept. 17, 1878.

27. *La Tribuna*, May 7, 1878. The names are obviously false, as both expressions are a play on words and have a double, saucy, meaning.

28. Cf. Carlos Heras, "El intento de reforma electoral de 1856 en la provincia de Buenos Aires," *Trabajos y Comunicaciones* (La Plata), no. 12 (1864) and "El proyecto de 1857."

29. The other two issues that occupied a central place in the legislative discussions were the creation of a civic register and the composition of the polling and scrutiny authorities. Cf. República Argentina, Congreso Nacional, *Diario de Sesiones de la Cámara de Diputados del año 1863* (Buenos Aires: Imprenta del Siglo, 1866).

30. República Argentina, *Diario de Sesiones, 1863*, pp. 706–7.

31. Provincia de Buenos Aires, *Diario de Sesiones de la Cámara de Diputados, 1864* (Buenos Aires: Imprenta de "La República," 1884), p. 118. The words are those of Rep. Dardo Rocha.

32. Ibid., pp. 116–24, 127–39, and 145–49.

33. República Argentina, Congreso Nacional, *Diario de Sesiones de la Honorable Cámara de Diputados. Año 1873*, pp. 609–11.

34. Some of these men later became extremely critical of the voting system they now defended. A new political regime was established in 1880 that set in motion a highly developed electoral machine that left the opposition with almost no chance of winning an election. Bernardo de Irigoyen and Aristóbulo del Valle, no longer in the official party, raised their voices against the electoral corruption of the regime and denounced the public vote as one of the pillars of the system. Cf., among others, Botana, *El orden conservador*.

35. República Argentina, *Diario de Sesiones, 1873*, pp. 619–21.

36. Ibid., pp. 660 ff.

37. *La Tribuna*, July 8, 1873.

38. República Argentina, *Diario de Sesiones, 1873*, p. 577.

39. See Provincia de Buenos Aires, *Actas de la Asamblea Constituyente de la Provincia de Buenos Aires* (Buenos Aires: 1870–73), vol. 2, pp. 85, 92.

40. Provincia de Buenos Aires, *Actas de la Asamblea Constituyente*, vol. 1, pp. 169 ff. Cf. Sabato y Palti, "¿Quién votaba en Buenos Aires?"; and Elías Palti, "Orden político y ciudadanía: problemas y debates en el liberalismo argentino del siglo XIX," *Estudios Interdisciplinarios de América Latina y el Caribe*, vol. 2 (1994).

41. Provincia de Buenos Aires, *Actas de la Asamblea Constituyente*, vol. 2, pp. 82–83.

42. Ibid., pp. 94–96.

43. The line belongs to representative Varela, and it was pronounced during

the debate on the provincial electoral law of 1864. Provincia de Buenos Aires, *Diario de Sesiones, 1864*, p. 117.

44. Provincia de Buenos Aires, *Actas de la Asamblea Constituyente*, vol. 2, p. 113.

45. Ibid., vol. 1, pp. 277–78.

46. Ibid., vol. 2, p. 246.

47. See, for example, the debates on the electoral laws that took place in the provincial legislature and in the press during 1875 and 1876.

Chapter 6: Political Citizenship and the Suffrage

1. Cf. Marshall, "Citizenship and Social Classes."

2. This point is superbly argued for the Anglo-Saxon case in Morgan, *Inventing the People*.

3. Botana, *El orden conservador*.

Chapter 7: The People Take to the Streets

1. See, for example, the now classic book by Sommi, *La Revolución del 90*.

2. *La Tribuna*, Mar. 8, 1873 (on the occasion of a meeting of university students).

3. *La Nación Argentina*, June 3, 1864.

4. *El Nacional*, May 30, 1864.

5. Ibid., May 31, 1864.

6. Ibid., June 1, 1864.

7. *El Pueblo*, June 1, 1864.

8. *La Tribuna*, June 4, 1864.

9. *El Nacional*, June 6, 1864.

10. *El Pueblo*, June 2, 1864.

11. *La Nación Argentina*, June 5, 1864.

12. Ibid., May 31, 1864.

13. *El Pueblo*, June 15, 20, and 28, 1864.

14. *La Nación*, Dec. 10, 1878.

15. Ibid., Dec. 15 and 17, 1878.

16. *La Prensa*, Dec. 18, 1878.

17. See, for example, *La Tribuna*, June 5, 1864; *La Nación*, Mar. 12, 1871; *La Tribuna*, Mar. 11, 1873; and *La Política*, Feb. 27, 1878.

18. *El Pueblo*, June 7, 1864.

19. Others were the Alegría, Coliseo, and Argentino. See Ricardo M. Llanes, *Teatros de Buenos Aires* (Buenos Aires: Municipalidad de la Ciudad de Buenos Aires, 1968).

20. *La Tribuna*, June 12 and 14, 1864.

21. Ibid., Sept. 16, 1870. The debate around the death penalty was recurrent in the press. In this case, the demonstration succeeded in its purpose, and the governor granted his pardon to the sentenced man.

22. Ibid., Mar. 1, 1875.

23. *El Porteño*, Dec. 19, 1878.

24. *La Nación*, Dec. 19, 1878.

25. Ibid., Dec. 19, 1878.

26. See Chapter 1. Also Aliata, "La ciudad regular," pp. 37–61; and Gorelik, *La grilla y el parque*.

27. *El Pueblo*, June 2, 1864; and *La Tribuna*, June 7, 1864.

28. *La Prensa*, Mar. 13, 1871. See also Miguel Angel Scenna, *Cuando murió Buenos Aires: 1871* (Buenos Aires: Ed. La Bastilla, 1974), pp. 236 ff.

29. *La Tribuna*, Mar. 1, 1875.

30. *La Nación, La Patria* and *El Porteño*, Dec. 19, 1878.

31. The newspapers mentioned the social condition of the participants only when they were reporting a political meeting. In those cases, they generally underlined the "distinguished" quality of the audience, which contrasted with plebeian elements present at the polls (see Chapter 5).

32. The data available on the participants of the demonstration of 1875 against the Jesuits corroborate this impression for that particular case (see Chapter 8). The available information on the mutual aid societies, the Masonic lodges, and the associations that nucleated the trades show that most of their membership was recruited among small and medium-size property owners involved in commerce, the service sector, and some of the professions, as well as white- and blue-collar workers and artisans. To a lesser extent, they also included journeymen, domestic servants, and other nonqualified workers. See Chapter 2.

33. Cutolo, *Nuevo diccionario biográfico*; Enrique Udaondo, *Diccionario biográfico argentino* (Buenos Aires: Coni, 1938); Jacinto Yaben, *Biografías argentinas y sudamericanas* (Buenos Aires: Metrópolis, 1938).

34. *La Tribuna*, July 13, 1867. Letter sent from Paris.

35. He made an ardent defense of the republics of the Americas that had been attacked in the speech of a "very rich property owner from Neuchatel, very aristocratic." *La Tribuna*, Oct. 30, 1867. Letter sent from Paris on Sept. 20, 1867.

36. *La Tribuna*, Mar. 12, 1875.

37. Ibid., Apr. 11, 1875.

38. Ibid., Sept. and Oct. 1870.

39. Ibid., Dec. 18, 1867, Sept. 16, 1868, and Dec. 22, 1869.

40. See Chapter 2, and Chamosa, "La 'sociabilidad festiva.'"

41. Puccia, *Breve historia del carnaval porteño*.

42. On Basilio Cittadini, see Cibotti, "Periodismo político y política periodística" and "1880–1890, una década de prensa italiana." On Enrique Romero Giménez, see A. and F. Herrero, "A propósito de la prensa"; and Montes, "*El Correo Español* y las prácticas."

43. See the above-mentioned works by Ema Cibotti.

44. Sabato and Cibotti, "Hacer política en Buenos Aires."

45. For example, all the Italian leadership had a prominent participation in the commemoration of the centenary birthday of San Martin in 1878. They also were among the members of the Peace Committee created in 1880 to stop the armed confrontation between the national forces and those of the province of Buenos Aires.

46. *La Tribuna*, July 6, 1870.

47. Ibid., July 7, 1870.

48. Chacabuco and Maipú were key battles won by San Martín in the war of Independence. *El Nacional*, June 3, 1864.

49. *La Tribuna, El Pueblo,* and *El Nacional*, June 7, 1864.

50. *La Tribuna*, June 14, 1864.

51. Scenna, *Cuando murió Buenos Aires*, p. 238.

52. *La Tribuna*, Dec. 23, 1873.

53. Ibid., Mar. 1, 1875.

54. *La Nación*, Dec. 19, 1878.

55. See political information published in *La Tribuna* during the month of May 1864.

56. Ibid., June 5 and 14, 1864.

57. *El Pueblo*, July 13, 1864.

58. *La Prensa*, Mar. and Apr., 1871; Scenna, *Cuando murió Buenos Aires*.

59. See Sabato and Cibotti, *Hacer política en Buenos Aires*.

Chapter 8: A Violent Episode

1. See, among others, Guillermo Furlong, S. J., *Historia del Colegio del Salvador y de sus irradiaciones culturales y espirituales en la Ciudad de Buenos Aires, 1617–1943*, vol. 1, part 1, 1868–1943 (Buenos Aires: Colegio del Salvador, 1944), esp. pp. 75–76.

2. Ibid.

3. Cayetano Bollini (pseudonym of Carlos Brocato), *¿Quién incendió la iglesia?* (Buenos Aires: Planeta, 1988).

4. Leandro Gutiérrez, "El Incendio del Colegio del Salvador, 1875: expresión de protesta social," mimeo, Buenos Aires, 1975. See also, Trinidad Delia Chianelli and Hugo R. Galmarini, "¿Una conspiración comunista en 1875?" *Todo es Historia*, no. 102 (1975): pp. 52–69; and Falcón, *Los orígenes del movimiento obrero*.

5. *El Católico Argentino* was founded on August 1, 1874, with the purpose of "disseminating the Catholic doctrine among the people, and sustaining that doctrine with all our might." It had the protection and support of the office of the archbishop. See Cayetano Bruno, S. D. B., *Historia de la Iglesia en la Argentina*, vol. 11 (Buenos Aires: Editorial Don Bosco, 1976), p. 100.

6. Furlong, *Historia del Colegio del Salvador*, p. 73.

7. *La Tribuna*, Jan. 27, 1875.

8. *El Nacional*, Feb. 13, 1875.

9. *La Tribuna*, Feb. 16, 1875.

10. Ibid., Feb. 16 and 22, 1875; *Il Gazzetino*, Feb. 12, 1875; *Le Courrier de la Plata*, quoted in *La Época*, Feb. 18, 1875; *El Nacional*, Feb. 18, 1875.

11. *El Nacional*, Feb. 16, 1875.

12. See, for example, *La Libertad*, Feb. 17, 1875; and *La Pampa*, Feb. 27, 1875.

13. Bruno, *Historia de la Iglesia*, pp. 108–9.

14. *La Libertad*, Feb. 17, 1875.

15. Ibid.; and *La Política*, Feb. 17, 1875.

16. *La Época*, Feb. 19, 21, and 25, 1875.

17. *La Política,* Feb. 21, 1875; *La Libertad,* Feb. 20, 1875; *El Comercial,* Feb. 20, 1875.

18. *La Época,* Feb. 17 and 19, 1875; *El Comercial,* Feb. 19, 1875; *La Libertad,* Feb. 20, 1875; *El Nacional,* Feb. 18, 1875; *La Política,* Feb. 25, 1875. On the creation of the University Club, see *El Comercial,* Feb. 3 and 5, 1875.

19. The postponement was apparently caused by the fact that the country was under state of siege, which had been established after the Revolution of 1874 and lasted until February 24, 1875.

20. *La Prensa,* Feb. 26, 1875.

21. *El Español,* Feb. 27, 1875; *La Pampa,* Feb. 27, 1875; *El Comercial,* Feb. 24, 1875; Furlong, *Historia del Colegio del Salvador,* pp. 75–76.

22. *La Tribuna,* Mar. 1, 1875.

23. *La Nación,* Mar. 1, 1875. On Bernardino Rivadavia, see chapter 2, note 1. He was the ideological and intellectual author of several liberal measures aimed at modernizing the institutions of the state, among them the abolition of the religious orders.

24. *La Tribuna,* Mar. 1, 1875.

25. *La Nación,* Mar. 1, 1875.

26. Ibid.

27. *La Tribuna,* Mar. 1, 1875.

28. Ibid.; *El Nacional,* Mar. 1, 1875; *La Prensa,* Mar. 2, 1875.

29. *El Nacional,* Mar. 1, 1875; *La Tribuna,* Mar. 1 and 2, 1875.

30. The official documents are reproduced in most newspapers of those days.

31. *El Católico Argentino,* Mar. 6, 1875.

32. *La Tribuna,* Mar. 1, 1875.

33. *La Nación,* Mar. 1, 1875; *La Tribuna,* Mar. 1 and 3, 1875; *La Prensa,* Mar. 2, 1875; *La Libertad,* Mar. 2, 1875.

34. Police notes reproduced in *El Nacional,* Mar. 3, 1875.

35. Ibid., Mar. 1, 2, and 3, 1875.

36. "La Inmigración y la Mala Policía," *La Pampa,* Mar. 10, 1875; "Las Clases Pobres y la Autoridad," *La Prensa,* Mar. 11, 1875; "El Nacional," *El Comercial del Plata,* Mar. 12, 1875; "Quién es Extrangero?" *El Comercial,* Mar. 12, 1875; "Una Protesta," "Protestamos," and "Vamos a Cuentas," *El Español,* Mar. 2, 3, and 10, 1875.

37. *El Español,* Mar. 2, 1875.

38. Reproduced in *La Tribuna,* Mar. 3, 1875, among others. The proposal was formulated by Senator Miguel Navarro Viola.

39. *La Prensa,* Mar. 4, 1875.

40. *El Nacional,* Mar. 2, 1875; *La Política,* Mar. 3, 1875; *Il Gazzetino,* Mar. 4, 1875; *La Tribuna,* Mar. 20, 1875; *La Prensa,* Mar. 20, 1875.

41. Moreno was replaced by Manuel Rocha, also an autonomist. He was a national guard commander and had fought in the War of the Triple Alliance against Paraguay. See *La Tribuna,* Mar. 2, 3, and 4, 1875; *La Prensa,* Mar. 2, 3, 4, and 6, 1875; *La Pampa,* Mar. 5, 1875; *La Libertad,* Mar. 2, 4, and 5, 1875; *La Unión Argentina,* Mar. 14, 1875; *El Nacional,* Mar. 3, 1875; *La Política,* Mar. 4 and 7, 1875.

42. *La Época,* Mar. 2 and 5, 1875; *La Tribuna,* Mar. 8, 1875; *La Pampa,* Mar. 3, 1875; *La Prensa,* Mar. 2 and 17, 1875; *Il Gazzetino,* Mar. 2 and 10, 1875.

43. *El Católico Argentino,* Mar. 6, 1875. There was also a crossfire of accusations between the different newspapers. See, for example, *La Pampa,* Mar. 4 and 10, 1875; and *La Política,* Mar. 3, 1875.

44. Bruno, *Historia de la Iglesia,* p. 118; and *La Época,* Mar. 2, 1875.

45. This allegation was refuted immediately by the *mitrista* leadership and press. See, among others, the official paper *La Unión Argentina,* Mar. 3, 1875.

46. See, for example, *Revista Masónica Americana,* no. 6, Mar. 30, 1875, p. 193.

47. This and the following sections are based mainly on the information found in the trial proceedings found in Archivo General de la Nación, *Tribunal Criminal,* files P10 and P11, 1875.

48. Among the eighty-eight men that were sent to jail, twenty-five were between fifteen and twenty years old; twenty-nine between twenty-one and twenty-nine; and twenty-eight were over thirty. For the remaining six, there is no information on age available. As to their national origins, thirty-nine were native Argentines and forty-two foreign born. No information is available on the remaining seven. Among the foreigners, thirty-nine were from various regions of Italy, fourteen from Spain, and nine from other countries (several came from Uruguay, two from Brazil, and one from France). This information is contained in the depositions of the arrested.

49. The data available for the city of Buenos Aires in 1869 and 1887 show that, among the adult (over fourteen years of age) male population, the foreign-born were from three to four times more numerous than the natives. See Sabato and Romero, *Los trabajadores de Buenos Aires,* appendix, table 10.

50. Archivo General de la Nación, *Tribunal Criminal,* P11, pp. 16–17.

51. Ibid., pp. 611v.–616.

52. Ibid., pp. 191–93.

53. Ibid., P10, p. 259. Other men arrested among the same group were Pedro Luvini or Lubinia, thirty-two-year-old watchmaker born in Italian Lombardia; Alejandro Medicina, thirty-eight-year-old turner from Livorno; José Armani, forty-year-old trader from Venice; Eduardo Galeano, nineteen-year-old Argentine student; José Torres, innkeeper born in Genoa; José de la Serna, fifty-six-year-old solicitor from Buenos Aires; Spiro Ungaro, thirty-two-year-old ship-builder from Sicily.

54. Archivo General de la Nación, *Tribunal Criminal,* P11, pp. 537 ff. The name Clemente XIV alluded to the pope from 1769 to 1774, who suppressed the order of the Jesuits. Other members of the club who were detained were Juan Storni, eighteen-year-old bookkeeper; Felipe González, nineteen-year-old clerk; Juan Arroqui, nineteen-year-old typographer; Manuel Celesia, twenty-two-year-old shopkeeper; Aristóbulo Cabrera, twenty-two; Alberto Jauregui, sixteen-year-old clerk, and Claro Acosta, thirty years old, employed at the customhouse. All of them were Argentines.

55. Archivo General de la Nación, *Tribunal Criminal,* P11, pp. 551, 651–52. Similar statements were formulated by Juan Podestá, twenty-year-old journeyman of the Parque station; Luis Parodi, thirty-five-year-old Italian bottle

seller; José Podestá, eighteen-year-old butcher from Italian Liguria; Timoteo Ortega, thirty-three-year-old native military; Pedro Carraquiri, fifteen-year-old
cobbler; Jacinto Pérez, twenty-six-year-old journeyman born in Tucumán, re-
putedly "a thief"; Luis Talavera, twenty-four-year-old Argentine typographer;
and José Ortega, twenty-seven-year-old illiterate painter, born in Buenos Aires.

56. Archivo General de la Nación, *Tribunal Criminal*, P11, pp. 34v ff.

57. Ibid., pp. 113v–14.

58. Ibid., pp. 37v ff.

59. The attorneys appointed initially to defend the accused were Marcelino
Aguirre, Leandro Alem, Faustino Alsina, Leopoldo del Campo, Daniel Cazón,
Jorge Echeverría, Baldomero García Quirno, Benigno Jardim, Bonifacio Lastra,
José G. López, Vicente Martínez, Martín Matheu, Angel Navarro, Aurelio Pala-
cios, Juan Panelo, V. Porcel de Peralta, Vicente Quesada, Dardo Rocha, José A.
Terry, Federico Tobal, José F. Torres, Lorenzo Torres; and Simón Zárraga. Not
all of them participated in the trial, and some of them were in charge of several
cases.

60. Archivo General de la Nación, *Tribunal Criminal*, P10, pp. 160v–61.

61. These words belong to the text by Aurelio Palacios, who defended several of the men arrested in La Boca. Other attorneys used similar expressions.
Ibid., pp. 247–50.

62. See, for example, *La Prensa*, Mar. 20, 1875.

63. *La Pampa*, Apr. 8, 1875.

64. See, among others, *La Tribuna*, Apr. 19, 1875; *El Nacional*, Apr. 20, 1875;
La Pampa, Apr. 20 and 22, 1875; *La Nación*, Apr. 21 and 27, 1875.

65. *La Tribuna*, Apr. 20, 1875.

66. Furlong, *Historia del Colegio del Salvador*, pp. 127–38.

67. *La Libertad*, Mar. 4, 1875.

68. Furlong, *Historia del Colegio del Salvador*, p. 142.

69. *La Época*, Mar. 5, 1875.

70. Ibid.

Chapter 9: On the Margins

1. *La Prensa*, Mar. 16, 1878.

2. In Europe, Raymond Wilmart had been a member of the International
since youth. In 1873 he was sent by that organization to Buenos Aires, where he
acted as its representative and also as the editor of a newspaper. In his letters to
Marx and other leaders, he complained about the difficulties of organizing the
workers in Argentina. He finally stayed in Buenos Aires but abandoned all political activism. Cf. the rigorous book by Falcón, *Los orígenes del movimiento
obrero*. See also his "Documentos para la historia de la Primera Internacional en
el Río de la Plata," *Apuntes para la historia del movimiento obrero latinoamericano*,
vol. 2, Jan.–Mar. 1980 (Amsterdam); and Chianelli and Galmarini, "¿Una conspiración comunista en 1875?"

3. This section is based on the documents found in Archivo General de la
Nación, *Tribunal Criminal*, L 1875 (7), Juzgado del Dr. Hudson.

4. *La Prensa*, Mar. 17, 1875.

5. Ibid., Apr. 16, 1875.

6. *La Tribuna*, Feb. 19, 1875.

7. *La Libertad*, Mar. 21, 1875.

8. *La Época*, Mar. 31, 1875.

9. Archivo General de la Nación, *Tribunal Criminal*, L 1875 (7), p. 70v (Apr. 14, 1875).

10. Ibid., p. 73.

11. The judge was Damián Hudson. The criminal prosecutor was Ventura Pondal, who had also participated in the proceedings originating in the violent episodes of Feb. 28.

12. Archivo General de la Nación, *Tribunal Criminal*, L 1875 (7), p. 75.

13. Ibid., pp. 76–79.

14. *La Nación*, Apr. 30, 1875.

15. Archivo General de la Nación, *Tribunal Criminal*, L 1875 (7), p. 55v.

16. The expression comes from the letter sent by the men arrested to the editor of *La Prensa* and published in the newspaper on April 16, 1875.

17. This information comes from Falcón, *Los orígenes del movimiento obrero*.

18. On the Sociedad Tipográfica Bonaerense and the Sociedad Unión Tipográfica, as well as on the first labor conflicts in Argentina, see Sebastián Marotta, *El movimiento sindical argentino*, vol. 1, chapter 2; Falcón, *Los orígenes del movimiento obrero*; and Badoza, "Typographical Workers and Their Mutualist Experience," pp. 72–90.

19. *El Correo Español*, Aug. 23, 1878.

20. *La Tribuna* and *El Nacional*, Aug. 31, 1878.

21. *La República*, Sept. 2 and 8, 1878; *La Patria*, Sept. 3, 1878.

22. *La Libertad*, Sept. 2, 1878.

23. Ibid.

24. *El Siglo*, Sept. 2, 1878. See also *La Patria*, Sept. 1 and 3, 1878.

25. *La República* and *La Libertad*, Sept. 2, 1878.

26. *El Correo Español*, Sept. 22 and 24, 1878.

27. In those days, the "hottest" issues were the reorganization of the municipalities following Article 200 of the latest provincial constitution, and the suspension of the municipal elections scheduled for that month. The papers devoted large spaces to these issues.

Chapter 10: A Culture of Mobilization

1. Cf. Colin Lucas, "The Crowd and Politics," Colin Lucas (ed.), *The Political Culture of the French Revolution* (Oxford: Pergamon Press, 1987).

2. Mona Ozouf, *La fête révolutionnaire: 1789–1799* (Paris: Gallimard, 1976), p. 91.

Index of Names

In this index an "f" after a number indicates a separate reference on the next page, and an "ff" indicates a separate reference on the next two pages. A continuous discussion over two or more pages is indicated by a span of page numbers, e.g., "57–59." *Passim* is used for a cluster of references in close but not consecutive sequence.